Graham MacLachlan

THE BIG BOOK OF KNOTS

The Complete Guide to Over 300 Knots for All Uses

ADLARD COLES

LONDON • OXFORD • NEW YORK • NEW DELHI • SYDNEY

ADLARD COLES
Bloomsbury Publishing Plc
50 Bedford Square, London, WC1B 3DP, UK
Bloomsbury Publishing Ireland Limited,
29 Earlsfort Terrace, Dublin 2, D02 AY28, Ireland

BLOOMSBURY, ADLARD COLES and the Adlard Coles logo are trademarks of
Bloomsbury Publishing Plc

First published as Le Grand Guide des Noeuds (979-1027103362)
First published in French by Vagnon, Paris, France – 2019
This edition published 2026

A catalogue record for this book is available from the British Library

Library of Congress Cataloguing-in-Publication data has been applied for

ISBN: PB: 978-1-3994-2985-6; ePDF: 978-1-3994-2984-9; eBook: 978-1-3994-2982-5

2 4 6 8 10 9 7 5 3 1

Designed by Austin Taylor

Typeset in Ballinger Condensed by Kirsty Hunter

Printed and bound in China by TOPPAN Leefung

FSC
www.fsc.org
MIX
Paper | Supporting
responsible forestry
FSC® C104723

Bloomsbury Publishing Plc makes every effort to ensure that the papers used in the manufacture of our books
are natural, recyclable products made from wood grown in well-managed forests. Our manufacturing
processes conform to the environmental regulations of the country of origin.

To find out more about our authors and books visit www.bloomsbury.com
and sign up for our newsletters

For product safety related questions contact productsafety@bloomsbury.com

BASIC KNOTS

INTRODUCTION TO BASIC KNOTS

This first chapter brings together all the basic knots: the simple, go-to knots that are useful in themselves, as well as forming the building blocks for other more complex knots.

Throughout the rest of this book, whenever you see the name of a knot in **bold**, you'll be able to find it explained in the following pages.

The fundamental elements of knots

The **turn** is the most basic knot form, as it involves just a single crossing. If you pass one of the ends through the turn, you get a knot with three crossings, known as an **overhand knot** (page 14), a **half-knot** (page 11), or a **half-hitch** (page 10), depending on how it is positioned in relation to a support.

These three knots are what we call the 'primary knots'.

The **round turn** (page 10) is a technique used to distribute the strain on the support (cleat, branch, ring), helping to reduce shearing stress on the rope.

Combined with two half-hitches or a **bowline** (page 18), the round turn is useful for pitching tents, setting up clotheslines, mooring lines, anchor points, and in any other situation where there's a high risk of wear.

Slipping a knot makes it easier to undo quickly.

This usually involves folding the working end back on itself (referred to as 'doubling the working end') before securing the knot.

Then, simply pulling on the end will undo the knot.

The **slip knot** (page 15) clearly demonstrates the principle behind the technique.

Another well-known example is the shoelace knot, which is a **reef knot** (page 17) with both ends slipped.

Most practical knots can be slipped. Finally, some knots and techniques allow you to repair and reinforce ropes, such as **hand-laying** (page 23) or applying a **whipping** (page 23).

Figure eight knot.

The different categories of knots

The stopper knot

A knot that increases the diameter of a rope is called a **stopper knot** or **button knot**.

It's also used to prevent a cut or damaged rope from fraying. The following knots fall into this category.

- The **overhand knot** (page 14), used to secure a sewing thread, create grip bumps on a climbing rope, or mark the intervals on the knotted cords used by medieval builders.
- The **slip knot** (page 15), used to quickly undo an overhand knot.
- The **double overhand knot** (page 14), used to increase the bulk of an overhand knot.
- The **figure eight knot** (page 15), used to stop a sailing sheet from slipping through a pulley. It forms the basis of many join-and-loop knots used by climbers.

The binding knot

A knot that wraps around an object to compress or tighten it is called a binding knot or seizing knot. The following knots fall into this category.

- The **half-knot** (page 11): the foundation of many knots, including the reef knot and the rosette. It is tied using both ends of the same rope, making it a binding knot. Also known as the safety knot among climbers.
- The **reef knot** (page 17), used to fasten all sorts of packages, secure a reef in a sail, or tie a practical and handy rope belt, though not recommended for joining two ropes together.
- The **granny knot** (page 17): a less popular variation of the reef knot. Its main

advantage is that it allows the ends to be positioned at a right angle to the binding part of the knot. The granny knot tends to loosen slightly before tightening and can be difficult to undo once pulled tight. It is highly unreliable, and even dangerous, when used as a join knot.

- The **surgeon's knot** (page 23), used to apply a binding in surgery. Its key advantage lies in the initial double half-knot, which makes it very stable from the outset, even when using a slippery thread.
- The **constrictor knot** (page 12), used to close a bag, secure another knot, or serve as whipping to prevent a rope from fraying. Characterised by a central turn that presses down on a half-knot, the constrictor knot is essentially an enhanced clove hitch. By reversing the direction of the half-knot, this important knot becomes the strangle knot. The slipped constrictor knot makes the constrictor knot easier to undo. However, even when slipped, it can still be difficult to remove.
- The **strangle knot** (page 12) is similar to the constrictor knot, but with the ends angled diagonally. It is, in fact, a double overhand knot tied around a support.

The hitch knot

A knot used to anchor a rope to a support is called a hitch or fastening knot.

The following knots fall into this category.

- The **half-hitch** (page 10): when the loop is made over its standing part, it forms a more secure hitch than the regular loop, as its end is trapped between the rope and the support. To protect it against sudden movement, you can wrap the

Clove hitch knot.

end several times around the part of the rope that encircles the support, or add a second half-hitch.

- The **timber hitch** (page 16) is used to start a lacing or a lashing, or to anchor a hauling knot. It is not suitable as an anchor knot in climbing.
- The **round turn and two half-hitches** (page 10) is used to attach a rope to any kind of support and is especially useful when the rope is under tension. Making a round turn on the support not only reduces wear by spreading the load, but also helps maintain rope tension so the knot can be finished under less strain. Possibly the most versatile, practical, and reliable knot of them all.

Fancy a twist? Check out the '**round turn and two reversed half-hitches**' on page 248. You simply turn that second half-hitch the opposite way, just like a cow hitch. You get all the grip of the classic version, although it is more difficult to undo.

- The **clove hitch** (page 21) is used to tie a fender to a guardrail, start a lashing, or close a bag. Note that the standing part and the working end come out on opposite sides of the knot.

- The **open-ended clove hitch** (page 11): this technique allows you to tie a clove hitch without using the ends of the rope.
- The **groundline hitch** (page 22) is similar to the clove hitch, but the result holds a little more firmly.
- The **cow hitch** (page 21) is used to tie a rope that might twist around its support, to stow a strap on a boat, or to fasten a sling for creating an anchor in climbing. Also known as the two reversed half-hitches, the cow hitch differs from the clove hitch in the way the ends are positioned, with both coming out on the same side of the knot.
- The **bale sling** (page 21) can be used to create an anchor point, sling a load for lifting, or distribute a load to reduce wear. Since the ends come out on the same side, the cow hitch is the ideal knot to prevent a rope loop from shifting sideways on its support.

The bend

A knot used to tie two ropes together is called a bend.

Here are some common examples of bends.

- The **overhand bend** (page 14) allows two ropes to be joined quickly and easily.

- The **water knot** (page 18) is used to close a rope loop or create an almost permanent join. It's identical in form to the overhand bend, except the standing parts exit on opposite sides of the knot. Known to climbers as the rethreaded overhand knot.
- The **tape knot** (page 18) is used to join two flat-ended sections. Its shape is identical to the water knot and the rethreaded overhand knot; only the tying method differs.
- The **sheet bend** (page 20) is used to join two ropes together, even those of different diameters, or to attach a rope to a loop (such as a spliced eye or a bowline). If the join is subject to sudden movement, the double sheet bend is preferable.
- The **double sheet bend** (page 20) has the same uses as the sheet bend, but offers greater resistance to jerks and sudden strain.

The loop

A knot that forms a loop at the end of a rope is called a loop or an eye.

Here are some common examples of fixed and sliding loops.

- The **overhand loop** (page 15) quickly forms a loop. Though not very elegant, it can be hard to untie once pulled tight. It's an overhand knot tied on the bight, also known as a thumb knot to sailors and a cow tail knot to climbers.
- The **bowline** (page 18) is used to moor a boat, lift a person in distress, or tow a car. This essential and widely known fixed loop knot is reliable, extremely versatile, and easy to undo, even after bearing heavy loads.
- The **Spanish bowline** (page 19) creates two fixed loops at the end or in the middle of a rope. Though known as a sailor's knot, it is rarely used on board, except to impress your crewmates.

- The **honda knot** (page 22) is an adjustable loop used to attach a rope to a bow or to make a lasso.
- The **noose knot** (page 12) is used to make a sliding loop with low holding strength.
- The **noose knot on a bight** (page 13) is a way to tie the simple slip knot without using the ends of the rope. A loop with easily adjustable size, but limited strength.
- The **slip noose** (page 13) is used to secure a slip knot that can be undone quickly, even from a distance.
- The **enhanced noose** (page 13) is used in any situation that calls for a sliding, compact loop. Stronger and more difficult to tie than the simple slip knot, the improved version rivals the poacher's knot in effectiveness.
- The **midshipman's hitch** (page 16) is used to tie off a rope without losing tension, using an adjustable loop.
- The **bale sling** (page 20) is an intermediary for mooring or lifting, used with a block and hook, carabiner, or anchor point. The join can be made using various knots, such as the double sheet bend, double fisherman's bend, water knot, or a short splice.

Storage

A knot used to store or temporarily shorten a rope.

For example, the **sheepshank** (page 22) is used to temporarily stow a rope in order to shorten a tow line or a telescopic mast stay without cutting it.

We should also mention coiling and flaking methods (see pages 265 to 270).

Round turn

Wrap the rope around
the support so that the
standing part and the
working end lie on the
same side.

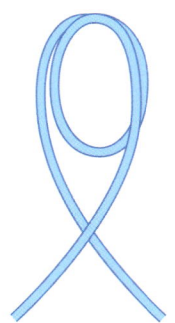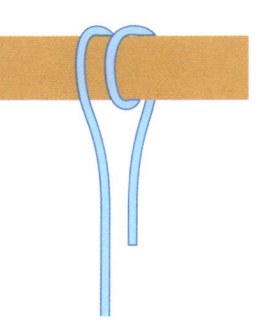

Single turn

A single turn is a rope looped once so that
the strands do not cross. Creating a turn
(folding an end into a single loop) allows
a knot to be undone quickly. Note: Do
not confuse a turn with a bight. (See, for
example, the slip knot on page 15).

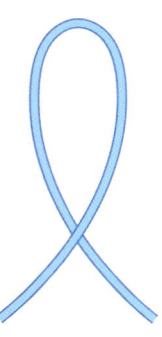

Half-hitch

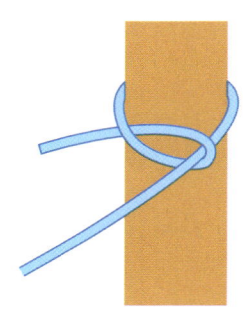

Round turn and two half-hitches

Make a **round turn** around the support (post, spar, ring, etc.) then secure the knot by tying
two half-hitches around the standing part.

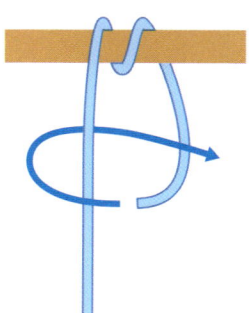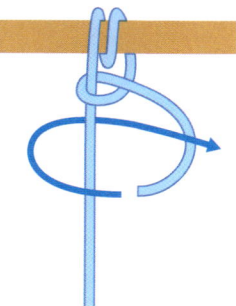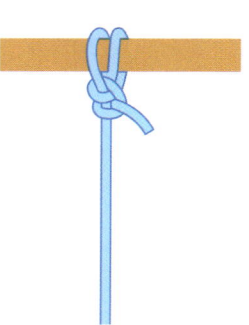

Open-ended clove hitch

Working from left to right, tie two identical half-hitches side by side, then place the left one over the right one. Attach the whole knot to the support.

Half-knot

Pass the rope around the support, then cross the ends and pass the one underneath over and under the other. It is also called the safety knot by climbers.

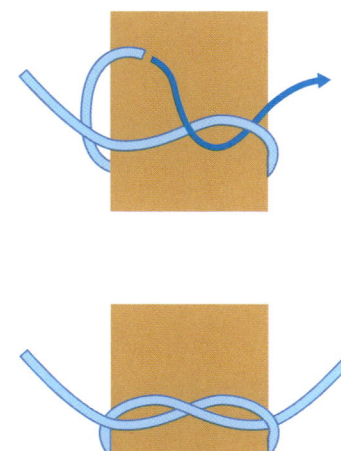

Constrictor knot

Wrap the rope around the support by passing it twice over the standing part, then under the standing part.

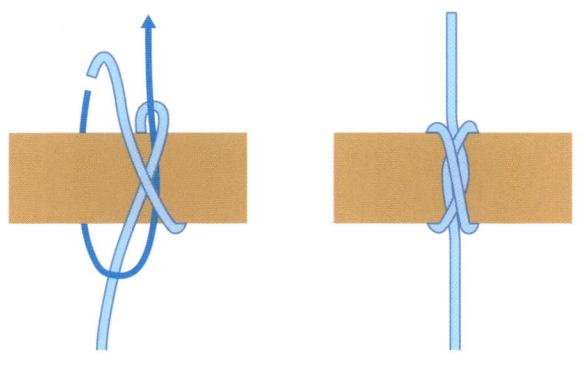

Strangle knot

Starting from the left, make a crossing twice around the support, then pass over the left strand and behind the crossing of the half-hitch.

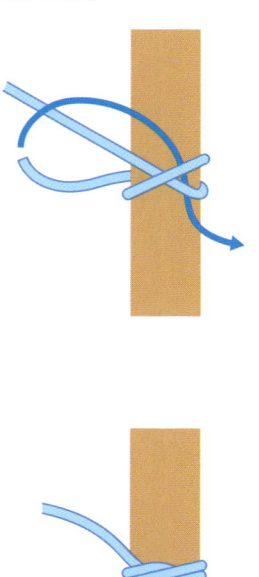

Noose knot

Form the loop, then tie an **overhand knot** around the standing part.

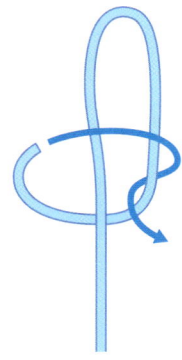

Noose on a bight

Tie a **loop** near the end of the rope, then pass the bight underneath and through this loop. Secure the loop by tightening the knot.

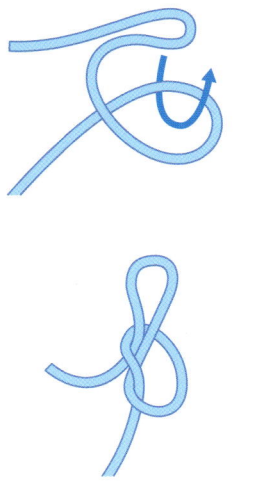

Enhanced noose

Form the loop, then tie a **constrictor knot** around the standing part.

Slip noose

Pass the rope through the attachment point (ring, carabiner, etc.), then tie a loop. Double the end and pass the resulting bight behind the standing part and through the **half-hitch**.

Tighten everything against the attachment point.

Pull on the working end to undo the knot.

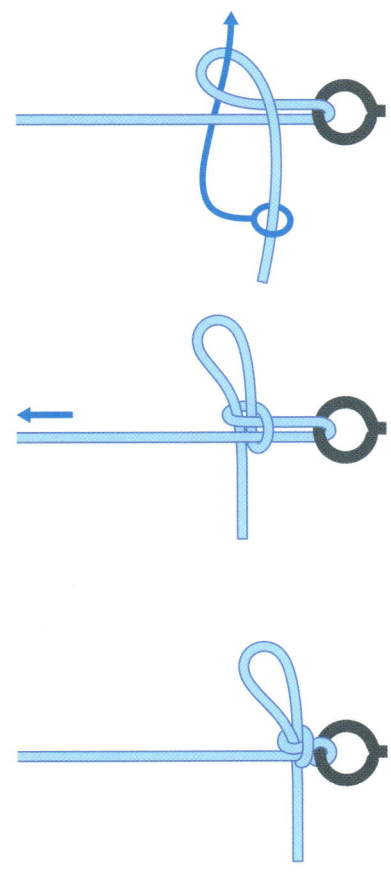

Overhand knot

Make a turn, pass the end through its loop, then tighten the knot on itself. You can create a series of overhand knots by lining them up, and you can tie a slipped overhand knot by doubling the working end before pulling it through the loop.

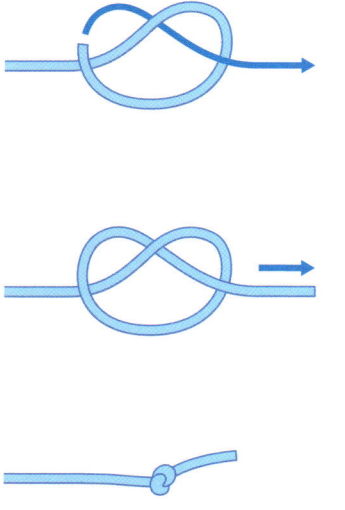

Double overhand knot

Tie an overhand knot, then pass the end through the loop again. Pull tight to form the stopper knot.

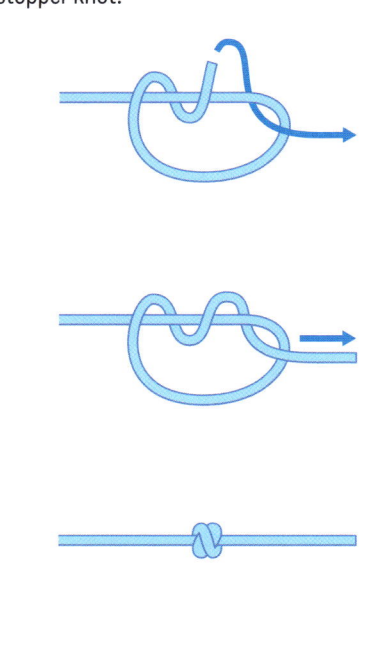

Overhand bend

Place the two ropes to be joined side by side, then tie an overhand knot.

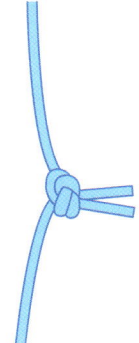

Slip knot

Make a turn over the standing part, then pass the working end behind it. Pull the strand through the turn without passing the end, forming the bight.

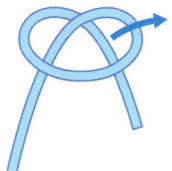

Overhand loop

Double the rope to form a bight, then tie an **overhand knot**. It is also known as the cow tail knot.

Figure eight knot

Make a turn, then pass the end around the standing part and through the loop.

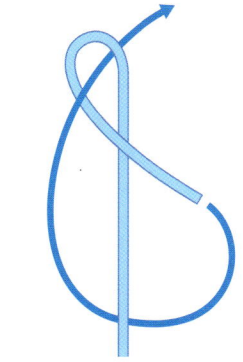

Timber hitch

Wrap the rope around the support and tie a **loop** around the standing part, then wrap the end around the loop's strand. Pull on the standing part to tighten. The end is trapped between the loop and the support.

Killick hitch

Add one or more **half-hitches** at a suitable distance from the **timber hitch**.

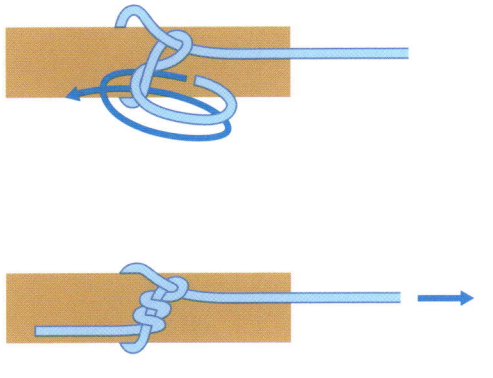
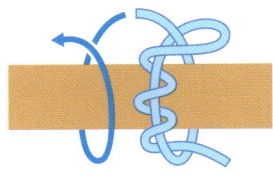
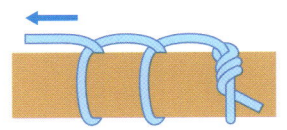

Midshipman's hitch

Pass the rope around the support (post, piton, tent peg, etc.) and put it under tension. Tie a **half-hitch** around the standing part, then make a second turn around the standing part, passing over the half-hitch and between it and the right strand of the loop. Secure with a **slipped half-hitch** tied around the standing part.

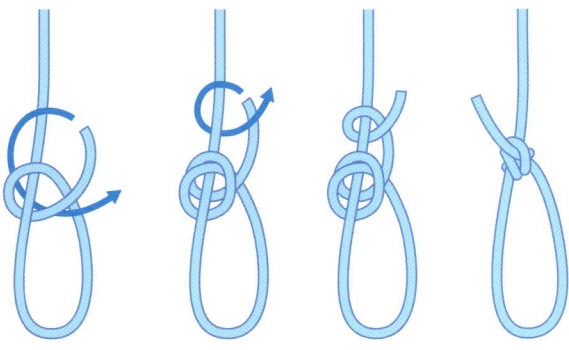

Reef knot

Tie a **half-knot**. Take the strand on top and lay it over the other. Pass the one underneath over and under the other, then tighten. Note that the knot is symmetrical and consists of two interlaced loops. To undo easily, pull the two strands of one loop in opposite directions. The other loop will transform into a cow hitch and can be loosened. A practical and useful knot, but not recommended for joining two ropes together. It is also called the square knot.

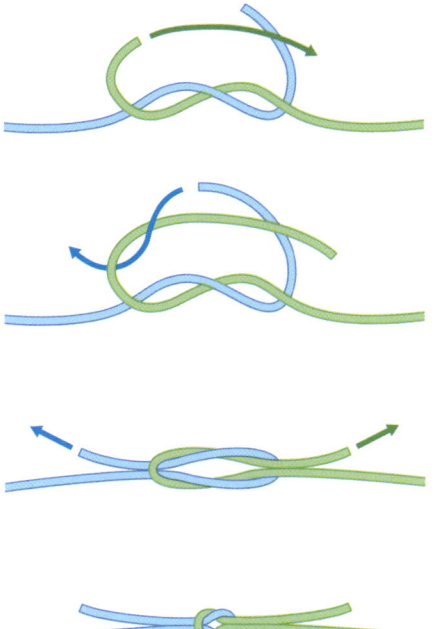

Granny knot

Tie a **half-knot**. Take the strand underneath and pass it over the other. Then pass the strand that is now underneath over and under the other, then tighten.

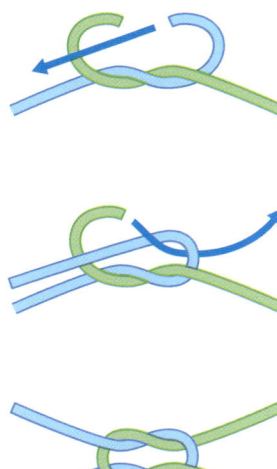

Tape knot

Tie an **overhand knot** in one end of the tape, then with the other end, follow the shape in the opposite direction.

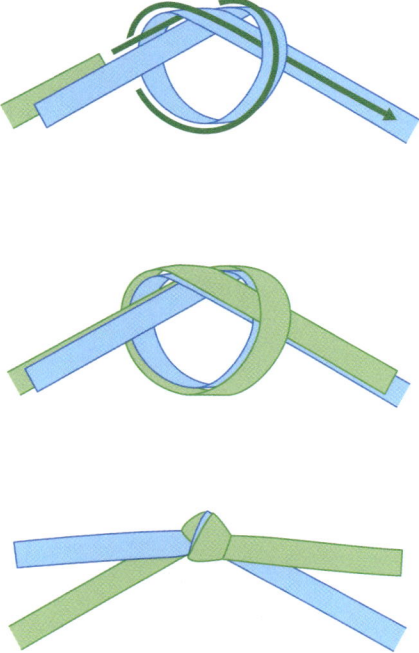

Water knot

Tie a **half-knot**, then cross the two strands. Next, pass the left end behind the standing part and through the centre of the knot. Do the same with the other strand and tighten.

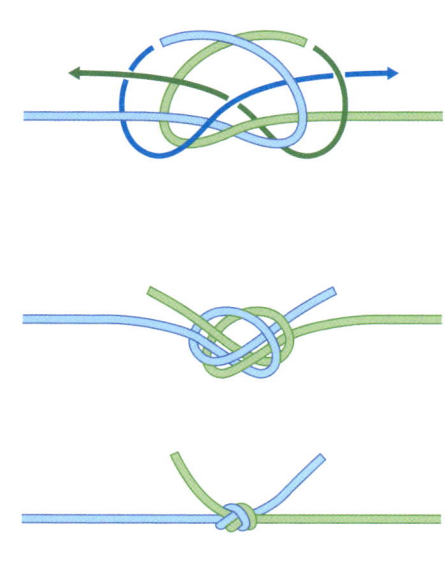

Bowline

Make a loop at some distance from the rope's end, then pass the working end through it, around the standing part, and back through the loop. To tighten the knot, pull the standing part with one hand and the two strands coming out of the loop with the other.

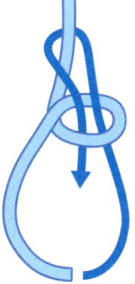 

Spanish bowline

Double the rope's end and fold the bight over the standing parts, then twist the small bights created toward the centre of the knot. Pass the left bight through the right one. Spread the bight at the start of the standing parts to enlarge it, then first pass its left side through the left bight. Repeat for the other side. Tighten the whole knot.

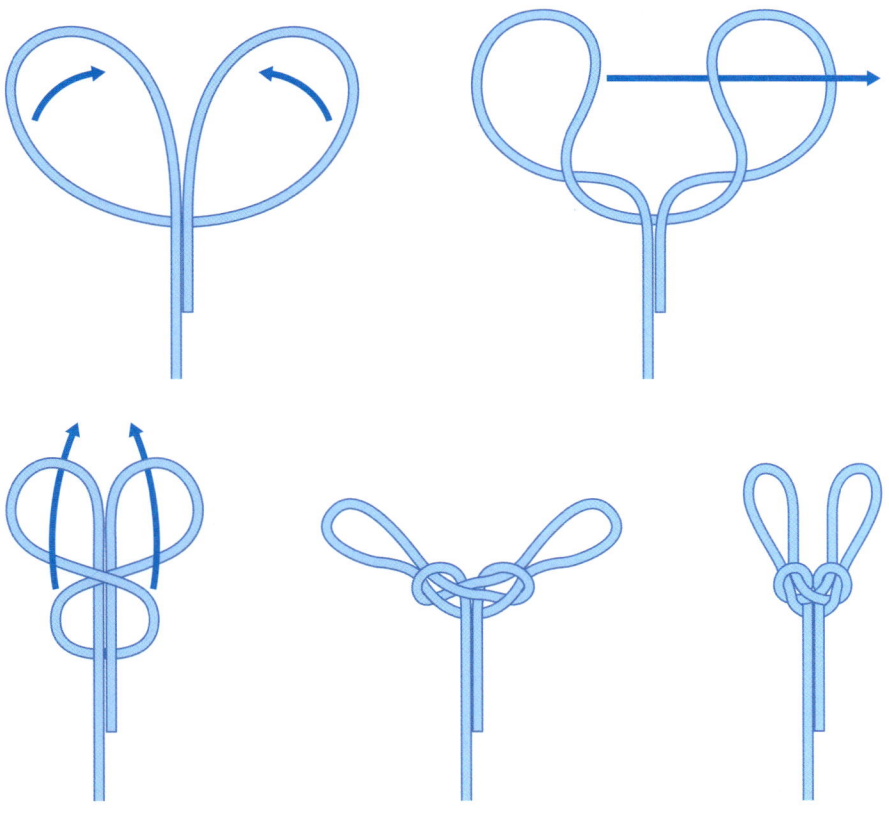

Sheet bend

This knot is used to join two ropes of different diameters. Double the end of the thicker rope to form a loop. Pass the thinner rope through the loop, around the two thick strands, then under itself. Tighten, leaving the ends protruding a few centimetres. Also known as the weaver's knot.

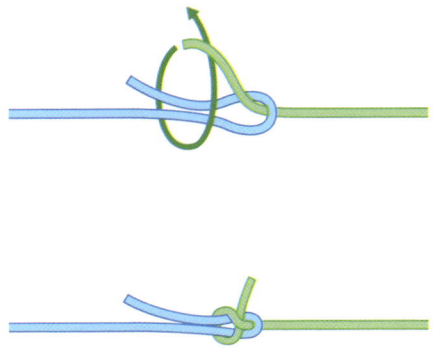

Double sheet bend

Tie a sheet bend and pass the smaller diameter rope a second time around the larger strands and under itself. Tighten, leaving the ends protruding a few centimetres.

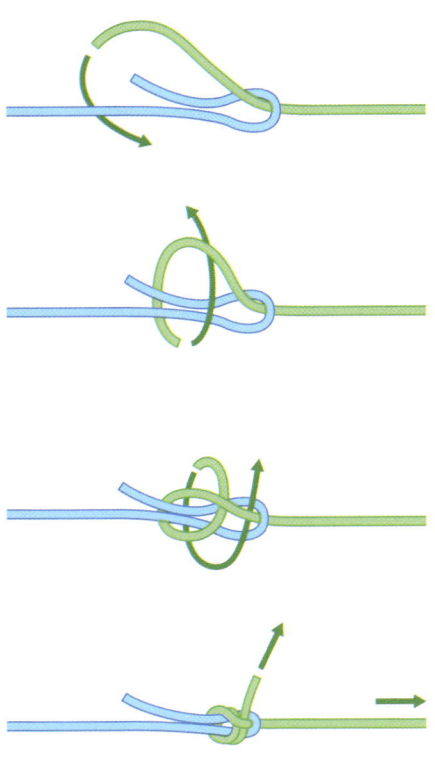

Sling

Tie the ends of the same rope, cord, or tape to create a textile loop of the desired size. Also known as a cordelette.

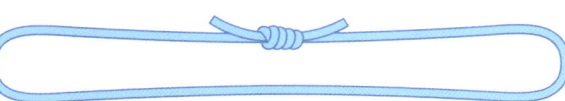

Bale sling

Wrap the rope or tape loop around the support, then pass one bight through the other. Attach the rope, hook, or carabiner to the protruding bight.

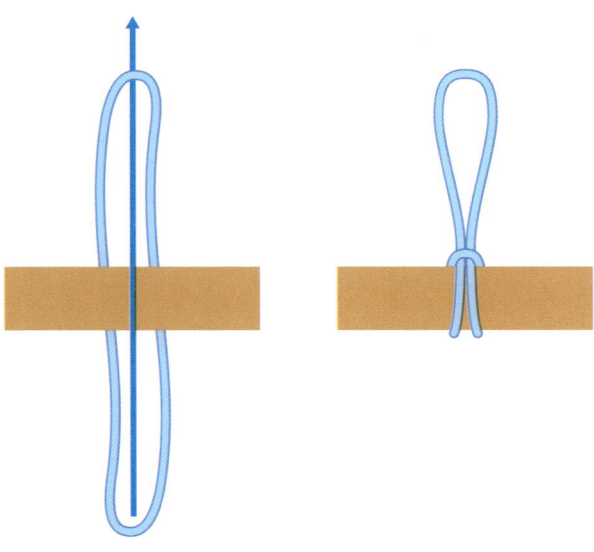

Cow hitch

Tie a turn around the support front-to-back, then a second one back-to-front.

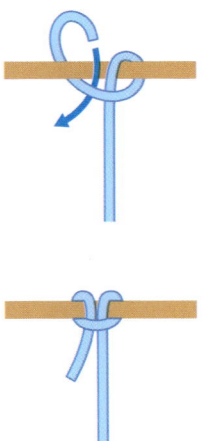

Clove hitch

Slip two turns directly onto the support, with the second positioned as a mirror image of the first.

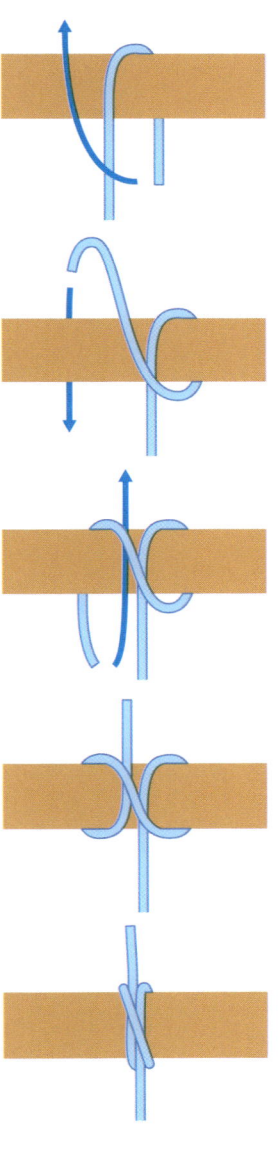

Honda knot

Tie an **overhand knot** fairly far from the end of the rope, then pass the working end through the knot, under the standing part. Tighten the overhand knot. Add a second overhand knot on the end to be able to lock the loop.

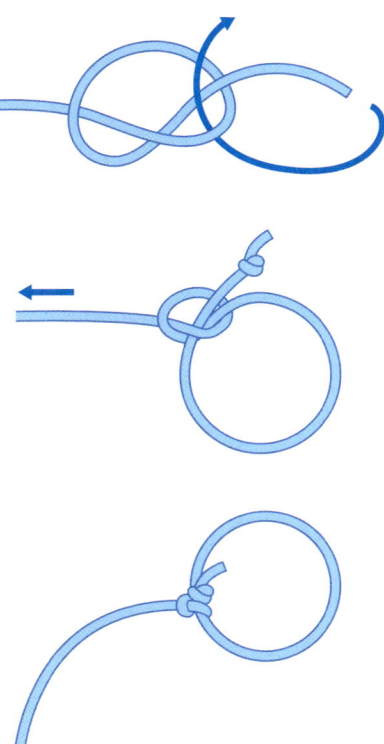

Groundline hitch

Make two turns with the second passing over itself and under the first. Pull on the standing part to tighten.

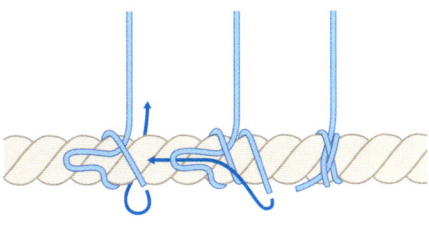

Sheepshank

Fold or coil the rope to the desired length to form the 'bundle' to be stowed. Twist one of the standing parts to make a loop, then pass one side of the bundle through the loop. Do the same with the other side of the bundle.

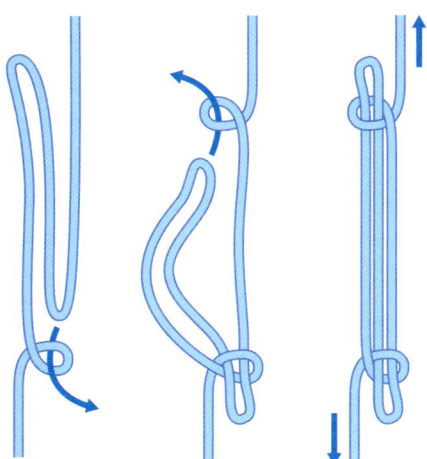

Surgeon's knot

Cross the working ends and tie a **half-knot** with each. Tighten, then secure with a third half-knot.

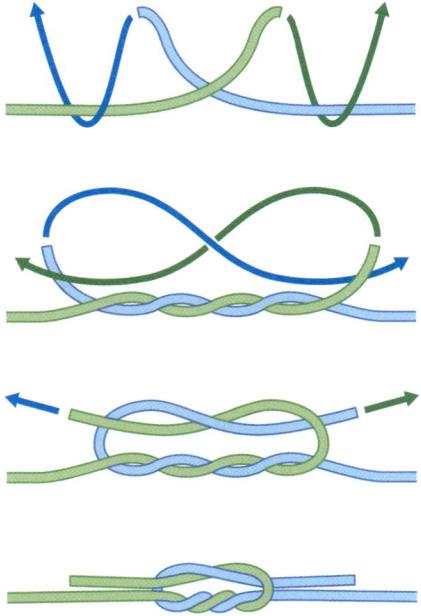

Whipping

Whipping is a type of **serving** (see the serving technique on page 263). Tuck the end of the twine under several turns, then pull the end tight to secure these initial wraps. Next, wrap the twine around the rope until you reach the desired number of turns. To finish, undo the last few turns, pass the end through, tighten the final wraps over the twine's end, then pull tight and cut off the excess.

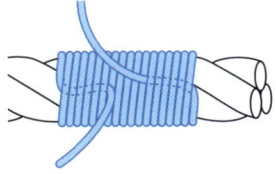

Hand-laying

Make a half-turn on itself following the twist direction of the yarns (usually clockwise) for each strand in turn, then place it next to the previous strand to reconstruct the rope. Repeat until the rope is rebuilt, then serve it.

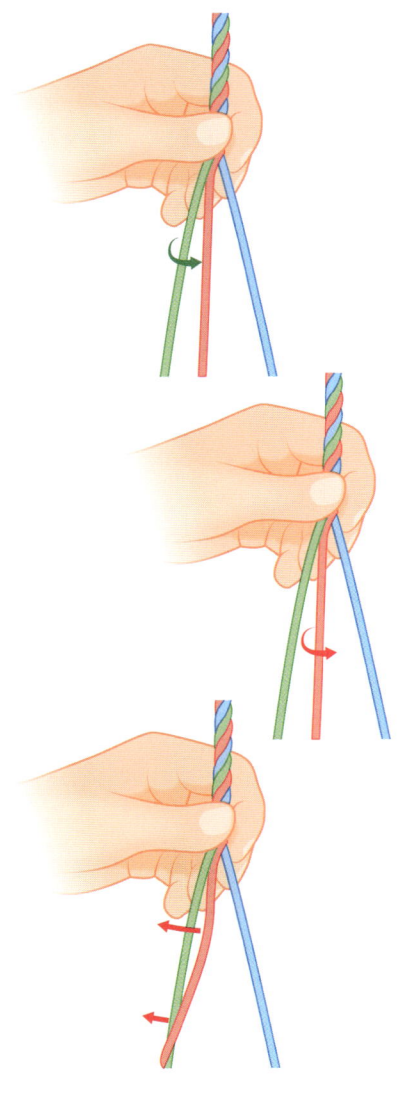

ARCHERY KNOTS

ARCHERY KNOTS

Traditional bowstring knot

Knot type: Fastening

Use: Attach the string to the bottom of the bow.

Method for tying the knot: Tie a **timber hitch** at one end of the string and slip the loop over the lower limb of the bow.

Perfect for a makeshift bow made with a hazel branch and twine for hay bales.

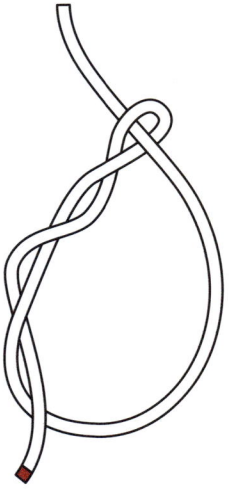

Traditional bowstring knot: alternative method

Knot type: Fastening

Use: Attach the rope to the bottom of the bow.

Method for tying the knot: Make **two slipped half-hitches** (in other words, an **open-ended clove hitch**) with one end of the rope, then slip the knot over the lower limb of the bow. Secure everything by tying the end around the standing part with two half-hitches.

Bowstring loop

Knot type: Fastening

Use: Attach the string to the top of the bow.

Method for tying the knot: Once the string is attached at the bottom of the bow, tie a **honda knot** at the other end. Slip the knot over the upper limb, then pull the working end to tighten it around the support.

💡 TIPS & TRICKS
....

Unlike the honda knot, this knot doesn't have an overhand knot on the end. However, if the string is slippery, it's better to add one.

Fletching

Fletching is a technique similar to the **bowstring serving** that attaches the feathers to the arrow. A very fine thread is used, preferably silk.

Bowstring serving

Knot type: Binding

Use: Protect the centre and the rope's eyelets.

Method for tying the knot: Apply a **serving** at the desired spot on the string. The string should be well tensioned before applying the thread wrap.

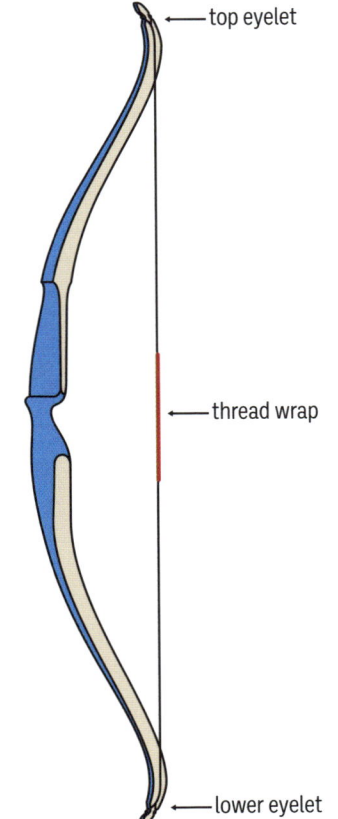

← top eyelet

← thread wrap

← lower eyelet

TOOLS
....

There is a tool that makes applying the thread easier: the bowstring serving tool.

Served bowstring eye

Knot type: Loop

Use: Attach the string to the limbs of the bow using fixed loops.

Method for tying the knot: Temporarily tie one end of the string to one of the loom points, then wrap the string around the four loom points to create the desired rope diameter. Untie the starting knot and tie the ends of the rope together with a **reef knot** (this knot will later be hidden under one of the thread wraps).

Whip a sufficiently long section of the string to form the eye, temporarily closing it with a half-hitch around the string. Align the four loom points and centre the whipped section on one of the points. Untie the **half-hitch** and continue whipping to bring the two string strands closer over the desired length.

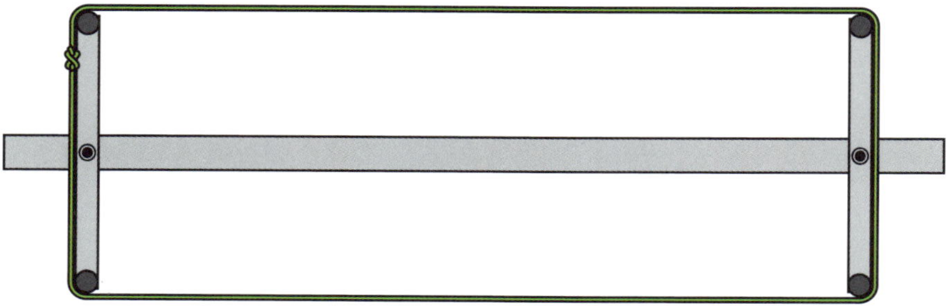

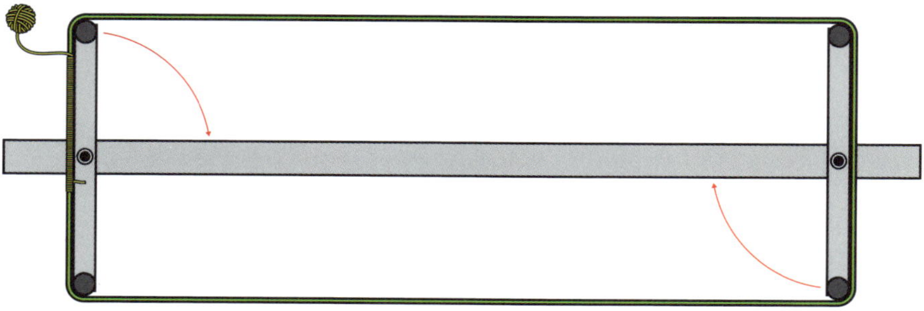

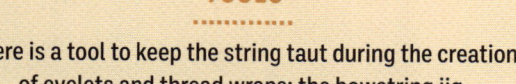

TOOLS

There is a tool to keep the string taut during the creation of eyelets and thread wraps: the bowstring jig.

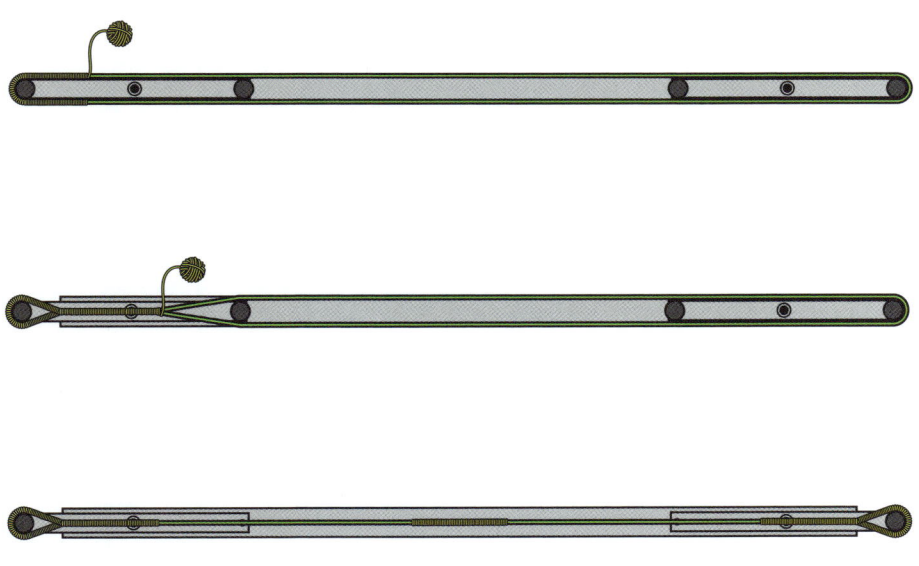

Twisted eyelet of two-strand bowstring

Knot type: Loop

Method for tying the knot: Determine the number of strands needed for the desired string diameter, then split them into two equal bundles (using a different strand colour for each bundle can make it easier to keep track).

At 20cm from the end, clamp the two bundles in a vice or similar device, and make a length of string long enough for the eyelet. To do this, take the bundle on the right between thumb and forefinger, twist it 180° clockwise, then pass the resulting strand to the left of the other bundle. Continue this process until the desired length is reached.

Next, fold the twisted part to form the eyelet and bring the strands together. Reduce the four strands to two by pairing a long strand with a short strand, and continue twisting them together for about 15cm.

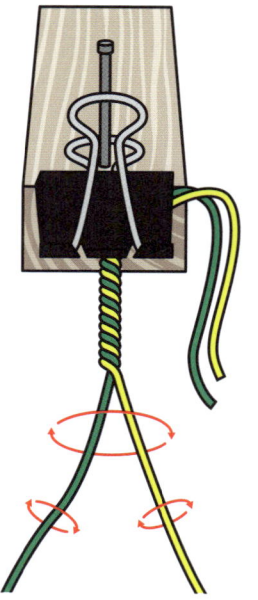
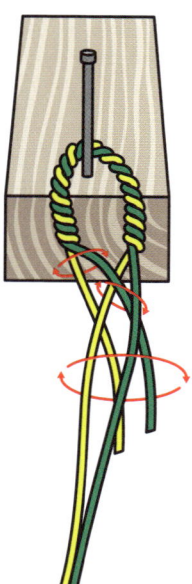

TIPS & TRICKS

If the number of strands is large, divide them into three bundles instead of two.

TOOLS

The twisted bowstring jig is used to give the twisted eyelet a tapered shape.

Spliced eyelet

See the method on page 126. To create a loop at each end of the rope, you can make two three-strand spliced eyes. This method is useful if the bowstring is already twisted.

Wrist strap

Knot type: Assembly

Use: Connect the bow to the archer's hand to prevent it from falling after a shot.

Method for tying the knot: Make a **noose** at each end of a cord.

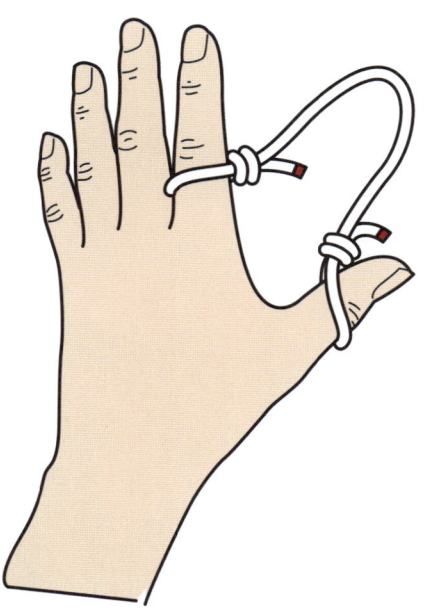

TIPS & TRICKS

The wrist strap is secured between the thumb and forefinger of the bow hand. Once the two loops are tightened around the fingers, adjust the length of the strap so you can hold the bow comfortably without it being too tight (about 10cm).

LASHING KNOTS

COMMON REUSABLE KNOTS

Lashings

Generally, a lashing is meant to hold together several sticks or wooden poles. It consists of knots and wraps. For scouts, lashings are used for camp constructions such as tripods to lift heavy water cans, support a basin for washing, build elevated platforms, and even bridges to cross streams!

TOOLS

To tighten the wraps and knots properly, use a **marlinspike hitch** (see page 262) or a frapping mallet.

Clove hitch

Use in lashings: To start or finish a lashing.

Although less discreet than the **timber hitch** and less elegant than the **constrictor knot**, the **clove hitch** is nevertheless useful because it's easy to untie, which makes it handy for adjusting, tightening or taking apart a lashing.

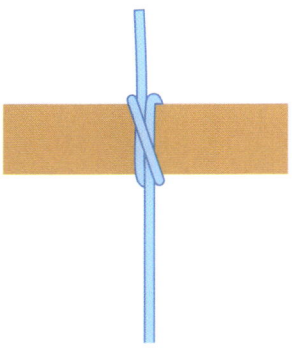

Timber hitch

Use in lashings: Start a lashing.

It's an effective and discreet way to start a lashing, as it can be 'hidden' under the wraps.

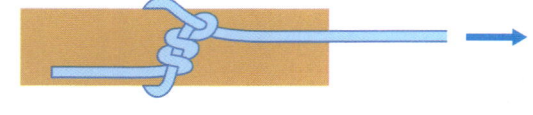

SPECIFIC LASHING KNOTS

Frapping knot

Knot type: Fastening

Use: Close a lashing.

Method for tying the knot: Bring the second **frapping turn** (see page 39) up to the centre, then pass the cord under the right strand and outward from the knot. Fold the cord to the left over the two strands of the frapping and pass it under the left strand toward the centre.

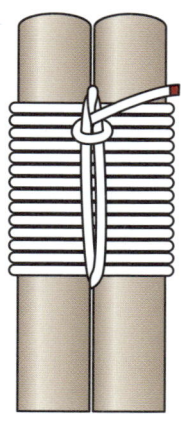

TIPS & TRICKS

Set the knot in place before tightening the frapping turns. A neater solution than the **clove hitch**, but very difficult to undo and requires frapping turns.

Lashing round turns

Knot type: Basic

Use: Structural element that gives the lashing its strength.

Method for tying the knot: Simply wrap the cord around the supports. This is the simplest way to join two supports together.

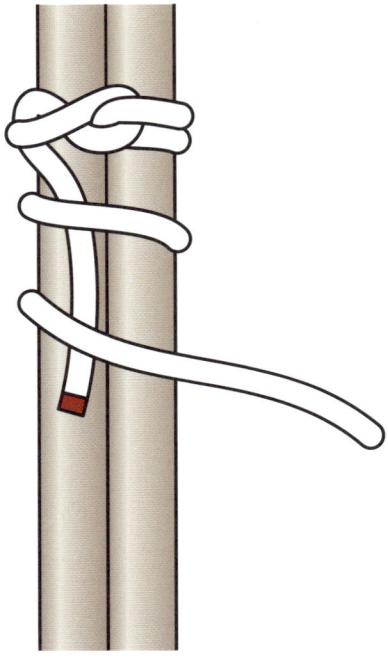

Figure eight lashing

Knot type: Basic

Use: Join multiple supports (such as a tripod lashing) or create any lashing that must withstand uneven tension on the supports.

Method for tying the knot: Wrap the cord in a figure eight around the supports. You can fill the gaps between the turns with wrapping turns.

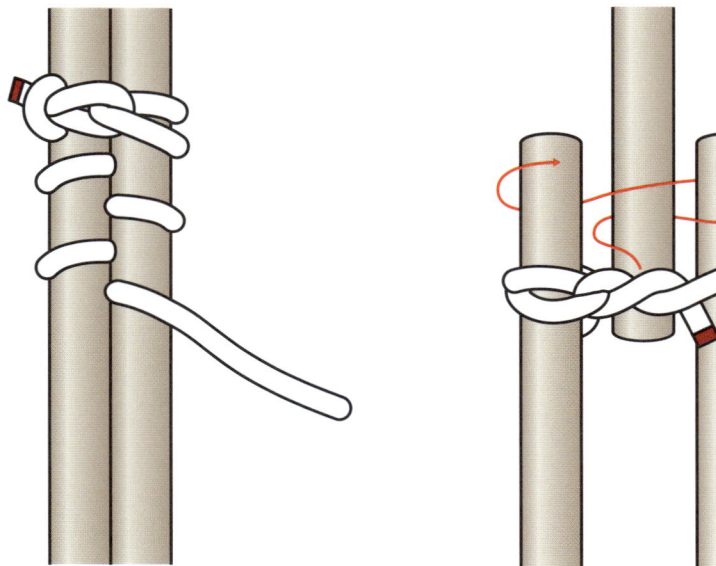

Wrapping turns

Knot type: Basic

Use: Strengthen a lashing, especially when there is a large difference between the size of the supports and the diameter of the rope used for the lashing.

Method for tying the knot: Wrap the cord a second time around the **round turns** or between the **figure eight turns**.

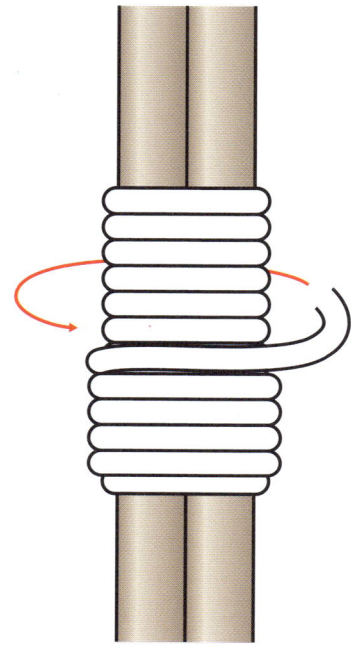

Frapping turns

Knot type: Basic

Use: Tighten the lashing further around the supports.

Method for tying the knot: Make two **round turns** around the centre of the lashing, between the supports.

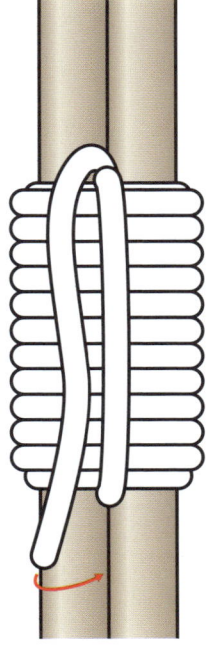

TOOLS

When the pulling forces on the supports are strong, use a **marlinspike** or a **frapping mallet** to tighten the turns properly.

End-to-end lashing

Knot type: Binding

Use: Join two or more sticks lengthwise. Reinforce a cracked stick.

Method for tying the knot: Start the lashing by tying a clove hitch or a **timber hitch** around the two sticks to be joined, then make a series of **round turns**. Finish the lashing with a **clove hitch** around the sticks.

TOOLS

Use a marlinspike or frapping mallet to tighten the turns and knots properly. End-to-end lashings come in pairs. The greater the distance between the two lashings, the stiffer the whole structure. Drive a wedge between the support and the lashing to make it even more rigid.

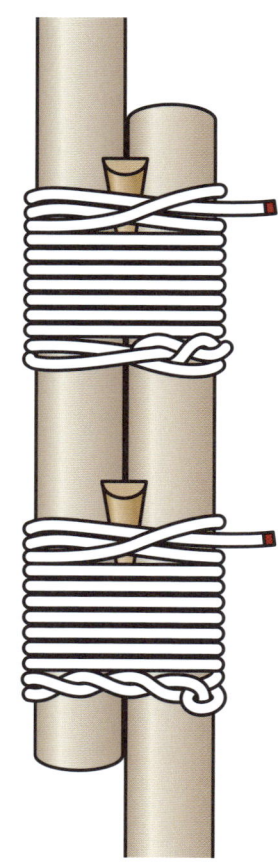

Square lashing

Knot type: Binding

Use: Join two sticks arranged perpendicular to each other.

Method for tying the knot: Start the lashing by tying a **clove hitch** around the vertical stick, just below the horizontal stick. Wrap the end around the rope, then make several **round turns** anticlockwise, alternating passes in front of and behind the sticks. Next, make a few round turns in the same direction but between the two sticks. Finish the lashing by tying a **clove hitch** on the horizontal stick.

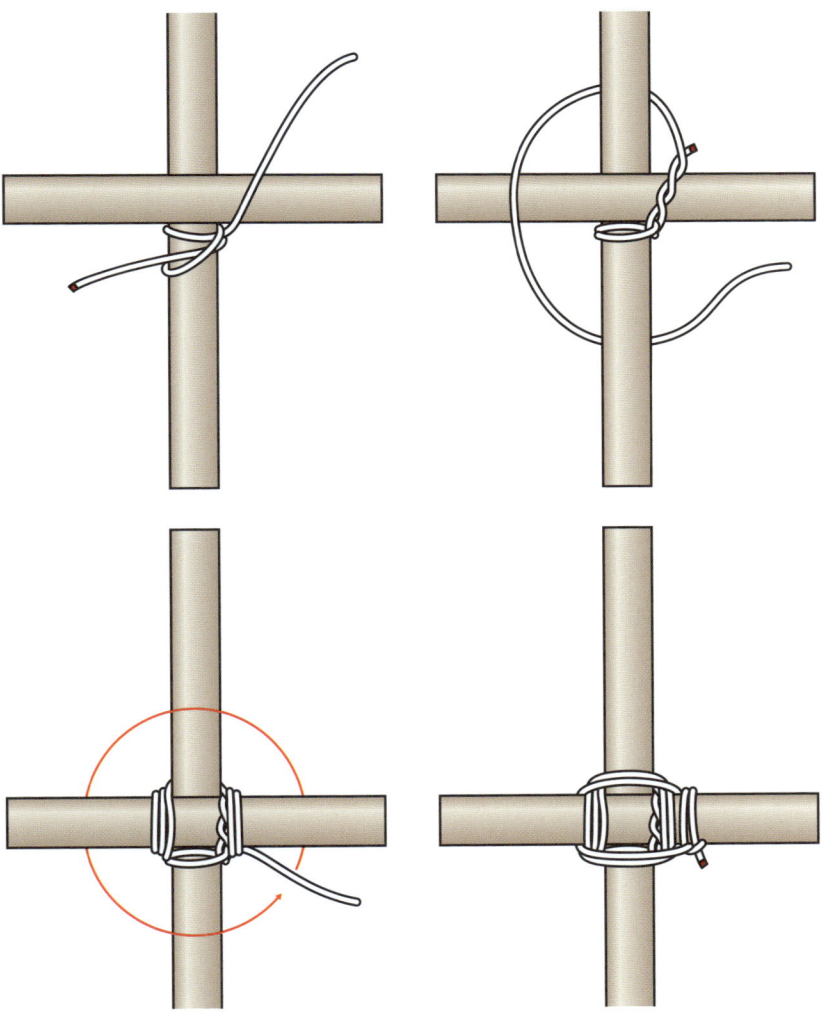

Diagonal lashing

Knot type: Binding

Use: Join two sticks crossed at a non-right angle.

Method for tying the knot: Tie a **timber hitch** around the two sticks, then make several **round turns** vertically, followed by horizontal turns. Finish the lashing by making a few turns between the two sticks and tying the end around one of the sticks with a **clove hitch**.

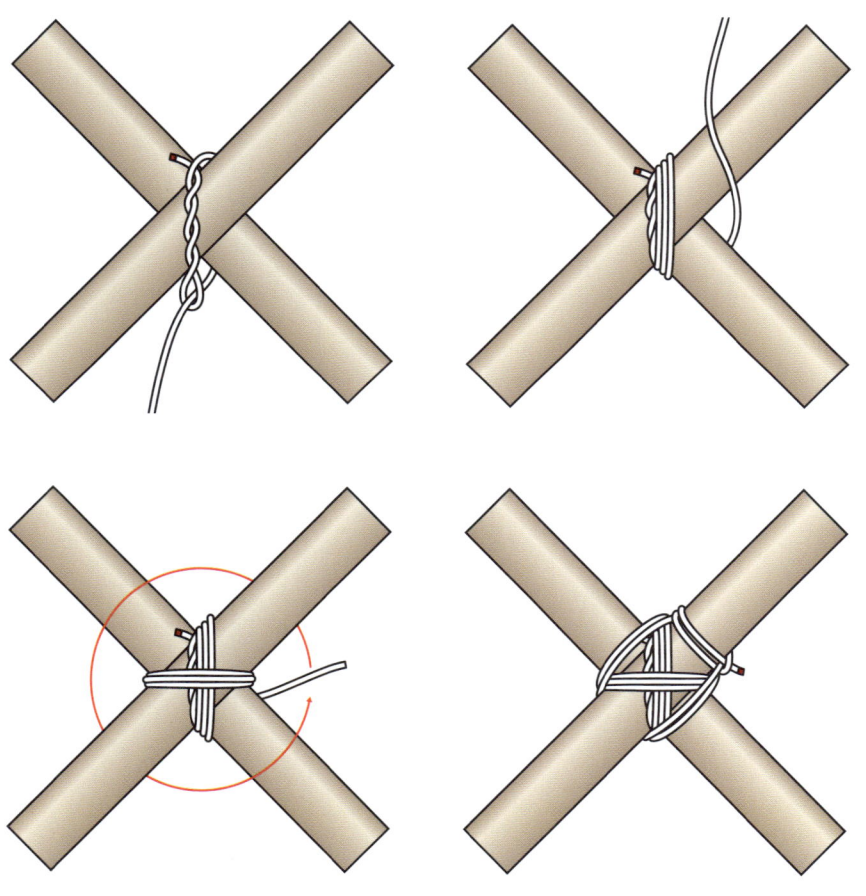

TOOLS FOR SQUARE AND DIAGONAL LASHINGS

Use a marlinspike or frapping mallet to tighten the turns and knots properly.

LASHING KNOTS
[42]

Shear lashing

Knot type: Binding

Use: Join two poles to make a lifting device or a support for a horizontal pole, for example, for a swing or a pergola.

Method for tying the knot: Attach the cord to one of the supports using a **clove hitch** or timber frapping hitch. Make a series of **round turns** around both supports, without tightening too much, and apply two **frapping turns** (see page 39). Finish by tying a **clove hitch** on one of the supports.

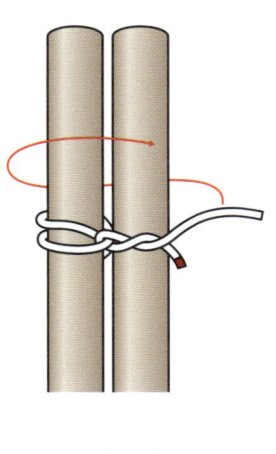
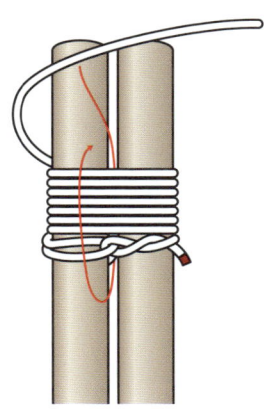
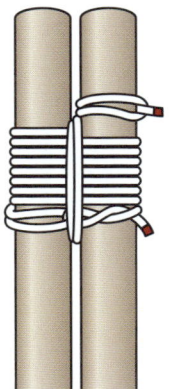

TIPS & TRICKS

No need to overtighten the lashing since the feet of the poles will be spread apart, which will help to stiffen the whole structure.

Tripod lashing

Knot type: Binding

Use: Join three sticks to create a lifting structure or a support for a basin.

Method for tying the knot: Arrange the sticks end to end. Attach the cord to one of the supports using a clove hitch or **timber hitch**, then make a series of **figure eight turns** (see page 37) around all three supports. Add two **frapping turns** (see page 39) between the left and centre sticks, then do the same on the right. Assemble the whole into a tripod shape.

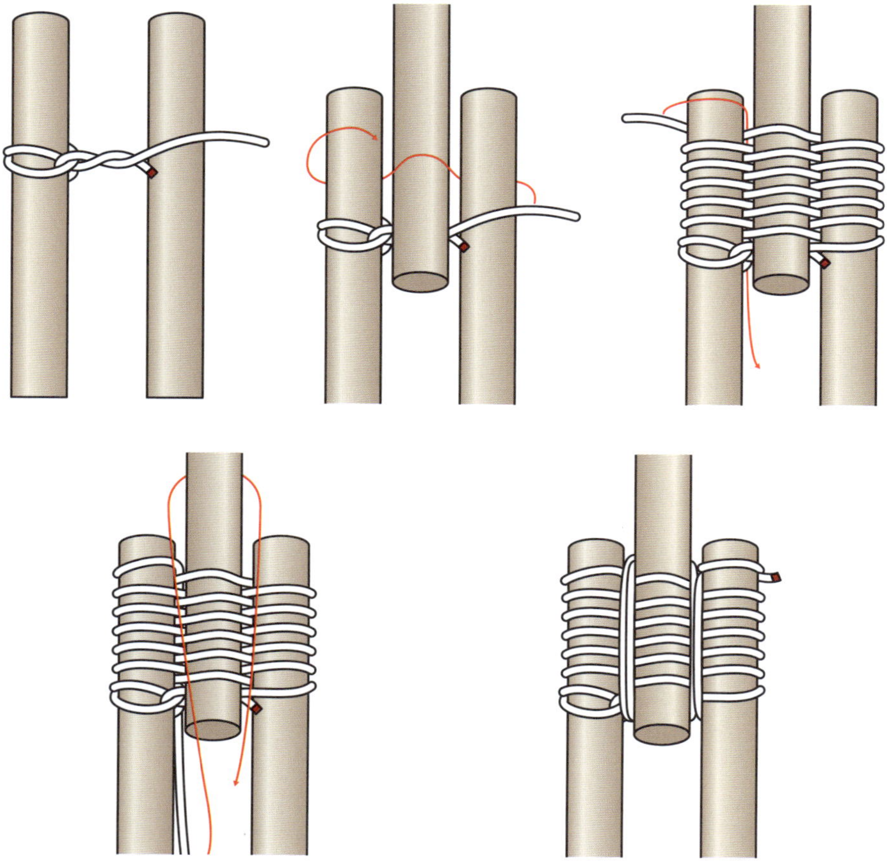

TIPS & TRICKS

No need to overtighten the lashing since the feet of the sticks will be spread apart, which helps to stiffen the entire structure.

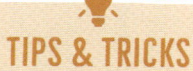

DIY
KNOTS

COMMON REUSABLE KNOTS

DIY

Many knots can be used by the skilled DIYer, especially for lifting and lowering materials, containers, and tools needed when working at height (scaffolding, trees, stairwells, etc.). A clever use of ropes can transform a ladder or wooden beam into a work platform for painting or masonry. For safety, it's crucial to secure the top of a ladder, and you should always follow safety guidelines for working at heights, including wearing a harness.

Sling

Use: The basic component of several knots used for lifting a load, as well as anchors. Ensure that the breaking strength of the rope or strap is at least three times the load to be lifted.

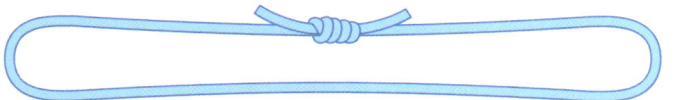

Tape knot

Use: Close a flat strap loop to sling materials for lifting onto scaffolding, etc. Leave the ends of the knot protruding about 10cm. Its shape is identical to the rethreaded overhand knot and **water knot** (page 18).

Granny knot

Use: Like the simple crossing of the **parcel lashing** (see page 63), the granny knot also allows you to change the direction of the strands . However, it is weaker than a square knot and should not be relied on for strength.

Round turn and two half-hitches

Use: Attach a rope to a container with a handle.

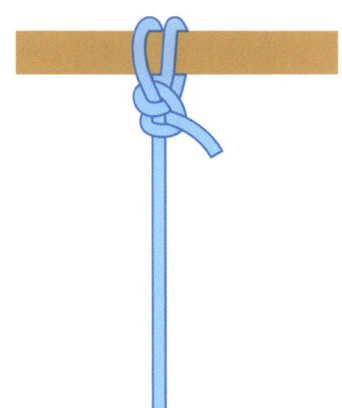

Killick hitch

Use: Raise a post, board, crowbar, etc. vertically. If the timber hitch doesn't hold well on a very smooth surface, use a **rung knot** (see page 60). Test the strength of the knots at the start of lifting.

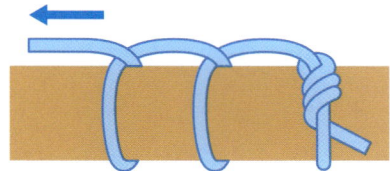

SPECIFIC DIY KNOTS

Keep your worksite neat

The stake and broom knots are used to keep a worksite clean and tidy.

Stake knot

Knot type: Fastening

Use: Temporarily mark off a worksite using red-and-white warning tape.

Method for tying the knot: Make a bight, then twist it a full turn clockwise. Slip the loop over the stake and tighten. Though not obvious at first, its construction is identical to that of the crossing knot.

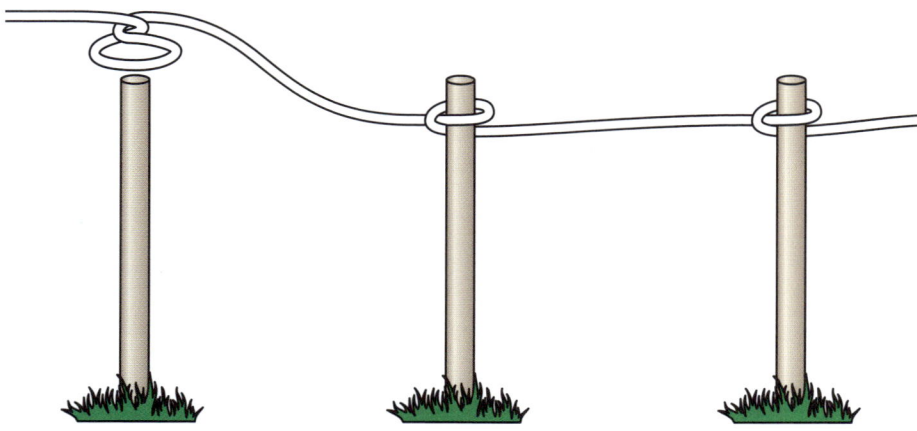

Broom knot

Knot type: Fastening

Use: Hang a broom to prevent its bristles from becoming flattened.

Method for tying the knot: Tie a **constrictor knot** around the handle, then join the ends with a **square knot**.

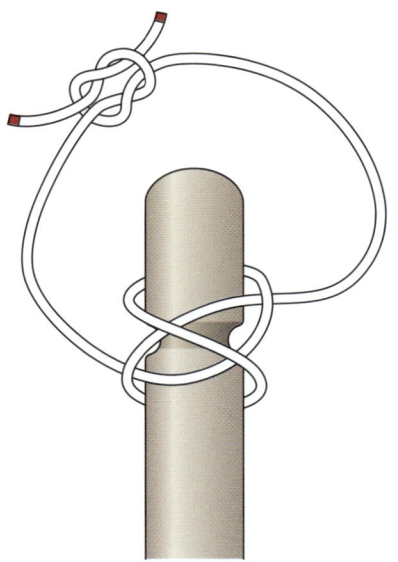

Plumb line knot

Knot type: Sliding loop

Use: Adjust the height of a plumb bob below ground level.

Method for tying the knot: Attach the standing part at the desired point to hang the plumb bob. Slip the plumb bob and tie a slipped overhand knot while positioning the plumb bob on the bight. Adjust the bight so that the plumb bob is at the correct height above the ground, then lock it by tying a **half-hitch** around the standing part.

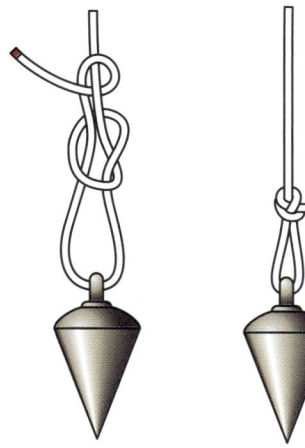

TIPS & TRICKS

If the constrictor knot slips, carve a groove into the handle using a wood file.

Plumb line knot with plate

Knot type: Stopper

Use: Create a stopper knot above the plate.

Method for tying the knot: Adjust the height of the plumb bob above the ground, then tie a slipped overhand knot to lock the line above the plate.

Lifting and lowering

The following knots are used for lifting or lowering tools, containers, packages, etc. Sometimes they are used with a hook.

Hammer knot

Knot type: Fastening

Use: This knot is used to raise or lower a hammer, mallet, sledgehammer, or any similar tool.

Method for tying the knot: For a light hammer, simply tie a **clove hitch** around the head. For a heavy sledgehammer, bring the crossing of the clove hitch over the top of the head and secure it with a bowline.

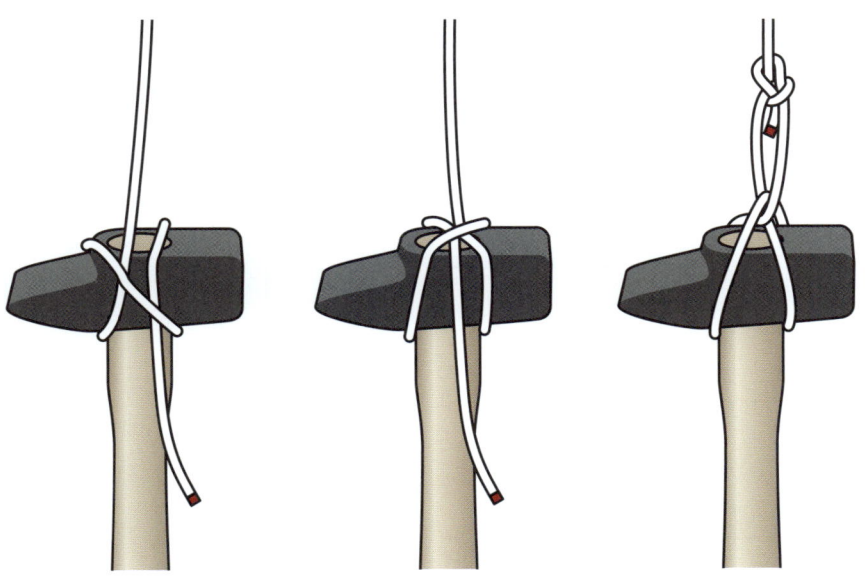

Axe knot

Don't confuse the hammer knot with the axe knot, which is used to lift an axe or other tool by the handle-first. For the axe knot, form a bowline or another fixed loop around the tool's handle, then pass the standing part around the blade and tie two spaced half-hitches on the handle. For heavy tools, such as sledgehammers or picks, the axe knot is more suitable than the hammer knot.

Bucket knot

Knot type: Fastening

Use: Retrieve the rope used to lower a bucket or other object with a handle.

Method for tying the knot: Double the rope, then pass the bight around the bucket handle. Near the handle, double one of the standing parts and tuck it between the strands of the bight and the other standing part, following the front-to-back directions. Pull on the slipped standing part to release the bucket.

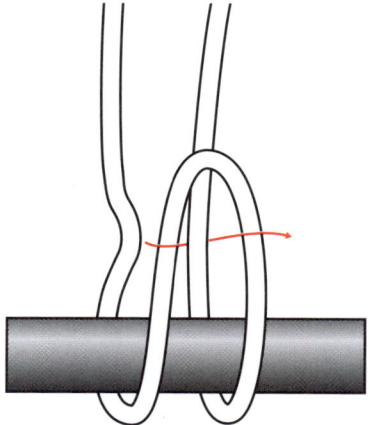

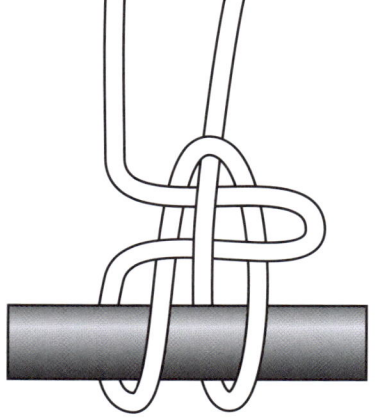

Barrel hitch

Knot type: Sling

Use: Lift a barrel, drum, bucket, or any other open container without a handle.

Method for tying the knot: Place the container on the rope, then tie a **half-hitch** above the opening. Open the half-hitch and slide a bight on each side of the container. Attach the end to the standing part using a **bowline**.

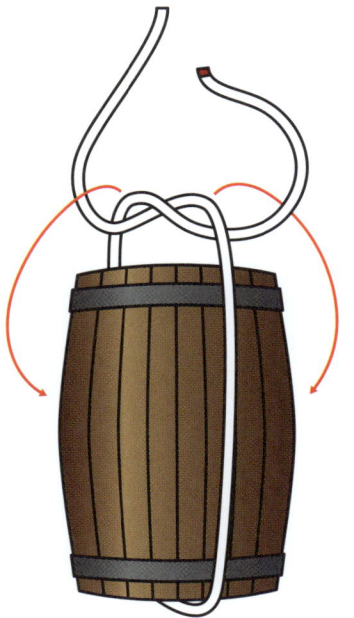

Package sling

Knot type: Sling

Use: Provide a bag, barrel, bale, or other object with an attachment point for a lifting device (block, crane, etc.).

Method for tying the knot: See **bale sling** (see page 21) in the basic knots section.

Blackwall hitch

Knot type: Fastening

Use: Put a rope under tension.

Method for tying the knot: Tie a **half-hitch** around the back of the hook. The loaded strand jams the working end against the base of the hook.

TIPS & TRICKS

To attach to a hook, use a **double cat's paw knot** (see page 58) if the sling is long enough.

TIPS & TRICKS

The rope must fill the hook properly to hold securely. Do not use this knot for lifting a load (preferably a **round turn and two half-hitches**).

Round turn and two half-hitches on a hook

Knot type: Fastening

Use: Put a rope under tension or lift a load.

Method for tying the knot: See **round turn and two half-hitches** (see page 49) in the common knots section. A reliable knot for all situations.

Cow hitch on a hook

Knot type: Fastening

Use: Secure a fixed loop or sling on a hook.

Method for tying the knot: Fold back the bight of the sling to be attached, then slip the loops over the hook.

Caution: It may be difficult to undo after lifting a heavy load.

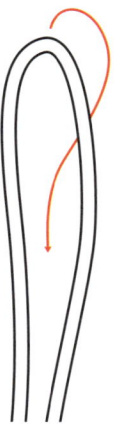
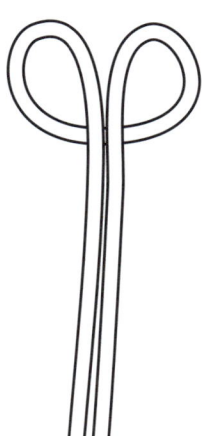
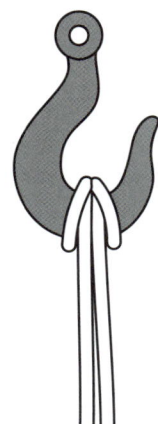

Double cat's paw

Knot type: Fastening

Method for tying the knot: Fold back the bight of the sling to be attached, as if making a **cow hitch**, then twist each loop towards the centre at least three times (540°). Slip the loops over the hook.

Caution: Even after lifting a heavy load, the knot comes undone easily.

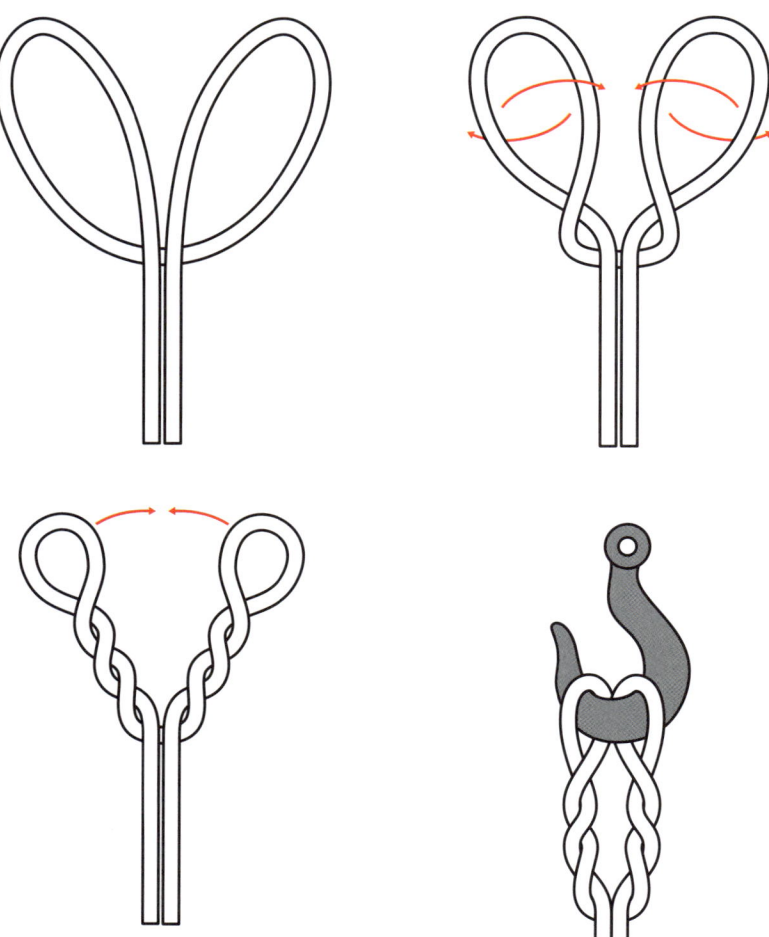

Bellringers knot

Knot type: Fastening

Use: Stow a hanging rope.

Method for tying the knot: Tie a **half-hitch** around the standing part, then insert the coil of rope. Add a second half-hitch to make it more secure. Bell ringers are said to have used this knot to keep the bell rope from dragging on the ground, hence its name. You could say it's a variation of the sheepshank.

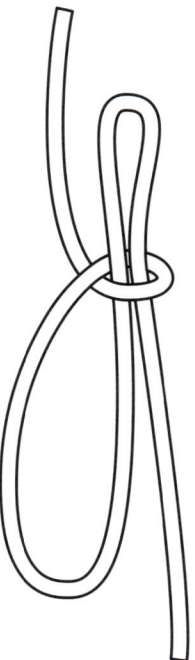 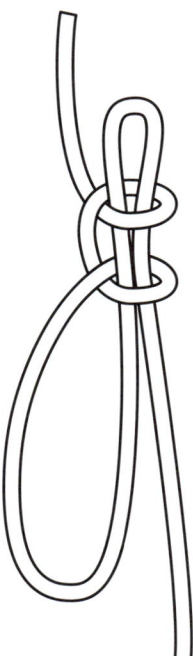

Ladders and platforms

The following knots allow you to create a platform for lifting objects or potentially working at height, or to secure a ladder.

Rung knot

Knot type: Fastening

Use: Attach the rope of a sliding ladder to the first rung and securely tie it to any roughly round-sectioned support.

Method for tying the knot: See **groundline hitch** (page 22)

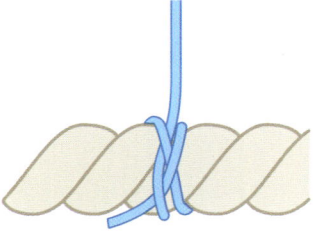

Mooring knot

Knot type: Fastening

Use: Secure the top of a ladder to prevent lateral movement or to lift it.

Method for tying the knot: Tie a **bowline** with the rope's end. Pass the loop through the ladder between the first and second rung, then slip the loop over the ladder's uprights. Secure the standing part to a safe anchor point. This knot was once used by firefighters.

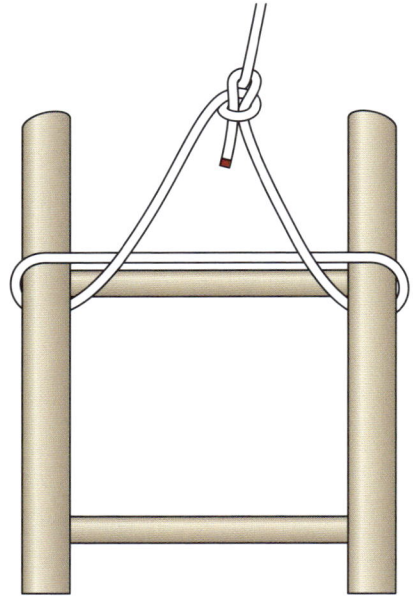

TIPS & TRICKS

For a temporary fastening, slip the end to make it easy to untie.

Ladder sling

Knot type: Loop

Use: Sling a ladder to create a platform.

Method for tying the knot: Tie a **sheepshank** at the end of the rope, flip the half-hitch with the lower strand, then bring the two half-hitches together to form two loops. Slip a loop over each of the ladder's side rails. Secure the shorter end to the standing part using a **bowline**.

TIPS & TRICKS

To prevent the loops from slipping off the ladder's side rails, pass each loop through the ladder before slipping it over. If the rope is slippery, it's better to use a Spanish bowline.

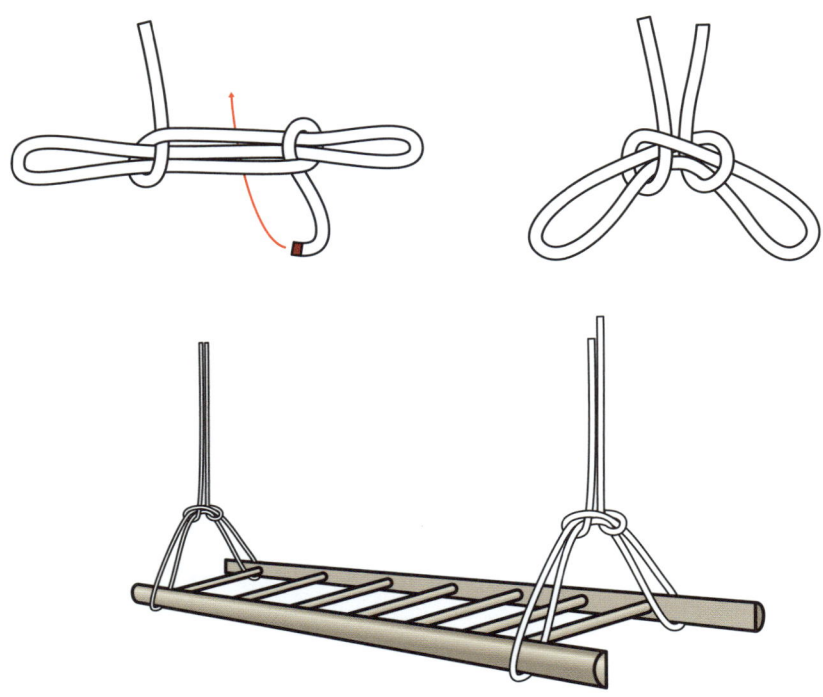

Plank sling

Knot type: Fastening

Use: Hang a board horizontally to use as a work platform or swing seat.

Method for tying the knot: Working from left to right, make **two round turns** around one end of the board, ensuring that the rope ends are on opposite sides of the board. Pass the left strand over the middle strand. Then, pass what is now the left strand over everything and around the end of the board. Secure the shorter end to the standing part with a **bowline**. Repeat the same at the other end of the board.

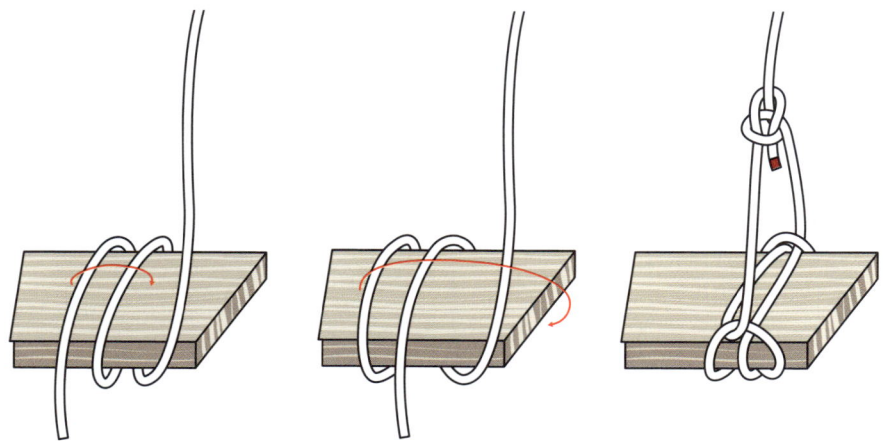

Wrapping

Using ribbons or twine, you can wrap a package decoratively without tape or glue.
DIYers can secure a large parcel, hold a protective cover on an object, etc.
Wrapping knots are essential whether brightening up your
gifts or ensuring a stress-free house move!

Parcel lashing

Knot type: Lacing

Method for tying the knot: Wrap the package in one direction and cross the strands.
Then pass one strand around the package in the other direction. Join the ends using a **reef knot**, a **packing knot**, or a **bow knot** (see the simple shoelace knot on page 240).

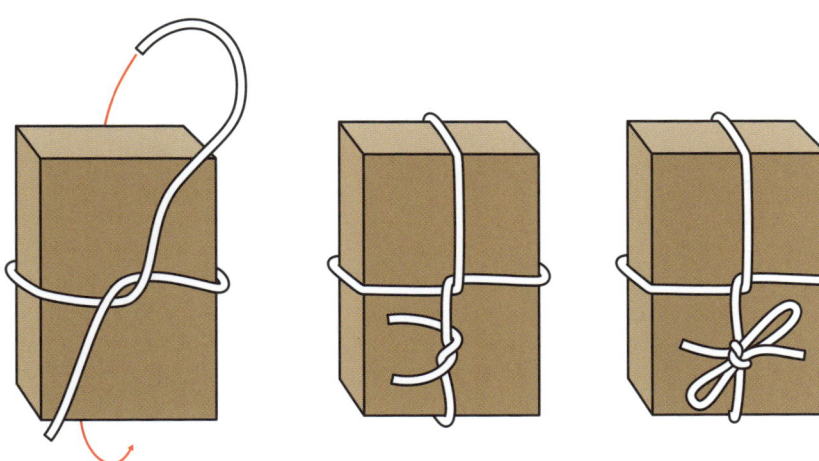

TIPS & TRICKS

The simplest method (above) allows you to offset the finishing knot. To make the
finishing knot at the centre of the package, pass the strand wrapping the package
over the central crossing and bring it back on itself to tie the two ends together.

Enhanced parcel lashing

Knot type: Lacing

Method for tying the knot: Wrap a corner of the package, then cross the strands on the underside. Pass each end through the part that surrounds the corner of the package and secure with a **reef knot** or a **bow knot** (see the simple shoelace knot on page 240).

Packing knot

Knot type: Fastening

Use: To lift a post, a board, a crowbar, etc. vertically.

Method for tying the knot: Anchor securely with a tight **timber hitch**, then apply **two half-hitches** on the upper half of the object to be lifted, spaced according to the length of the support. If the standing part is inaccessible because it is tied off or runs through a pulley, start with the half-hitches and finish with the anchor knot.

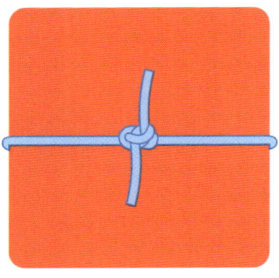

TIPS & TRICKS

If the timber hitch doesn't hold well on a very smooth support, use a **ladder rung knot** instead. Test the strength of the knots before lifting.

Crossing knot

Knot type: Fastening

Method for tying the knot: Pass once around the support so that it crosses itself on the front. Then lead it under the support and over the standing part. Pull up to tighten the twine, then pull down. Repeat if necessary.

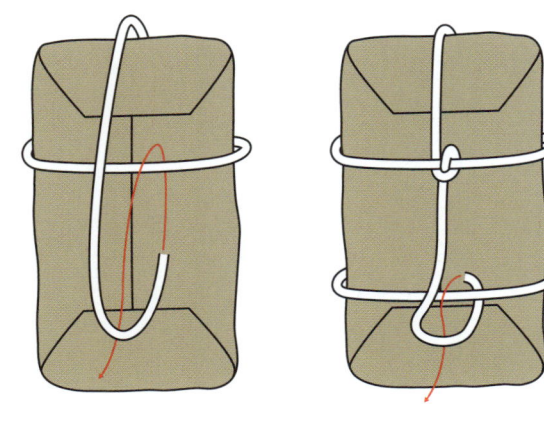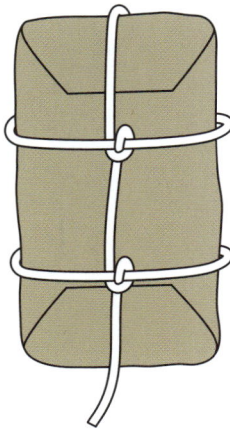

TIPS & TRICKS

Start tying the package with a **packing knot** around it, then send the working end to the opposite side of the package, turning in the other direction. This knot represents an important technique in rope work and can be adapted to many situations. See, for example, the **stake knot** (page 50).

Bow knot

The bow knot, a finishing knot with two loops, is probably the most famous decorative knot in the world. (See the **shoelace knot** on page 240.)

CAMPING KNOTS

COMMON REUSABLE KNOTS

Camping

An outdoors lifestyle. Using tension and anchor knots, you can make your own Canadian-style tent from tarps and ropes to shelter the camp's kitchen and dining tables. With a ladder made from bamboo rungs and cords, you can create access to a cabin or a hideout in a tree. Or, you can add a handle to a bottle to carry water around the camp or on a short hike. Knots are useful for everything!

Clove hitch

Use: Tie a rope to a support, start a lashing, close a bag.

Caution: Quick to tie and easy to undo, the clove hitch can, however, perform poorly under heavy strain. The clove hitch, like the **timber hitch** and the **round turn and two half-hitches**, is an anchoring knot (used on stakes, posts, tree trunks, etc.).

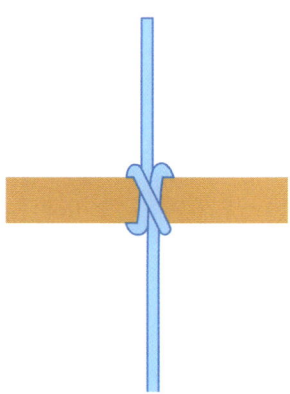

Timber hitch

Use: Anchor the ridge rope of a Canadian-style tent or a simple clothesline to a tree.

Caution: The timber hitch is unsuitable as an anchoring knot for a knotted rope or ladder. Note: The **killick hitch** can be used to climb vertically any construction element at height. However, a **groundline hitch** is preferred when the support is very smooth.

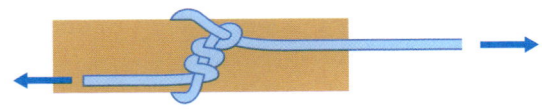

Round turn and two half-hitches

Use: Secure any kind of rope under tension, from a clothesline to a zip line. It is extremely reliable and adapts to every situation.

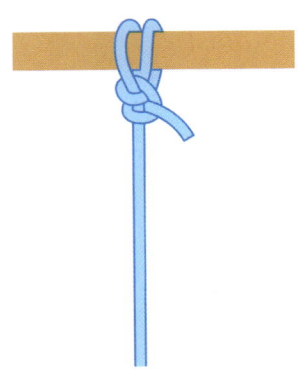

SPECIFIC CAMPING KNOTS

Anchor knots

The bowline knot, the harness knot, and the tent guyline knot are all used for anchoring – on stakes, posts, tree trunks, etc.

Bowline with running

Knot type: Loop

Use: Attach a rope to a tree or other support to start a clothesline, a tent ridgepole, or a zip line anchor point. This knot is the most suitable fastening method for many situations. It's easy to move along its support and can be quickly untied.

Method for tying the knot: Tie a **bowline knot**, then pull the standing part through the loop to create a sliding loop. (It's not necessary to pass the entire length of the rope through the loop.)

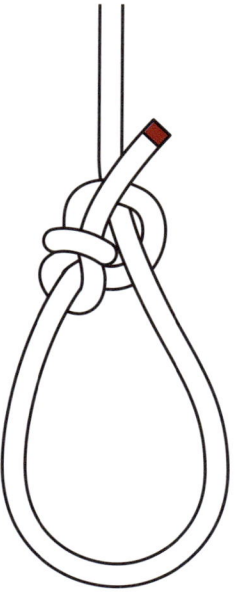

Harness loop

Knot type: Loop

Use: Make a loop in a rope without using the ends, to create an attachment point.

Method for tying the knot: Tie a **half-hitch** around the standing part, then pass the standing part under this half-hitch. Pass the bight of the half-hitch under the standing part and over itself to form the loop. Tighten the knot. A classic hauling knot, it was once used to tow cannons.

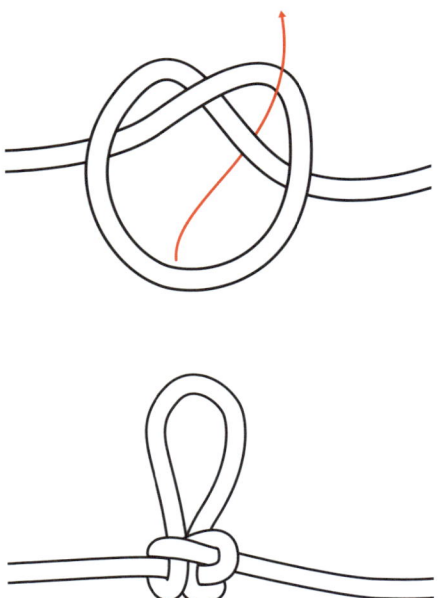

Tent guyline knot

Knot type: Fastening

Use: Attach a guyline to your tent or any other rope to a loop, using the **double sheet bend**. It's a very secure knot designed to withstand all kinds of weather conditions.

Method for tying the knot: Using the guyline cord, tie a **double sheet bend** on the sewn loop attached to the tent.

Tension knots

The midshipman's hitch, tautline hitch trucker's knot, slipped sheet bend, wet weather hitch, and hump bend are all tension knots used for guylines and ridge ropes.

Midshipman's hitch

Knot type: Loop

Use: Tighten a tent guyline, a sunshade, or even an improvised clothesline.

Method for tying the knot: Proceed in the same way as described on page 16. You can slip the locking half-hitch to undo the knot more quickly.

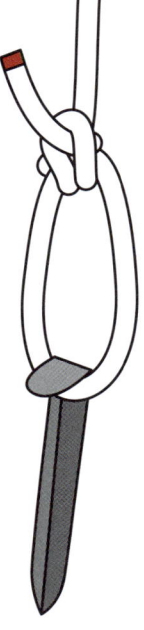

Tautline hitch

Knot type: Loop

Use: Tighten the guylines of Canadian tents and other shelters.

Method for tying the knot: Wrap the rope around the anchor point (post, peg, etc.), then tie a tautline hitch on the standing part. Adjust the tension by sliding the knot along the standing part. This knot is quite similar to the midshipman's hitch but is better suited for thicker ropes.

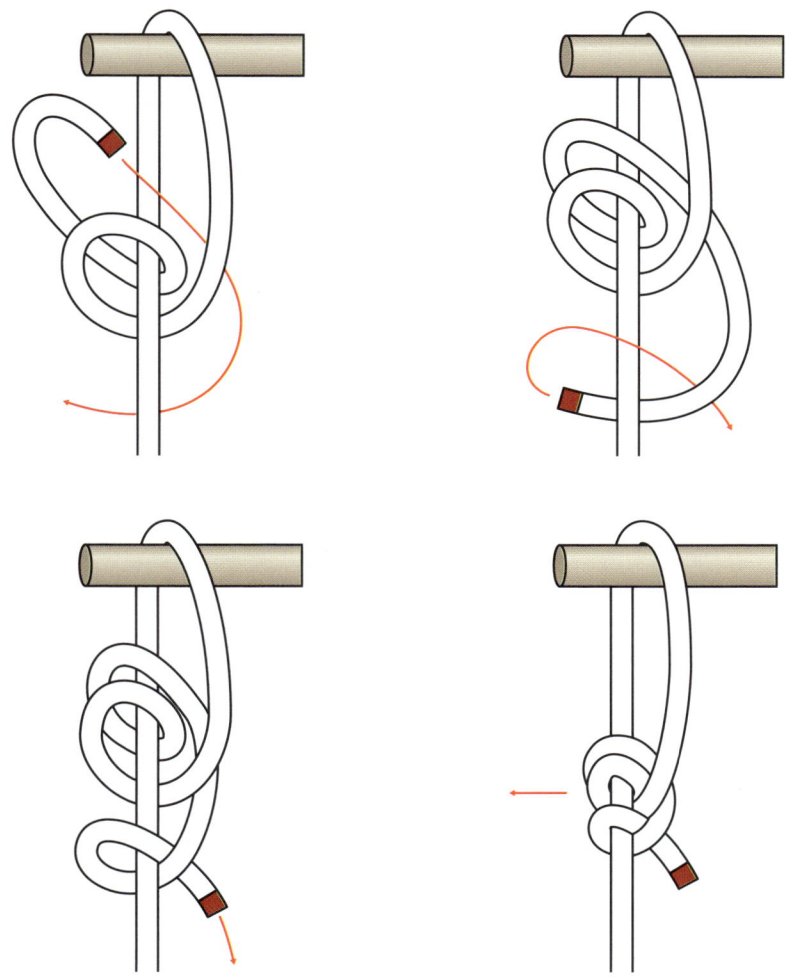

Trucker's knot

Knot type: Assembly

Use: Makeshift pulley for tightening ropes very tightly.

Method for tying the knot: Create a loop at a suitable distance from the end of the rope (see **figure eight loop on a bight** or **alpine butterfly loop** on pages 161 or 166). Pass the end through the anchor point (ring, post, etc.) and then through the rope loop. Temporarily secure the knot by tying a **slipped half-hitch** around the two strands of the pulley. Make several **half-hitches** for a durable lock. The knot's name comes from its effectiveness in tightening the ropes used to secure a load on a truck or trailer bed.

Caution: Friction between the ropes greatly reduces its efficiency compared to a pulley equipped with sheaves.

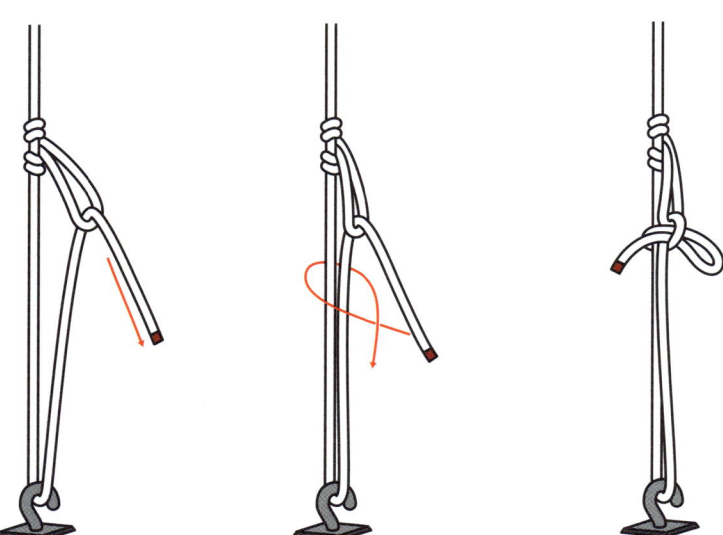

Slipped sheet bend

Knot type: Bend

Use: Join two ropes together temporarily in a way that allows for quick untying. This is especially well suited to setting up a large tent or marquee. Practical when one end has a fixed loop (**spliced eye, bowline**).

Method for tying the knot: Tie a **simple sheet bend**, but before making the final tuck, double the end to form a bight.

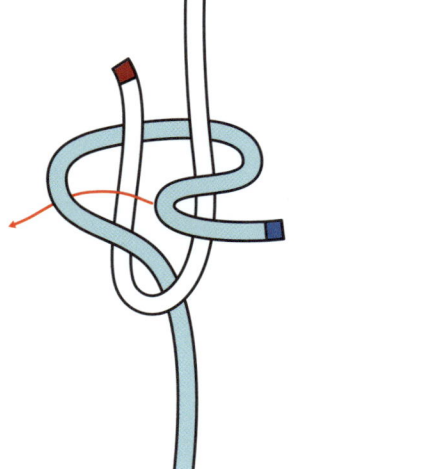

Wet weather hitch knot

Knot type: Fastening

Use: Secure a rope to an anchor point that needs to be retightened regularly, such as a Canadian tent guyline.

Method for tying the knot: Make a **turn** around the support, then pass over the standing part and make another turn. Next, double the end and tie a **half-hitch** around the standing part. Tighten the slipped half-hitch close to the anchor point.

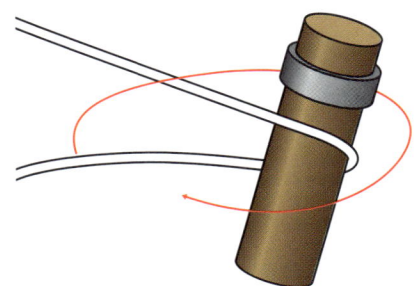

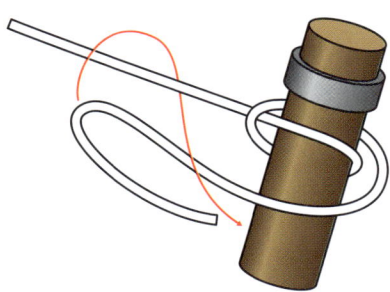

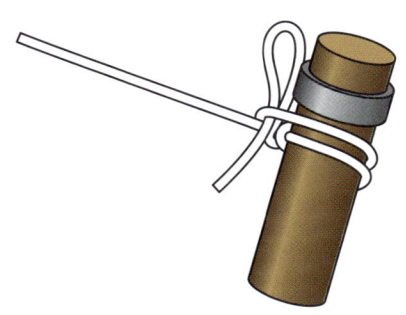

Adjustable bend

Knot type: Bend

Use: Join two ropes together in an adjustable way, especially for setting up Canadian-style tents but also for securing a load. It's certainly the best tension knot for rope-to-rope applications.

Method for tying the knot: Tie a **rolling hitch** (see page 258) with each rope end around the standing part of the other rope.

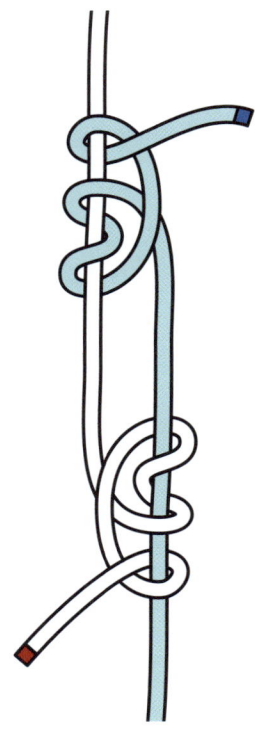

Climbing trees

The harness knot rope, ladder assembly, ladder knot, and ladder rung splice provide reliable ways to get up high.

Harness knot rope

Knot type: Assembly

Use: Add loops to a rope to make climbing easier. Similar to the simple knot rope, this version is easier to climb because it has loops.

Method for tying the knot: Tie **harness loops** (see page 71) at regular intervals suited to the climbers' size. Alternatively, tie **alpine butterfly loops** (page 166). Securely attach the top end of the rope with a **round turn and two half-hitches** or a secured **bowline**.

TIPS & TRICKS

Anchoring the bottom end of the rope will make climbing easier. Use a rope designed for climbing.

Ladder assembly

Knot type: Assembly

Use: Climb a tree or a camp structure.

Method for tying the knot: Double the rope, then attach the rungs at equal distances using a **temporary ladder knot** (see page 80) or a **fixed ladder rung splice** (see page 81). Use a file to carve a notch all around each rung (a few centimetres at each end) to hold the rope.

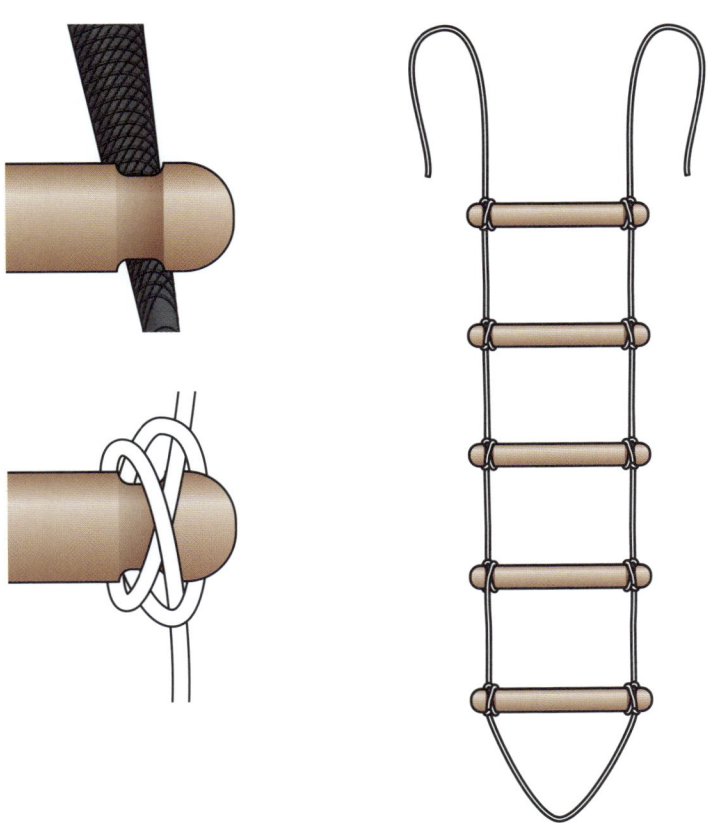

TIPS & TRICKS

To prevent the ladder from twisting, make sure that the anchor points are spaced a rung's width apart.

Ladder knot

Knot type: Assembly

Use: Secure a wooden rung or step to a rope to make a ladder. For a more durable method, opt for the **fixed ladder rung splice**.

Method for tying the knot: Fold the rope in half and make a full twist. Pass the first crossing through the loop while keeping the standing parts apart. Place the rung in the centre of the knot (the 'x' in the diagram) and tighten. The standing parts should be positioned directly opposite each other.

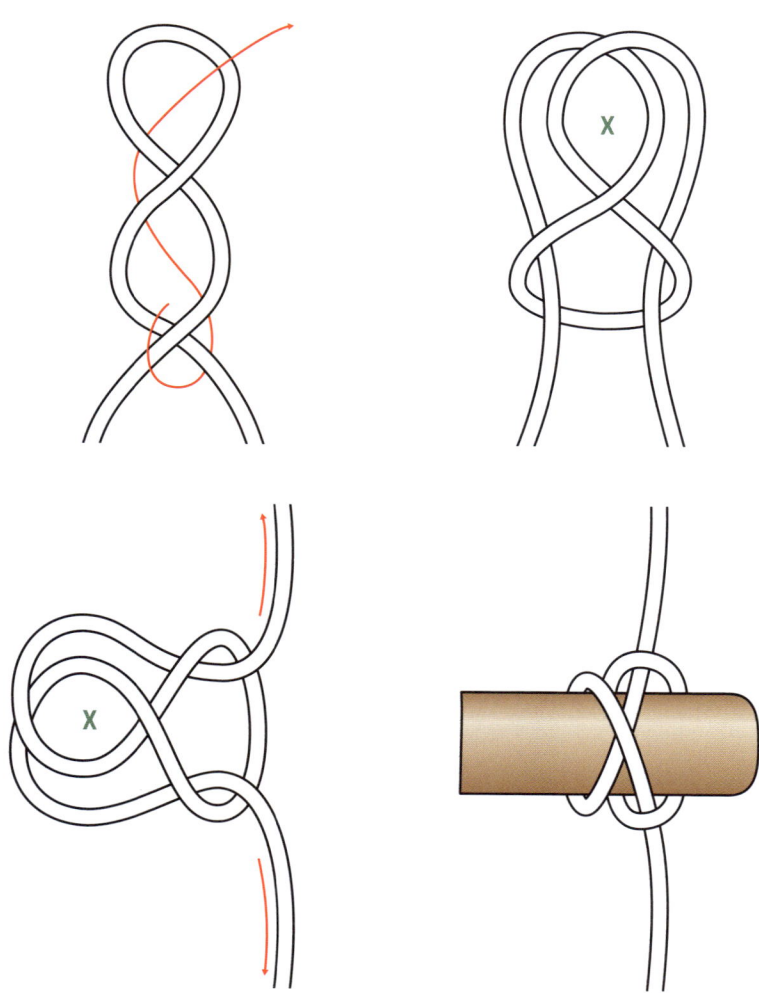

Ladder rung splice

Knot type: Assembly

Method for tying the knot: Preferably use a four-strand rope. Separate the strands and insert the rung into the opening. Apply **serving** or (better) a **Turk's head knot** (see page 120) to each side of the rung to secure it.

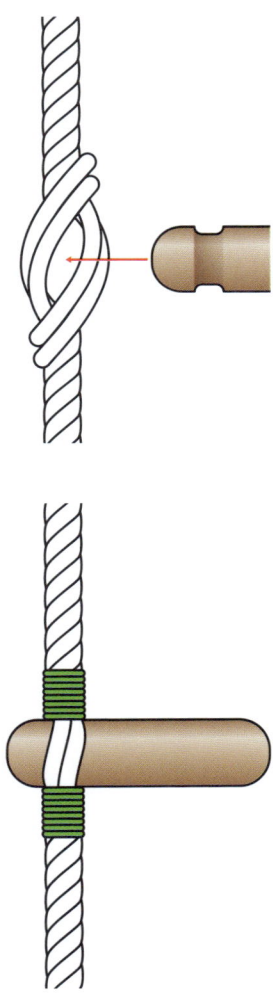

Making a swing

To make the most of your camping fun!

Swing knot

Knot type: Fastening

Use: Attach a swing rope to a tree branch or other support in a way that significantly reduces friction.

Method for tying the knot: Pass the end behind and over the support, then tie a **clove hitch**. Next, pass the end behind the standing part and under the first crossing. Leave at least 30cm of the end protruding.

Caution: Regularly check the attachment point for wear and slippage.

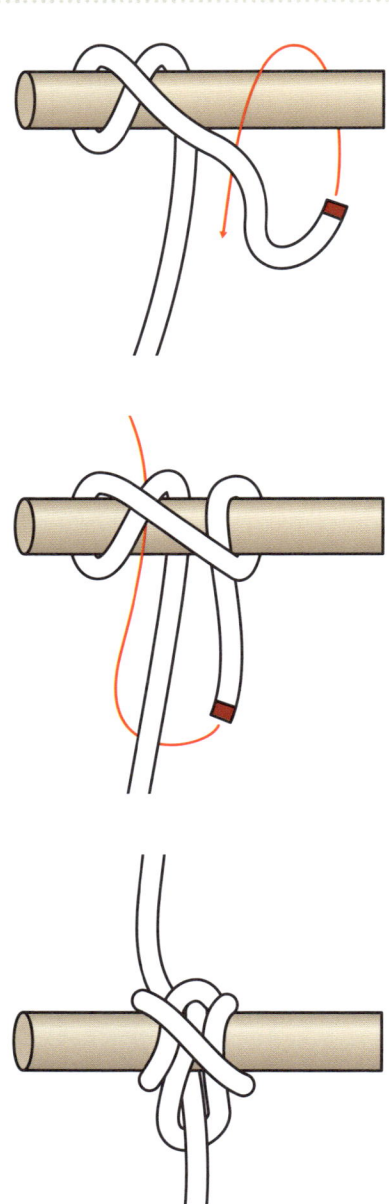

Swing seat

Knot type: Assembly

Use: Make a seat for a swing, a hoist, or a chair for working at height.

Method for tying the knot: Take a wooden plank of suitable length and drill four holes with diameters large enough for the rope to pass through. Fold the rope in half and – starting from underneath the seat – pass the ends through the corresponding holes. Join the ends under the seat using a **single sheet bend**, **double sheet bend** or a **splice**. Form the upper eye by adding a **lashing** around the four gathered strands. Make a second lashing around the crossing beneath the seat. Test the seat's strength before use.

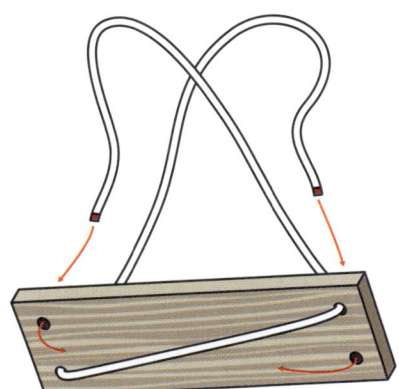 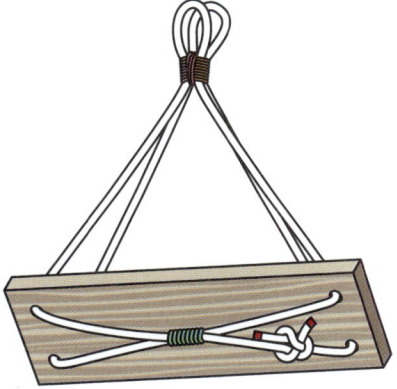

TIPS & TRICKS

Attach the swing rope to the seat using a **double sheet bend**, and the swing to a sturdy branch using the **swing knot** (see page 82). For a makeshift seat, tie a log of the right length to the rope using a **constrictor knot** secured with a **bowline**.

Repairing worn ropes

The plain whipping, the Zeppelin bend, and the hunter's
bend are used to repair worn ropes.

Plain whipping

Knot type: Binding

Use: Prevent the end of a rope from fraying or unravelling.

Method for tying the knot: Place a loop of the twine on the rope to be whipped, then make several turns, 'pinching' the loop. Pass the end of the twine through the loop, then pull the other end to 'bury the join' beneath the whipping turns. The whipping should be as wide as the diameter of the rope it's applied to.

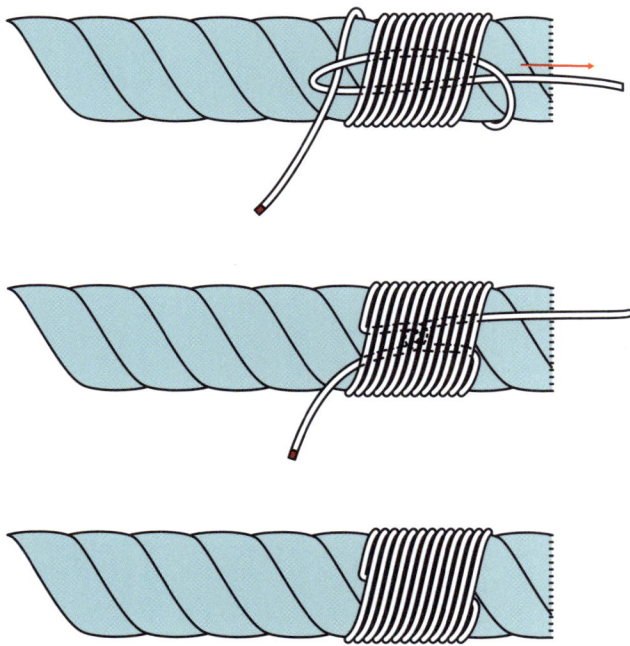

Zeppelin bend

Knot type: Bend

Use: Join the two ends of a broken – or cut, if about to break – rope.

Method for tying the knot: Tie a loop in each end to be joined, making sure that one is shaped like the number 6 and the other like the number 9. Note that the standing part of the 6 is underneath, while that of the 9 is on top. Place the 6 over the 9, then pass the end of the 6 through the centre of the knot from underneath, and the end of the 9 over the top. The result is two interlocking overhand knots. Tighten gradually by alternately pulling on the standing parts and the ends. Surprisingly little known for such a strong knot, it is compact and easy to tie. It is also called the Rosendahl bend.

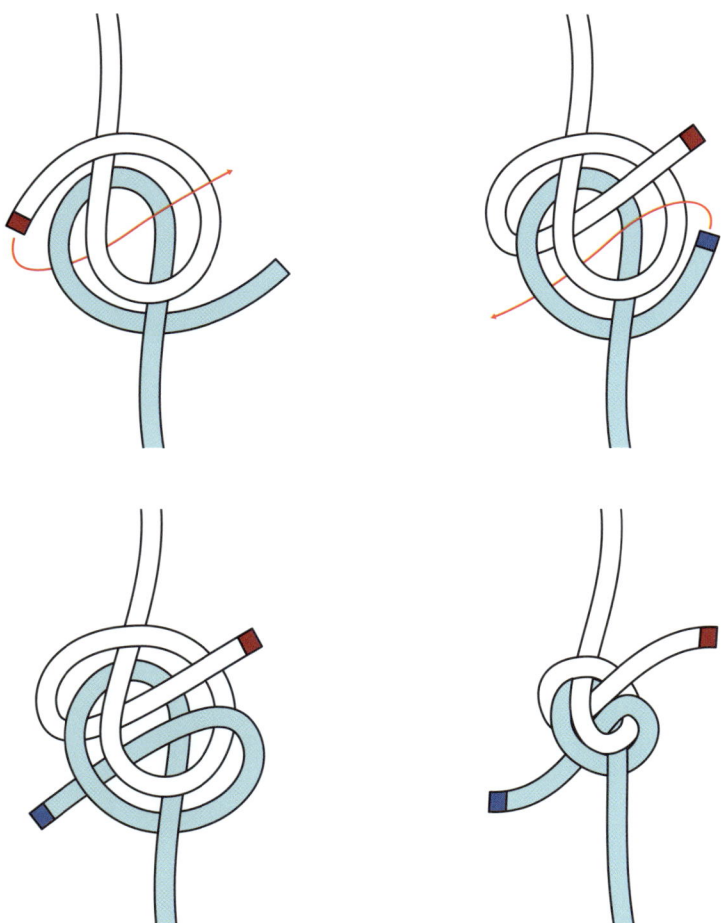

Hunter's bend

Knot type: Bend

Method for tying the knot: Tie a loop on each rope to be joined – one with the end underneath, the other with it on top. Place the first over the second and pass the ends through the centre of the knot. Ensure that the lower strand passes through the top knot from top to bottom and that the other strand passes the opposite way.

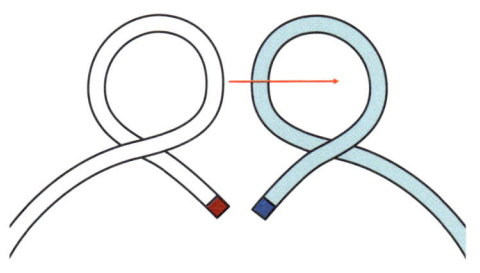

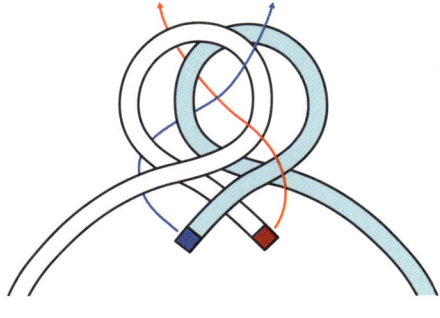

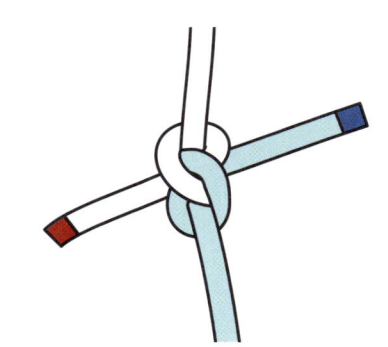

Sharing a drink with friends with the bottle sling knot

Knot type: Binding

Use: Create a handle to hang a jug, bottle, or any other container with a bulge around the neck.

Method for tying the knot: Tie a **slip knot**, then form a loop within its loop. Place this loop over and around the central **half-knot**. Pass the original slip loop once over and once under to exit through the middle of the knot (where the 'x' is) and tighten. Before tying the ends together with a **sheet bend**, pass one end through the opposite loop to create the handle. It is also called the bottle knot.

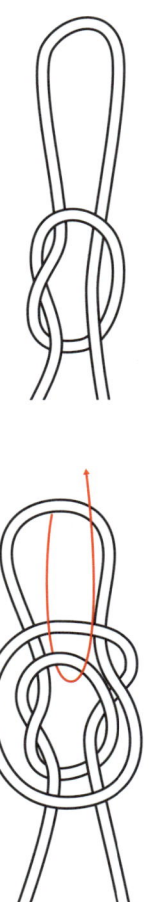
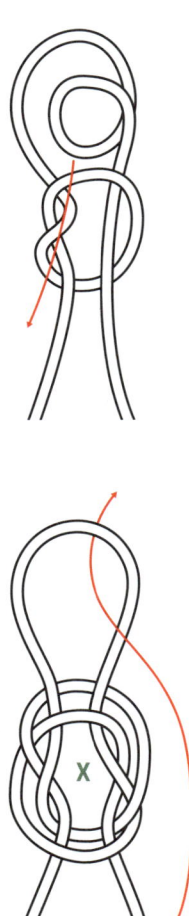

DECORATIVE KNOTS

DECORATIVE KNOTS

Stopper knots

Among the many knots with one, two, or three loops, here's a selection
of the most well-known and attractive for creating coat buttons,
closing a collar, tying a bracelet, or making a decorative net.

Love knot

Knot type: Loop

Use: Join two strands into a button shape
to form a loop, close a collar or bracelet,
or create a decorative net.

Method for tying the knot: Tie an overhand
knot, then pass a strand through this first
overhand knot. Make sure the standing part
of the first strand and the working end of
the second strand pass over the loop of the
knot. Next, form a second overhand knot
whose loop surrounds the crossing of the
first. Tighten by pulling simultaneously
on both strands on each side of the knot.
There are several knots known as love knots,
all characterised by two interlaced overhand
knots. The version presented here is based
on the sailor's cross knot.

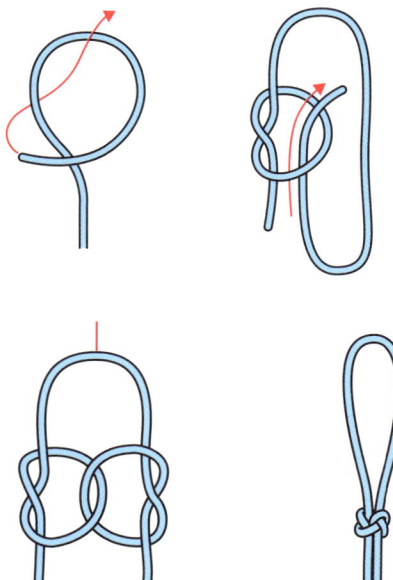

Love knot: alternative method

An alternative method involves tying a two-strand wall knot.

Sailor's cross

Knot type: Loop

Use: Create a triple, or even quadruple, loop by knotting the standing parts, as a starting point for a mesh bag or a macramé project.

Method for tying the knot: Form a first overhand knot with the working end passing over its loop. Bring the working end back into the loop of the first overhand knot, making sure it passes from bottom to top, then under and over the loop. Tighten by holding both ends in one hand and the loop in the other. At this point, you have created a **love knot**. Next, pull each loop through the crossing of the opposite overhand knot. Tighten and even out the loop sizes.

Variation: by omitting the top loop, the knot can be made with just two strands.

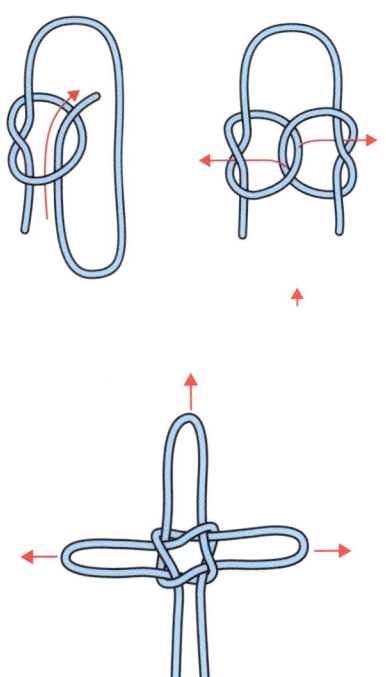

Triskelion knot

Knot type: Loop

Method for tying the knot: Fold the rope in half and form two loops in the centre to create three branches. Fold each strand over its neighbour, as in a **Turk's head knot**. Turn the knot over and tie another Turk's head knot.

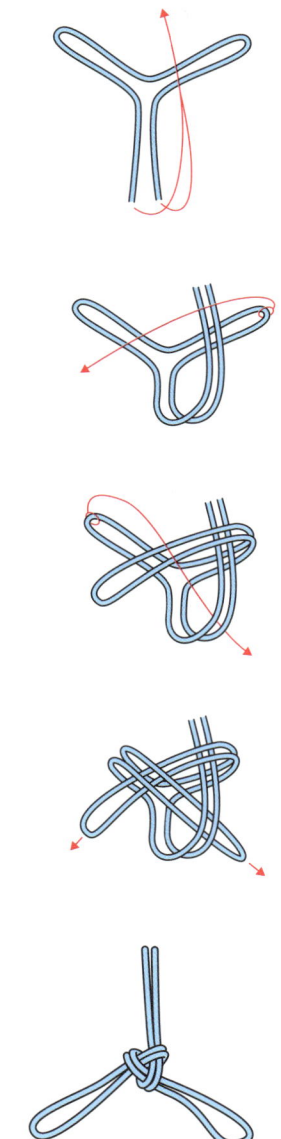

Bosun's whistle lanyard knot

Knot type: Loop

Use: Make a fixed loop with a braided button effect to attach a pendant to a necklace or a whistle, for example.

Method for tying the knot: Wrap the rope around the palm, then around the thumb of the same hand. Slide the thumb strand over the strand around the hand, creating a loop. Pass the left strand under the other strand, then under itself while passing over the loop. Next, pass the ends over the strand that goes around the hand and through the centre of the knot, from underneath. Tighten by holding the loop and pulling the ends in opposite directions.

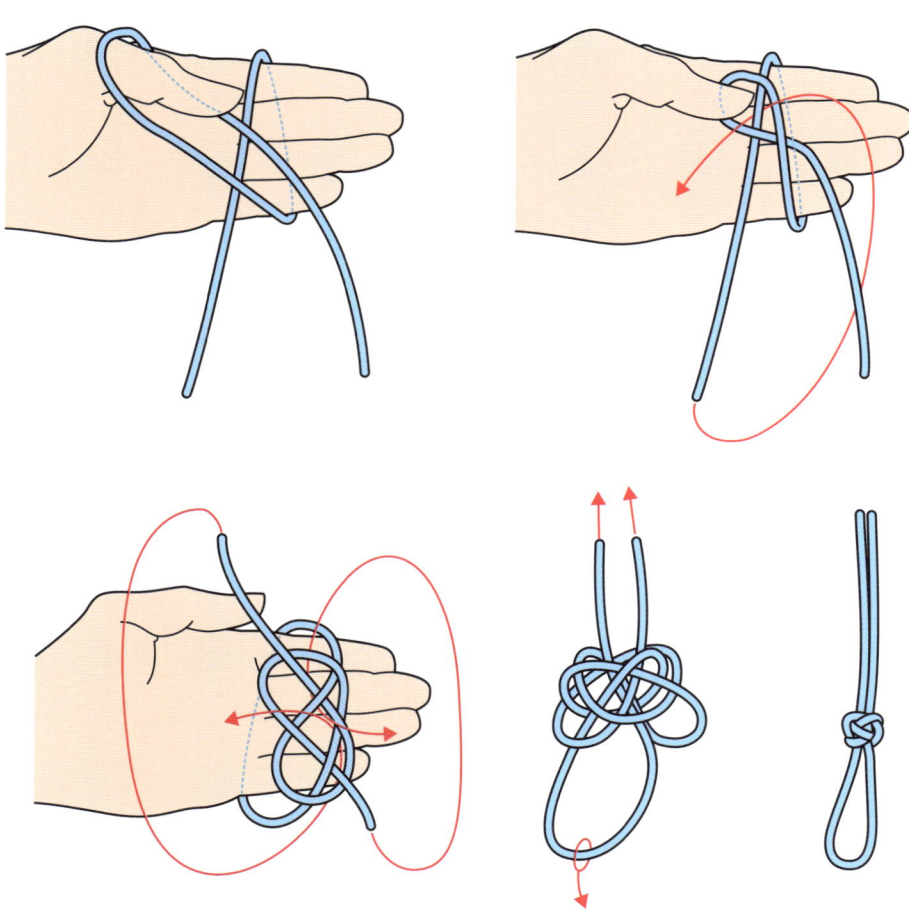

Macramé

Macramé involves creating textile works such as plant hangers, decorative wall panels, bags, bracelets, and even sandals. The technique is similar to lace-making. You can find plenty of patterns and ideas online.

Tatting knot

Knot type: Binding

Use: The first basic knot in macramé.

Method for tying the knot: Tie a **half-hitch** around the support.

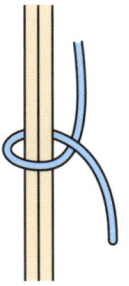

Half-square knot

Knot type: Binding

Use: Second basic knot in macramé.

Method for tying the knot: Place one strand through the support, then pass the other strand over the working end of the first, under the support, and over the standing part of the first strand. This is a **two-strand Turk's head knot**.

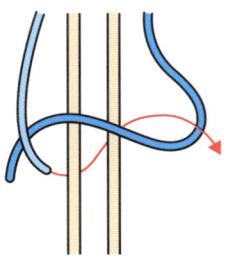

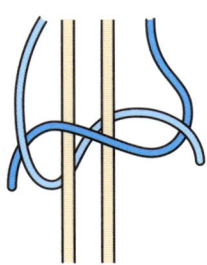

Square knot

knot type: Binding

Use: Third basic knot in macramé.

Method for tying the knot: Tie a **half-square knot** around the support. Then, tie a second cross knot, ensuring that each strand follows the same path: the strand that started on the right passes over the fixed strands, while the other strand passes over, then under, then over again.

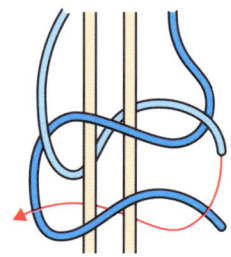

Corkscrew bar

Knot type: Binding

Use: Macramé strings are used to create patterns around a stick, fashion a tool handle, or make a bracelet.

Method for tying the knot: Tie a series of **half-hitches** around the support, always knotting in the same direction to create a spiral pattern.

Buttonhole bar

Knot type: Assembly

Method for tying the knot: Tie a series of **half-hitches** around the support, aligning the half-hitches one beneath the other to create a straight pattern. To align the half-hitches, first tighten the knot, then pull it backwards to counter its tendency to twist around the support.

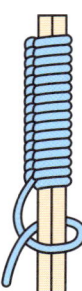

Single tatted bar

Knot type: Assembly

Method for tying the knot: Tie a series of **half-hitches** around the support, ensuring the working end passes over the support, then twice under, twice over, and so on. A double buttonhole knot creates a pattern shaped like a **cow hitch**.

Solomon bar

knot type: Assembly

Method for tying the knot: Tie a series of **square knots** around the support, making sure that one strand always passes over the support and the other always passes under. This knot is very popular for making bracelets.

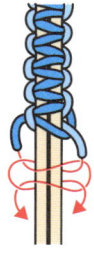

TIPS & TRICKS

To make a string of half-square knots, tie a series of half-square knots around the support, ensuring that the same strand passes once over the support, once under the support, once over again, and so on.

Thump knots and loops

All of the following knots can be used as small mats, doormats, trivets, coasters, or patches. For trivets, choose a non-flammable rope, such as hemp, coir, or sisal.

Flat Turk's head

Knot type: Mat-style

Method for tying the knot: Tie a loop, then place the working end over its loop. Pass the working end under the standing part and lock the loops together by passing over and under twice. Bring the working end next to the standing part and double the pattern, following the over-and-under path. This knot creates a circular mat. It's the flat Turk's head with three turns and four bights.

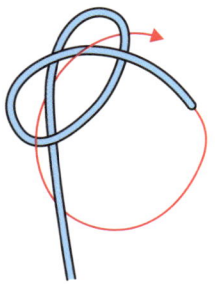
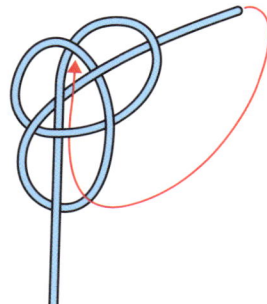

Thump mat

Knot type: Mat-style

Method for tying the knot: Tie a loop, then pass the working end over twice. Next, tie a second loop, then pass the working end through the upper right loop, over the second loop twice, and under the standing part. Lock everything by alternating passes over and under. Follow the initial pattern to double or triple the design. This circular mat was used by sailors to cover metal fittings to muffle the noise of pulleys banging on the deck.

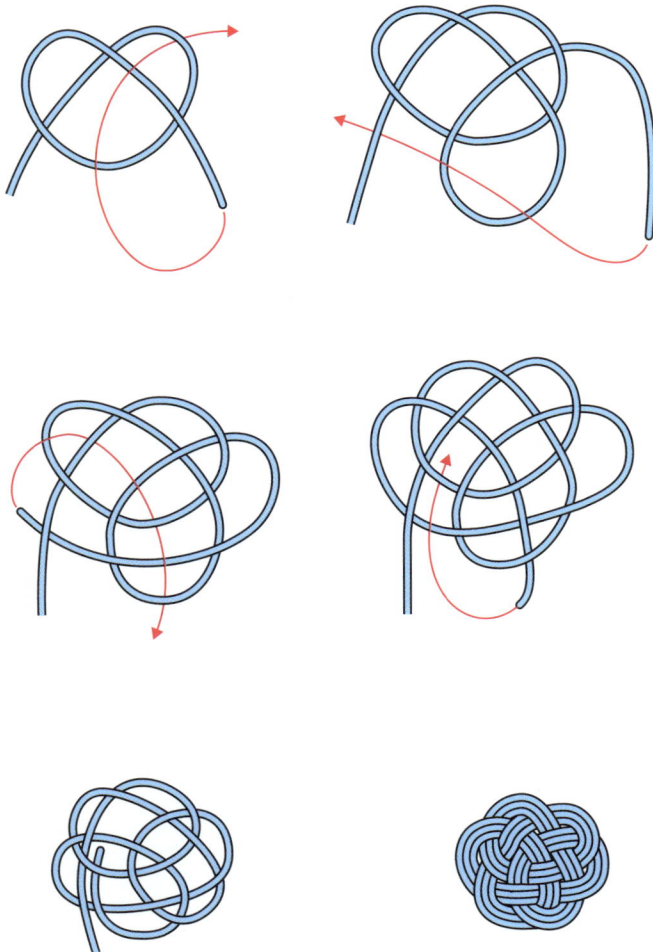

Mat: four-strand extended braid

Knot type: Mat-style

Method for tying the knot: In the middle of the rope, tie a loop with the crossing facing upwards. Place the left strand over the turn twice over, then lock everything with the right strand. Next, pull the starting turn down to extend it, and twist to the left to form a new turn. Repeat the steps shown in the first figure. Once at the desired length, double or triple the braid to make it wider. This rather rectangular knot extends infinitely, depending on the length of the cord and the patience of the person tying it. It's especially well suited for filling a narrow space, such as the edge of a table, shelf, or picture frame.

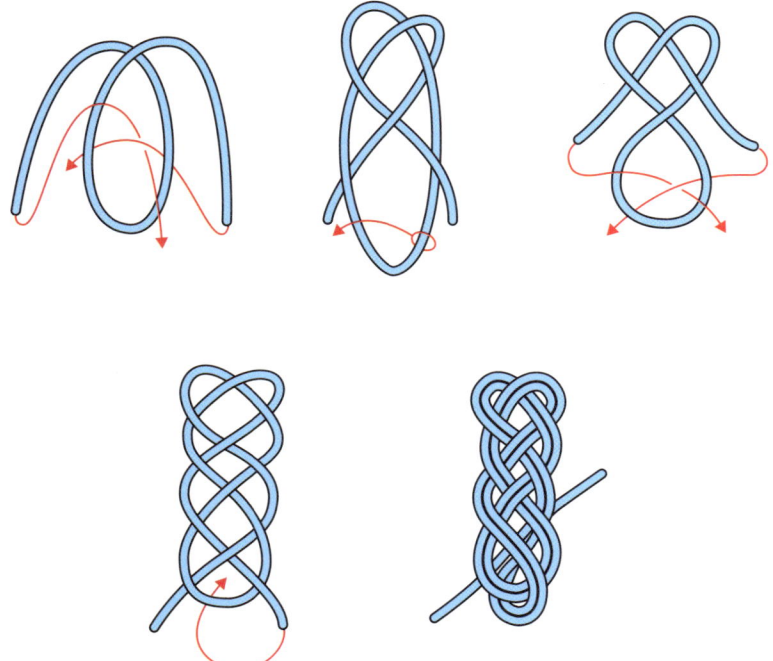

Mat: six-strand extended braid

Knot type: Mat-style

Method for tying the knot: Find the centre of the cord and tie two large loops clockwise, then place the left one over the right. Weave the right strand under, twice over, and under again, then the left strand over and under twice. Next, enlarge the initial loops downward. Twist the two bights to form loops and again place the left one over the other. Weave the strands as in steps 2 and 3. Extend the knot further by repeating steps 5, 6, and 7. Finish the knot by passing the right working end beside the left (or vice versa). Double or triple the pattern as desired.

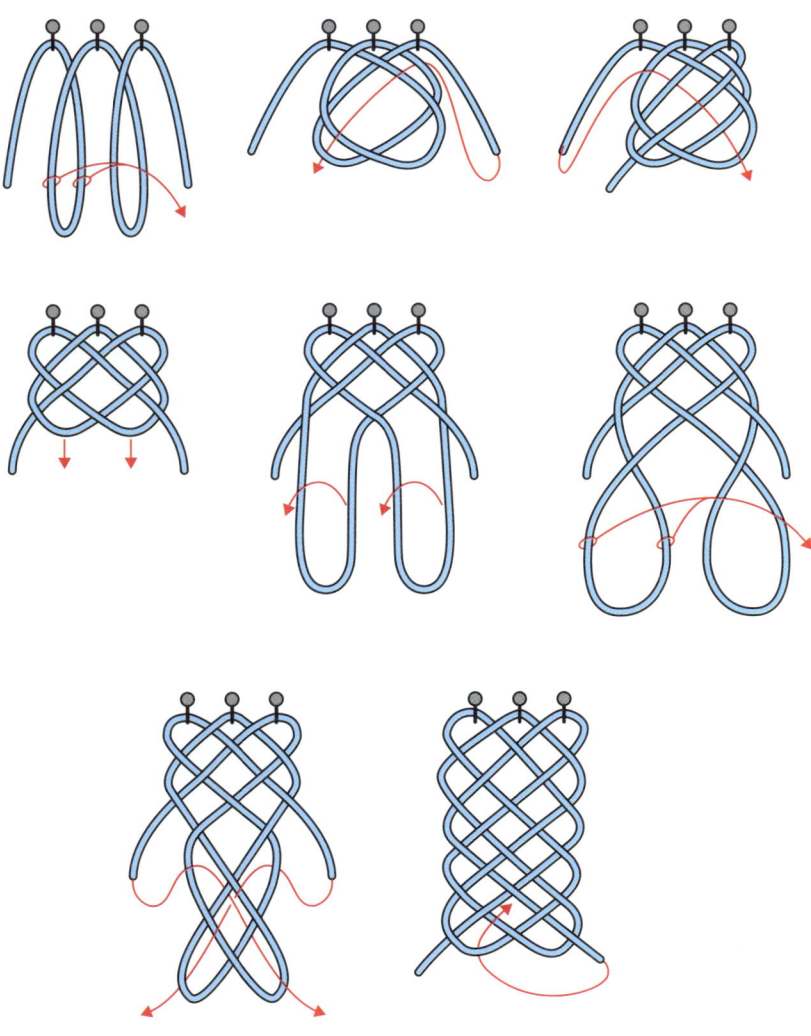

Rectangular mat

Knot type: Mat-style

Method for tying the knot: Follow the diagram step by step without tightening too much. Use pins or small nails to hold the strands in place while forming the pattern. Finish the knot by passing the right working end beside the left (or vice versa). Double or triple the pattern as desired.

Caution: The knot will tend to twist when tightening, so be careful to maintain its rectangular shape by tightening gradually.

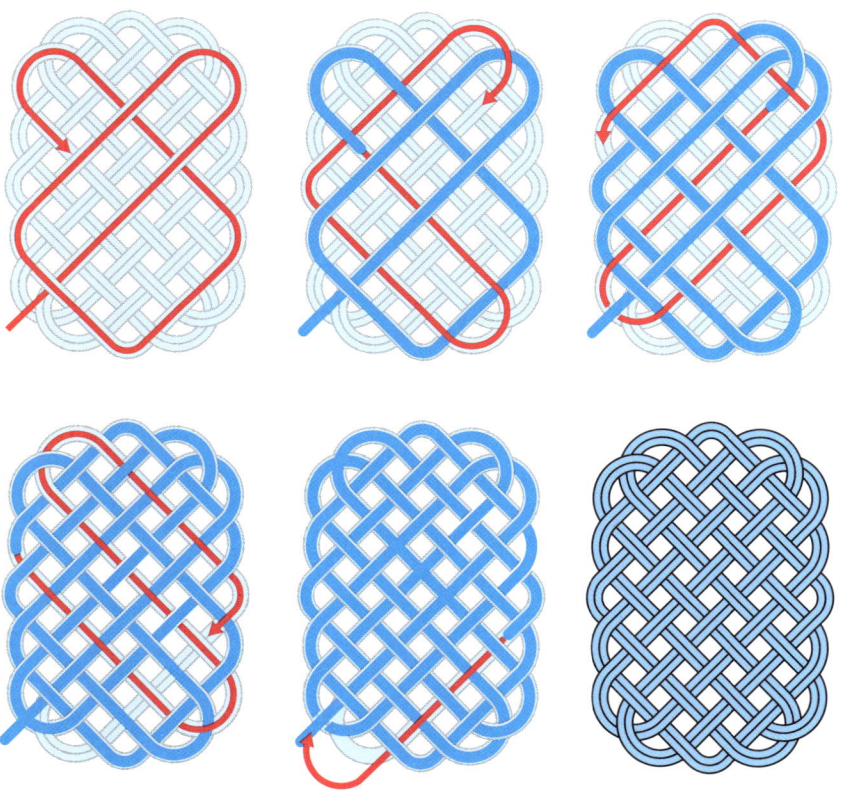

Oval mat

Knot type: Mat-style

Method for tying the knot: Follow the diagram step by step, without tightening too much. Use pins or small nails to hold the strands in place while forming the pattern.

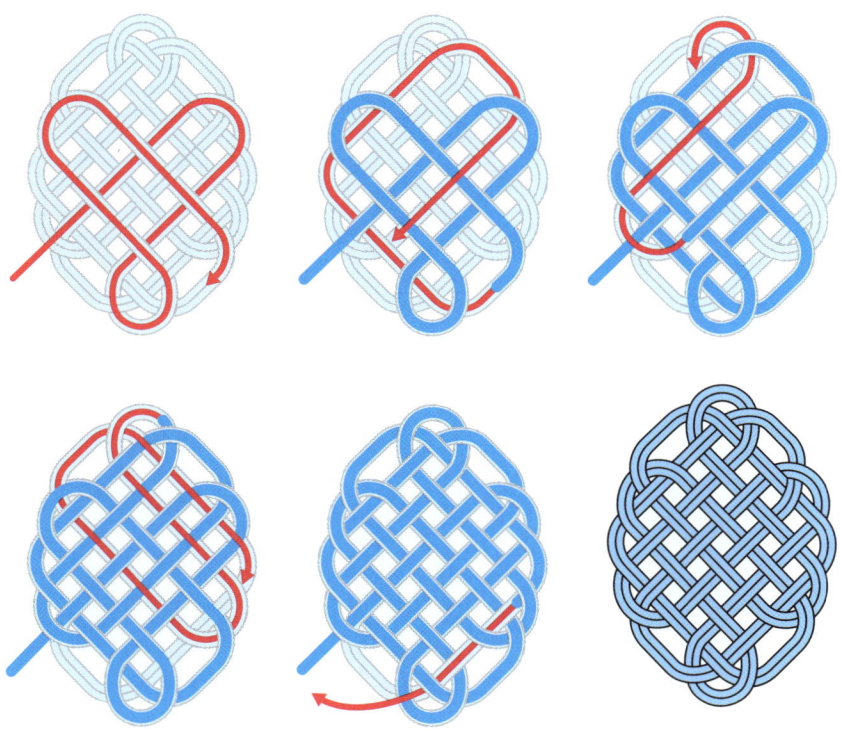

ONE MORE KNOT:

Thief's knot

It is said that a sailor would seal his bag with this knot. If a thief went through the bag, they'd be likely to close it back up with a simple reef knot and thus be exposed. This knot's perfect for joining ropes laid out diagonally (think decorative nets, wall hangings, or mats). To tie it, fold one end into a loop, then thread the other end through that loop, wrap it around the strands, and back through the loop again. Just make sure that the ends slip out diagonally.

Ocean plait mat

Knot type: Mat-style

Method for tying the knot: Tie a simple knot with the ends pointing upwards and enlarge the bights formed on each side of the crossing. Twist these bights to the left, then place the left loop over the right. Weave the right strand under, twice over, and under again. Lock the knot with the other strand. Double or triple the pattern as desired to make the knot wider.

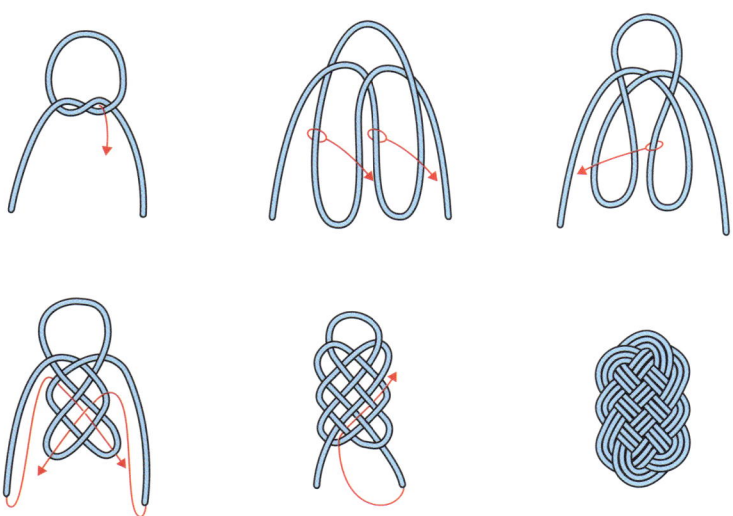

Scoubidous

Made up of a series of knots sailors call the Celtic button knot, the scoubidou is a three-dimensional braid used for making bell ropes, keychains, zipper pulls, or just entertaining kids while improving their dexterity!

The method is always the same for scoubidous tied in one direction.

Arrange the strands like a star. Then, lay each strand anticlockwise over its neighbour. The last strand will pass through the loop formed by the first strand. Tighten and repeat the process until you reach the desired length.

The method is always the same for scoubidous tied in alternating directions. Start as you would with a one-way Celtic button braid, meaning with a left-handed (anticlockwise) Celtic button knot. Then, make the second Celtic button knot in a right-handed (clockwise) direction. Tighten each step and repeat the left/right process until you reach the desired length.

In all cases, the three-strand scoubidou has a triangular cross-section, the four-strand forms a square, and the six-strand version is more circular.

Three-strand scoubidou tied in one direction: Celtic button knot

Knot type: Braid

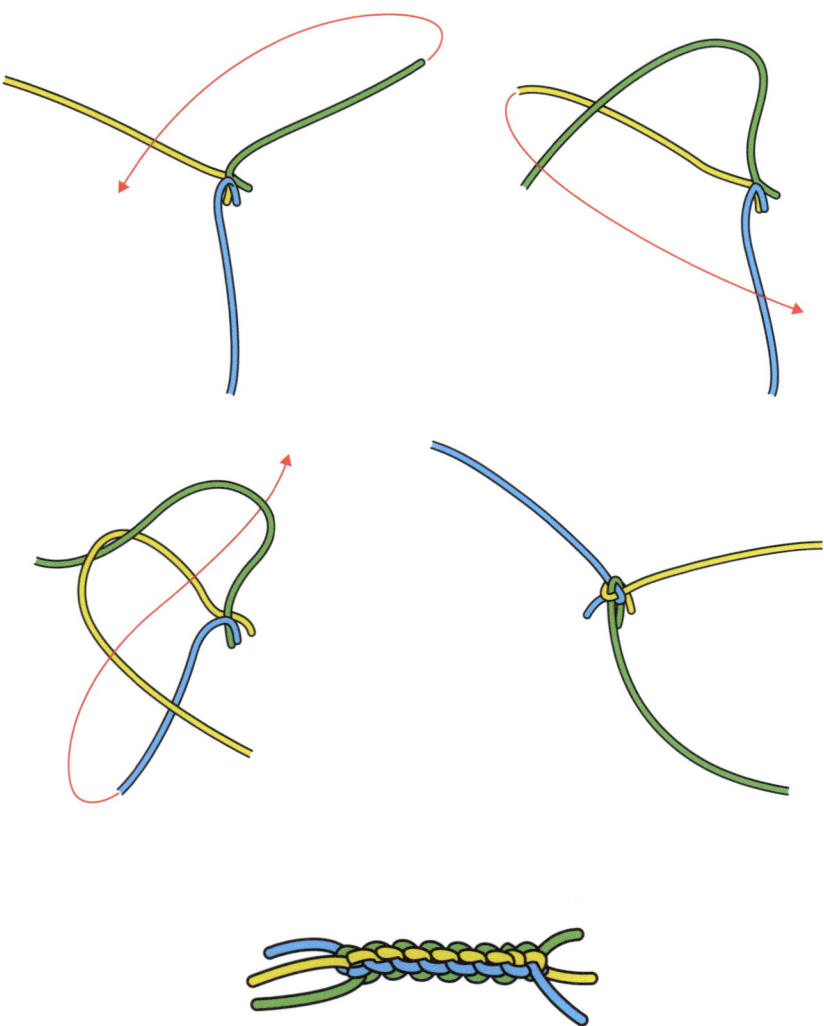

Four-strand scoubidou tied in one direction

Knot type: Braid

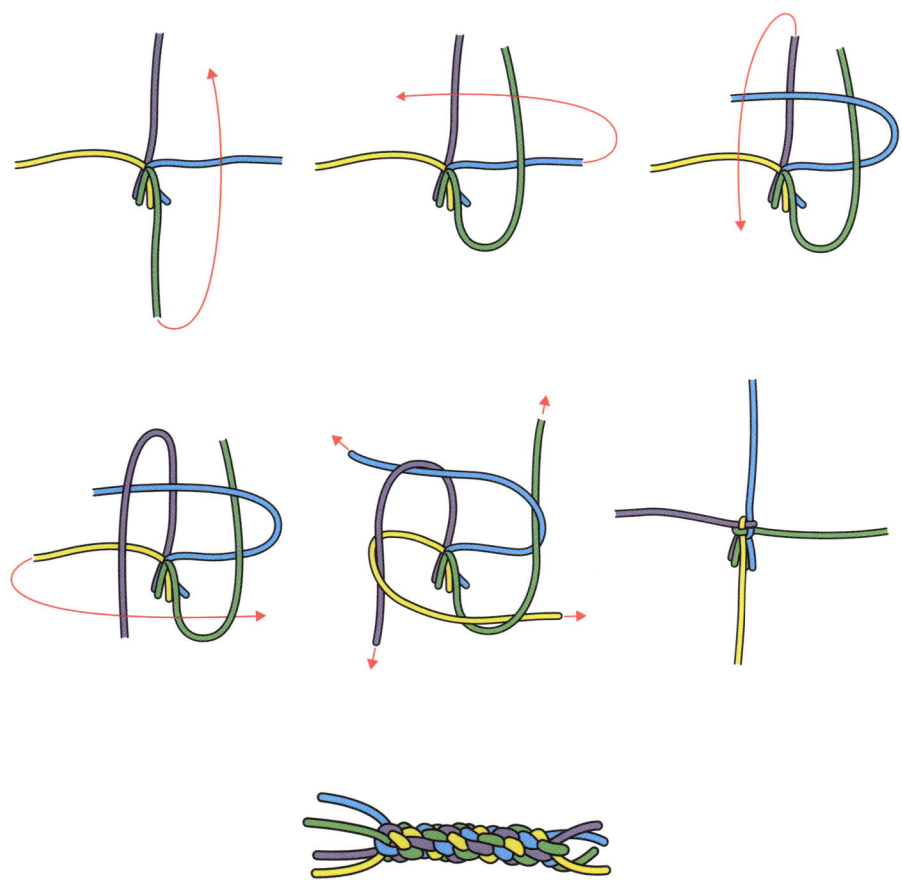

Six-strand scoubidou tied in one direction

Knot type: Braid

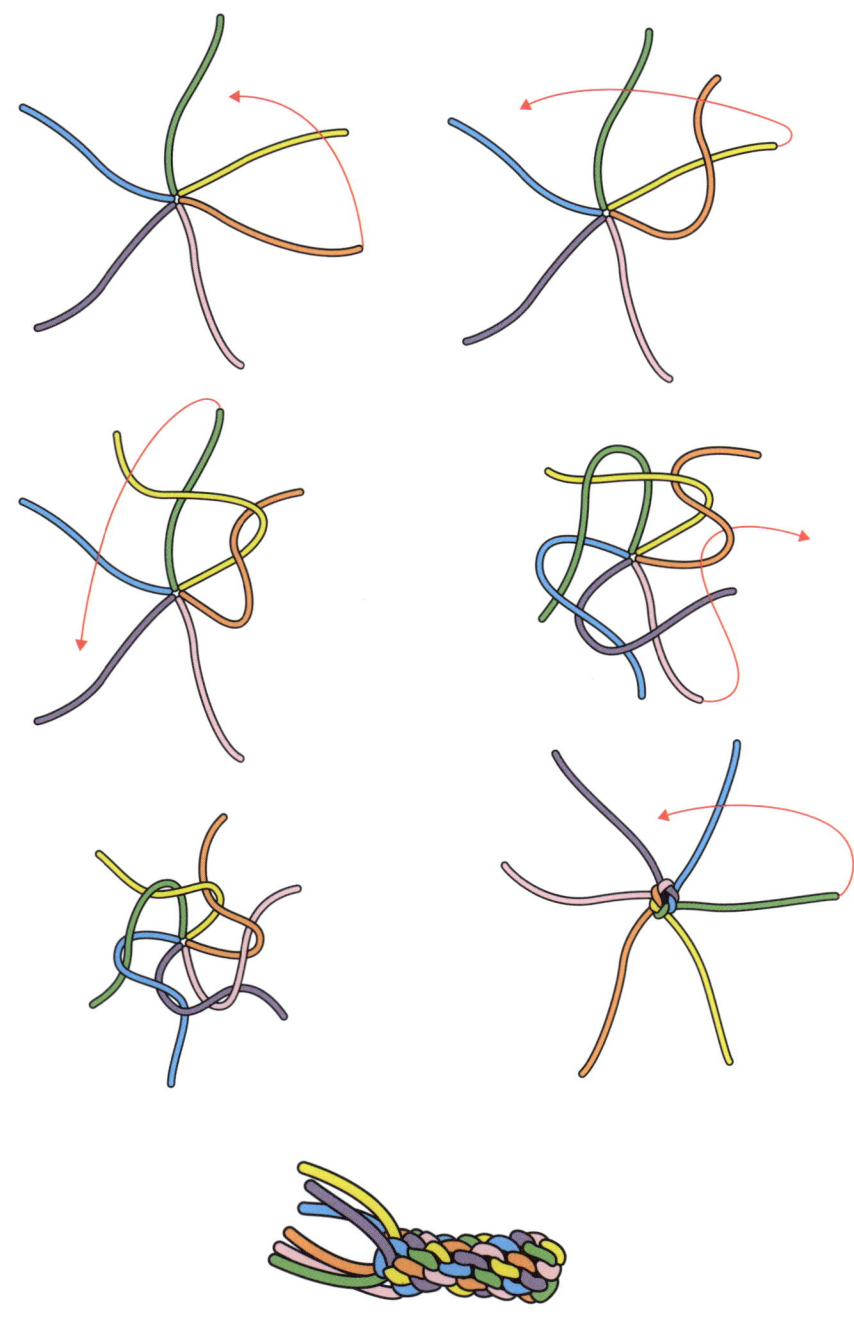

Three-strand scoubidou tied in alternating directions

Knot type: Braid

Method for tying the knot: This starts with a **Celtic button knot** (page 103).

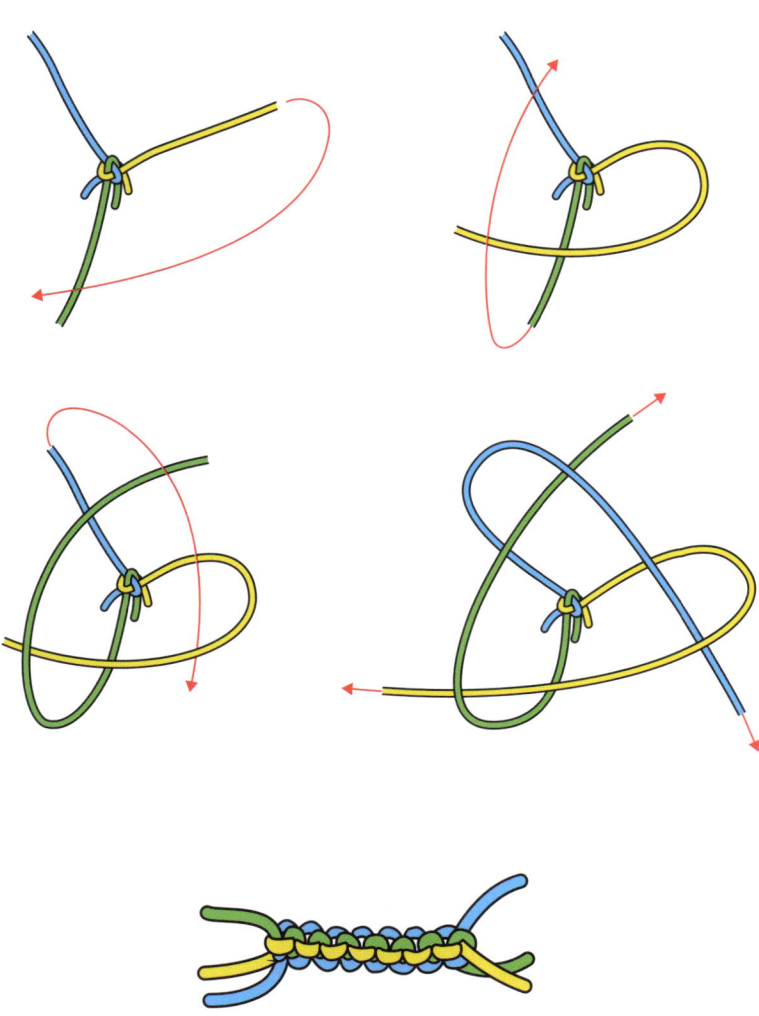

Four-strand scoubidou tied in alternating directions

Knot type: Braid

Method for tying the knot: This starts with a **Celtic button knot** (page 103).

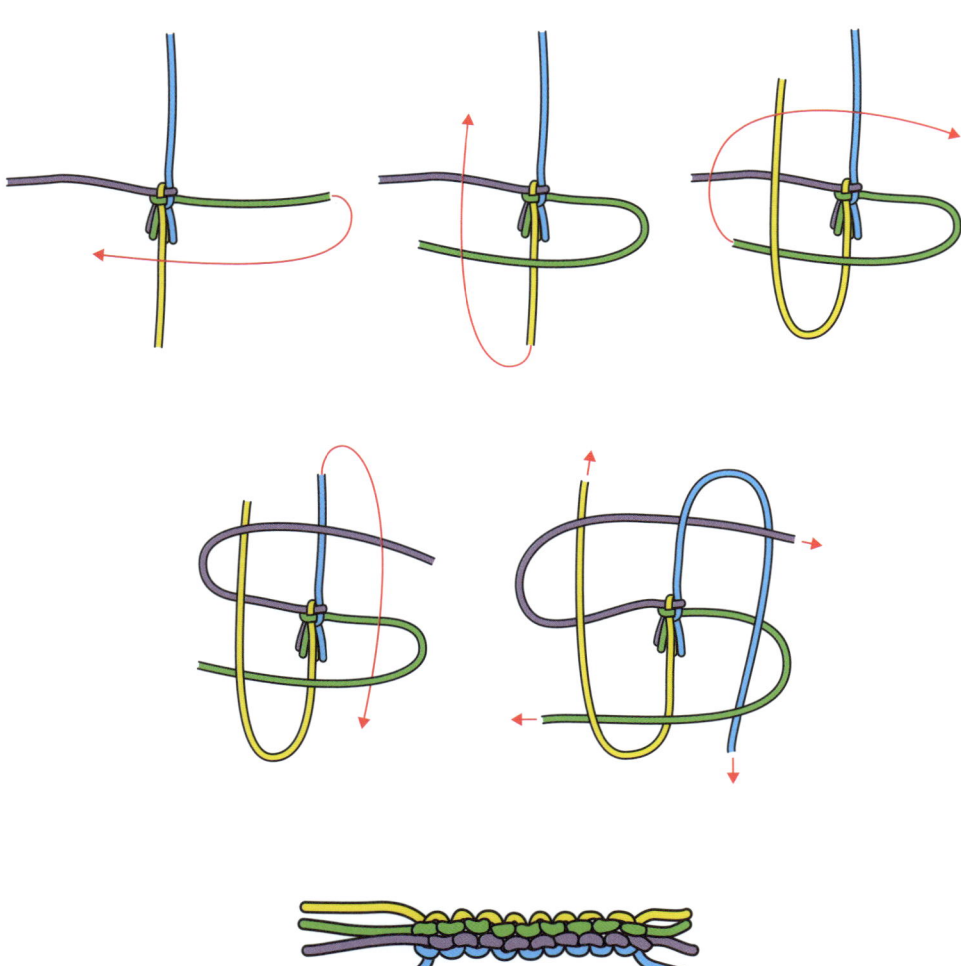

Six-strand scoubidou tied in alternating directions

Knot type: Braid

Method for tying the knot: This starts with a **Celtic button knot** (page 103).

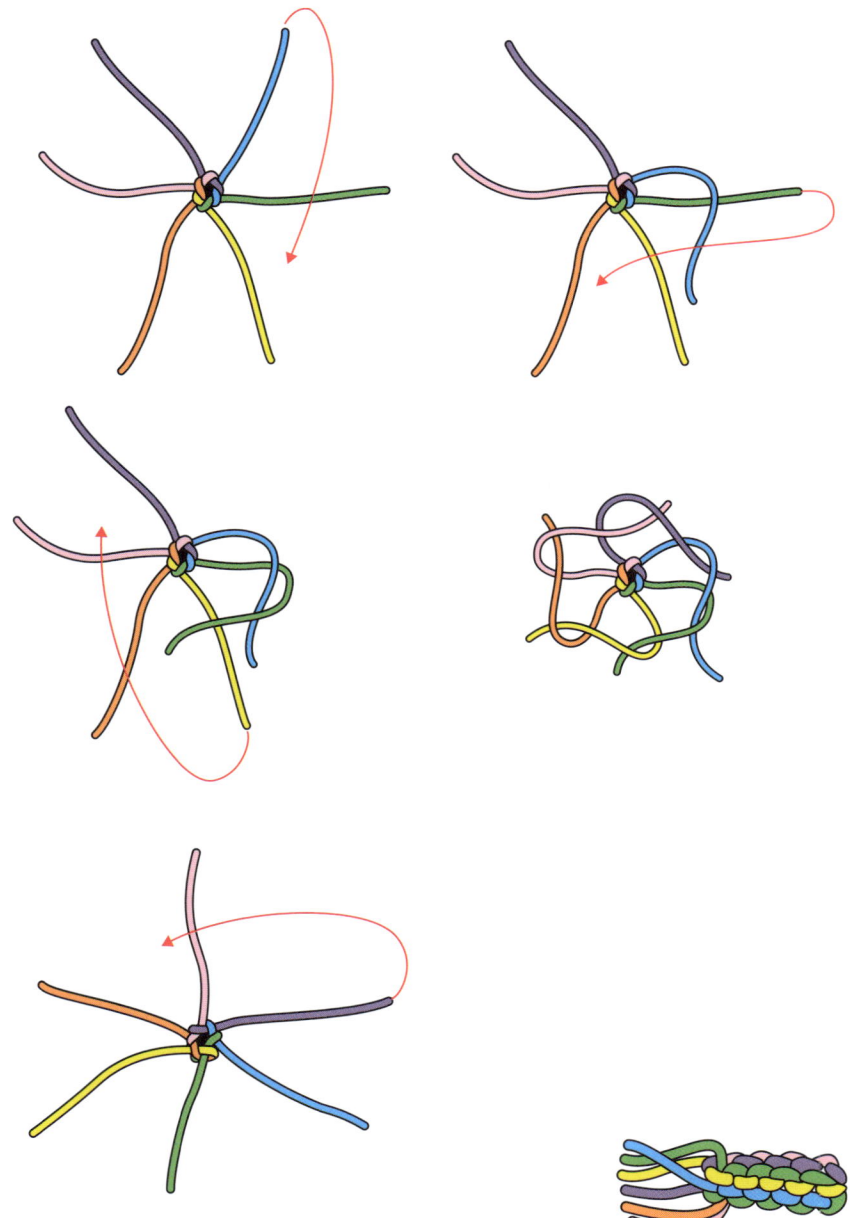

Single- or multi-strand button knots

Beyond its practical use of increasing a rope's diameter or preventing fraying, the button knot is an elegant way to finish a rope stair railing, make a keychain, or stop shoelaces from slipping out of eyelets. Combined with other decorative knots, it becomes part of complex bell ropes, keychains, handbag handles, and more. Some buttons are made with multiple strands.

Capuchin knot

Knot type: Stopper

Method for tying the knot: Tie a **double overhand knot**, then pass the end back through the loop. When tightening, make sure the strand forming the loop of the overhand knot stays at the centre of the knot. Learn to tie the double overhand knot first. It's said to be the knot that finished the rope belts of the Capuchin monks.

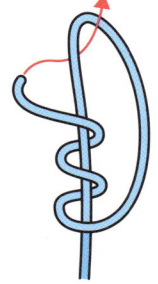

Monkey's fist knot

Knot type: Stopper

Method for tying the knot: Wrap the twine three times around your hand, then fold it at a right angle and wrap three more times around the first coils. Remove the bundle from your hand, being careful not to undo the coils. Lock everything in place by wrapping the twine three times around the second set of coils. Optionally, add a bead or ball of suitable size at the centre of the knot, then gradually tighten. Originally used to add weight to the end of a throwing line (see also the **stevedore knot** on page 251), this is the key ring knot known by every scout and budding sailor!

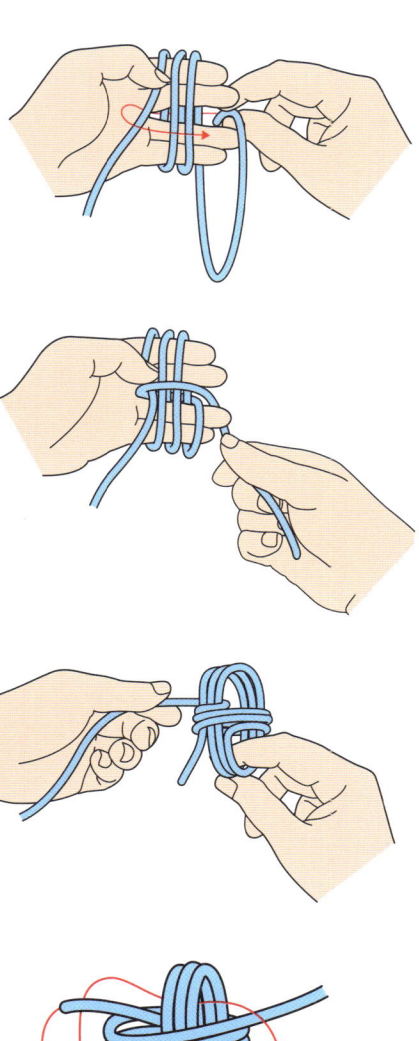

TIPS & TRICKS

Increase or decrease the number of wraps according to the size of the spherical object.

Enhanced monkey's fist knot

Knot type: Stopper

Method for tying the knot: Wrap the twine three times around your hand, then cross the working ends and wrap the lower working end three times around these initial coils. Lock everything in place by wrapping the other working end three times around the second set of coils. Optionally, add a bead or ball of suitable size at the centre of the knot, then gradually tighten. Note that, compared to the classic monkey's fist, the changes in direction are hidden inside the knot.

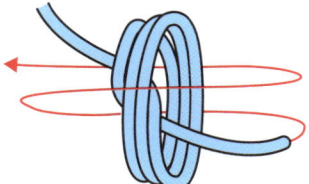

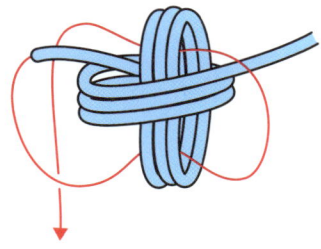

Manrope knot

Knot type: Multi-strand stopper

Method for tying the knot: Tie a **simple wall knot**, then tie a **Celtic button knot** over it (see page 103). Next, double the pattern by having each strand pass under a strand of the wall knot and then under a strand of the Celtic button knot. Once doubled, pass the ends through the centre of the knot. Tighten the knot gradually.

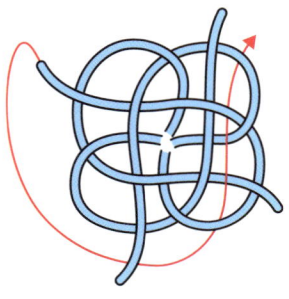

Simple wall knot

Knot type: Multi-strand stopper

Use: Wall knots gather several strands and can serve as transitions: for example, between different parts of a bell rope.

Method for tying the knot: Arrange the strands in a star shape, then – moving anticlockwise – tuck each strand under its neighbour. The second strand will go under two strands. The last strand will pass through a loop formed by the first strand. Next, weave each strand through the loop to its right, always from underneath. There's no limit to the number of strands you can gather in a wall knot. Adding an extra weave with each strand creates a double wall knot, another pass makes a triple wall knot, and so on.

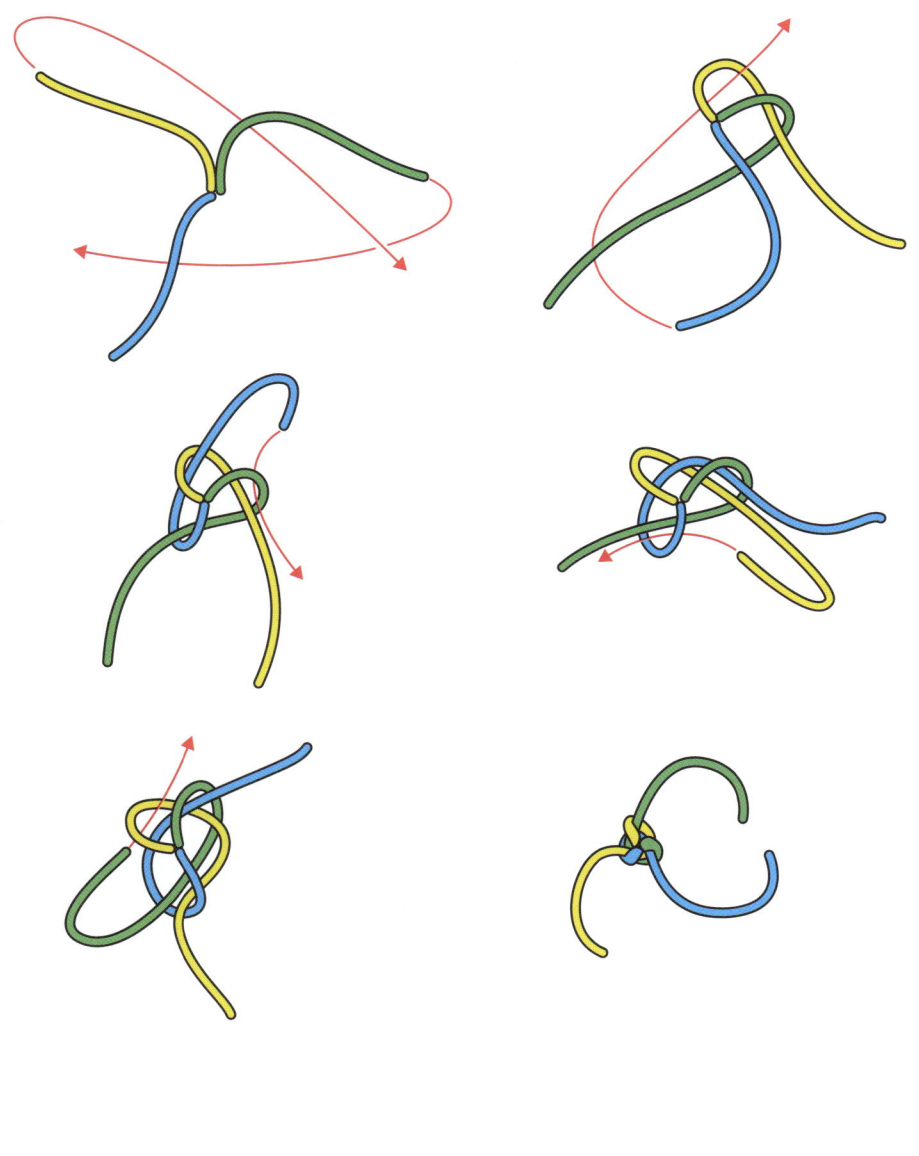

Double wall knot

Knot type: Multi-strand stopper

Method for tying the knot: To tie a double wall knot directly without going through the **wall knot** step, start by tying a **half-hitch** around the standing part with one strand. Do the same with the next strand, making sure its end also passes through the first half-hitch. Repeat with the third strand, but this time pass it through both the first and second half-hitches. Tighten gradually.

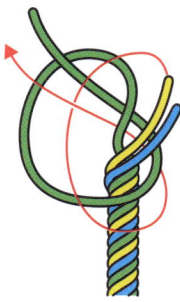  

Star knot

Knot type: Multi-strand stopper

Method for tying the knot: Bind the strands together with a **constrictor knot** and arrange them like spokes. Tie a loop in one strand, with the working end underneath. Pass the neighbouring left strand through the first loop from below, then twist this strand to form the next loop. Repeat this with all strands. Next, fold each strand clockwise so it is trapped under its neighbour, then fold each strand anticlockwise, passing it under itself, over, and through the loop of its 'front neighbour'. Turn the knot over and pass each strand through the gap to the left of the previous spoke. To finish, pass each strand again through its outer loop.

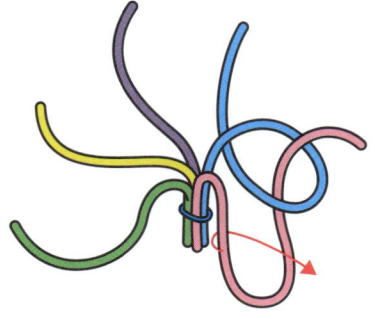

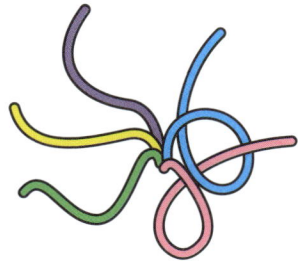

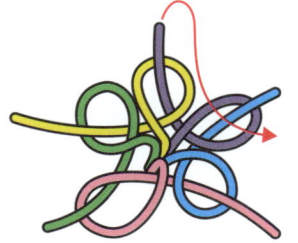

BRAIDS

For braiding hair, but also for making straps, bands, bracelets, bag shoulder straps, drum straps

Flat braid

Knot type: Braid

Method for tying the knot: Place the strands side by side. The left strand passes over the middle one and becomes the new middle strand. Then the right strand passes over the middle one and becomes the new middle strand. Repeat the left/right movements until the braid reaches the desired length. Secure with an elastic band or whipping around the strands.

Reverse flat braid

Knot type: Braid

Method for tying the knot: Follow the instructions for a **flat braid**, except the strands pass under the middle strand. This is a reverse-style flat braid.

Four-strand flat braid

Knot type: Braid

Method for tying the knot: Arrange the strands side by side, then divide them into two groups of three strands and one single strand. Follow the method for a **flat braid**, except that the outer strand on one side passes over two strands, and the other passes over one strand. This method produces an asymmetrical braid and can also be applied to **six strands** (five strands plus one strand or four strands plus two strands).

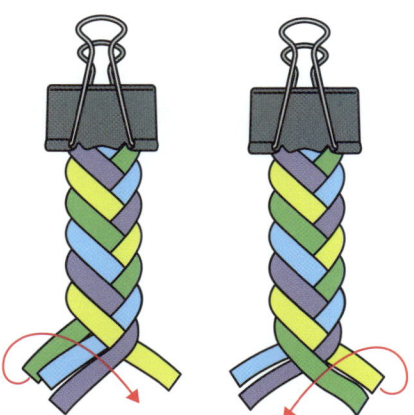

Five-strand flat braid

Knot type: Braid

Method for tying the knot: Arrange the strands side by side, then divide them into two groups of three and two strands. Follow the method for a **flat braid**, except that the outer strand passes over two strands each time. This method can be applied to **seven strands**.

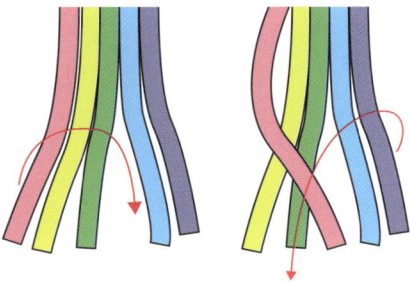

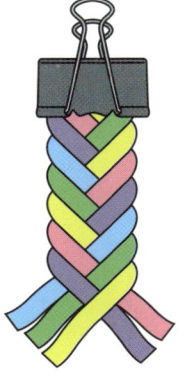

Flat braid, odd number of strands

Knot type: Braid

Method for tying the knot: Arrange the strands side by side, then divide them into two groups: for example, four strands and three strands. Pass the outer strand of the four-strand group under, over, and under its neighbours within the same group. It now becomes the fourth strand of the other group. Do the same with the outer strand of the group that now contains four strands, and so on. This method also applies to five strands (three plus two strands), nine strands (five plus four strands), etc.

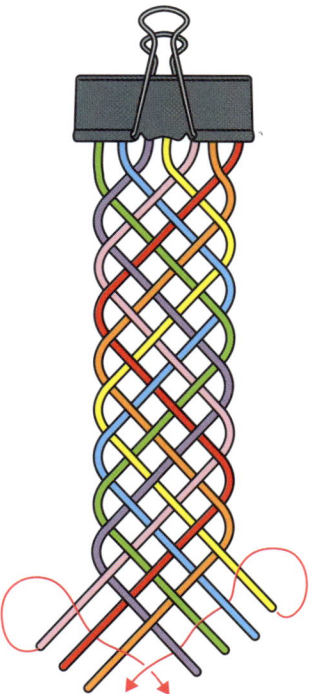

Flat braid, even number of strands

Knot type: Braid

Method for tying the knot: Arrange the strands side by side, then divide them into two groups of, for example, three strands. Pass the outer strand of the first group of three over and under its neighbours within the same group. It now becomes the fourth strand of the other group. Pass the outer strand of the group that now contains four strands under, over, and under. Repeat the process. This method also applies to eight strands (two groups of four strands), ten strands (two groups of five strands), etc.

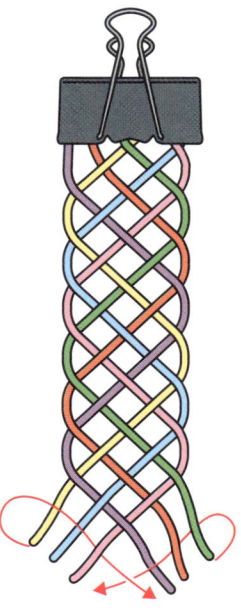

Chain stitch

Knot type: Braid

Method for tying the knot: Make a loop with the working end passing under the standing part. Double the working end to form a loop, and pass this loop through the loop of the half-hitch. Repeat until the chain stitch reaches the desired length. Lock the knot by passing the working end, without doubling, through the last loop. The chain stitch can be considered a one-strand braid. When used as a shoulder strap or drum sling, note that one side has an edge that may be uncomfortable when resting on the shoulder. It can also be used to shorten a rope.

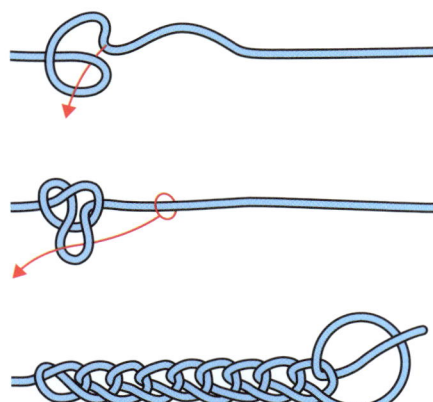

TURK'S HEAD KNOTS

A Turk's head knot is a continuous braid wrapped around a support. There are many types, described by the number of turns and bights. A turn is one full wrap around the support; a bight is the intersection where several turns cross. To understand this, look at a flat Turk's head knot with three turns and four bights (see page 96). Starting from the centre and moving outwards, in any direction, the number of strands a line would cut through gives the number of turns (in this case, three). To find the number of bights, simply count the loops around the knot (in this case, four).

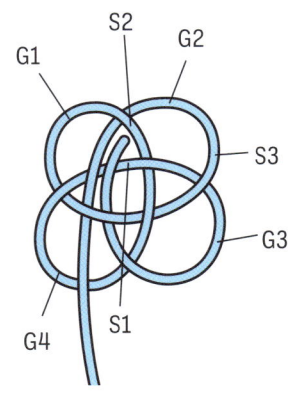

Turk's head knot, three turns and four bights

Knot type: Binding

Method for tying the knot: Wrap the rope around your hand, cross the strands, make a second turn around the hand to the left of the standing part, and then pass the end over and under the strands. On the back of your hand, slide the left strand over the right strand. Pass the end under the strand now on the left and return to the starting point. Double or triple the pattern as desired, then tighten it around a support. The Turk's head knot with three turns and four bights is probably the most well known of its kind.

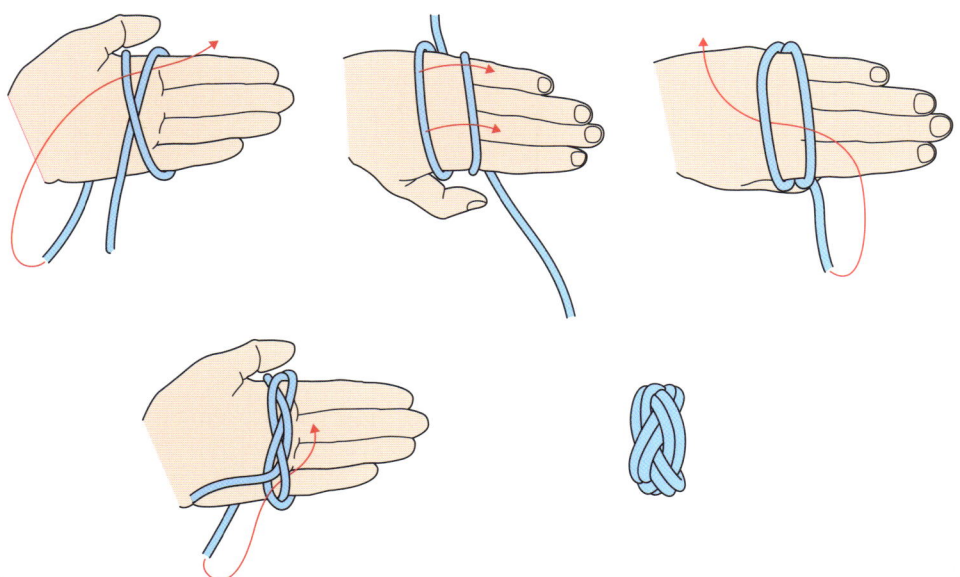

Turk's head knot, three turns and two bights

Knot type: Binding

Method for tying the knot: Start as for a Turk's head knot with three turns and four bights, but after the second turn around the hand, pass to the right of the standing part and weave the end over and under the strands. Make another turn around the hand and return to the starting point.

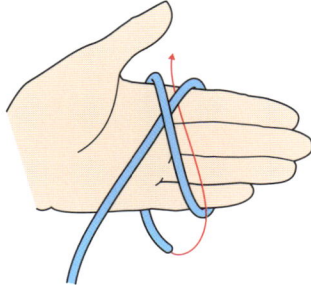

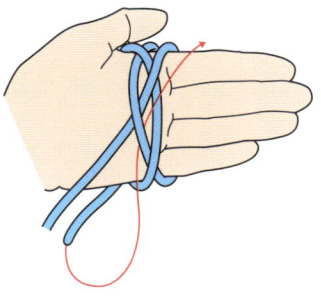

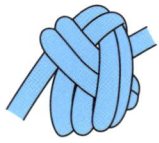

Turk's head knot, three turns and five bights

Knot type: Binding

Method for tying the knot: Tie a **Turk's head knot with three turns and two bights**, but instead of returning to the start, slide the left strand over the right. Next, to the right, pass the end under and over the strands. Now slide the right strand over the left and weave the end to the left, passing under and over. Return to the starting point and double or triple the pattern as desired.

Turk's head knot, four turns and three bights

Knot type: Binding

Method for tying the knot: Start with a **half-hitch**, then wrap around the support passing under and over. Wrap around again, then pass the strand under itself. Next, weave the end over, under, and over, returning to the starting point. Double or triple the pattern as desired, then tighten gradually.

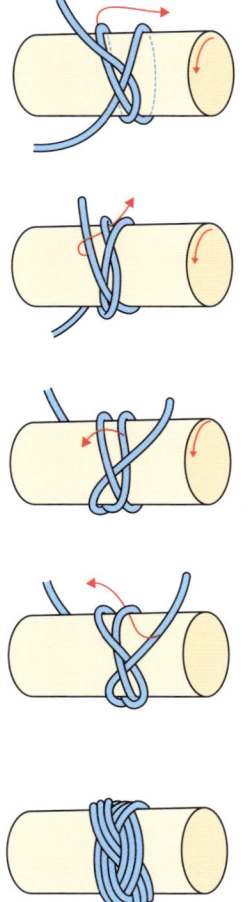

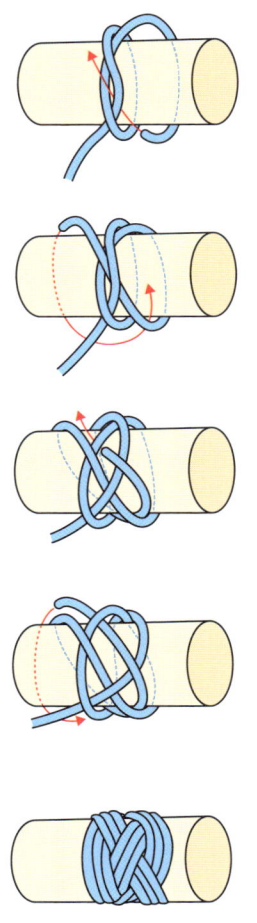

Turk's head knot, six turns and five bights

Knot type: Binding

Method for tying the knot: Tie a **Turk's head knot with four turns and three bights**, then begin doubling the pattern by weaving under, over, under. Now, instead of following the four turns and three bights pattern, pass under, over, and under. Once back at the start, continue as usual, alternating over and under. This is called 'opening the pairs'. At the start again, double or triple the pattern as desired.

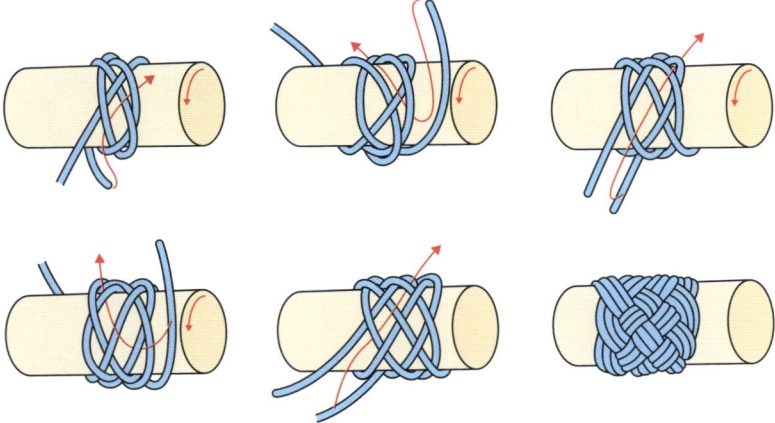

SPLICING

SPLICING ON TRADITIONAL ROPES

Three-strand splicing

Knot type: Loop

Use: Create a permanent loop at the end of a rope.

Method: Unlay the rope for a few centimetres and whip the ends of the strands to prevent them from untwisting. Fold the rope back on itself to form the eye of the desired size. During all the following steps, to keep a good reference point, hold the whole between your thumb and index finger at the intersection of the two parts of the eye.

Turn the eye a quarter-turn to the right so that the short end of the rope is on top. Unlay this short part up to the thumb to reveal the three strands. Note that one of these strands will be behind the other two: it sits on the left. The middle strand stays in the middle, and the third strand sits on the right.

Insert the marlinspike into the long part of the rope (the standing part), under the first strand (the one in front of the thumb). Going from right to left, pass the middle strand through the space opened by the marlinspike. Remove the marlinspike and tighten the middle strand in the opposite direction of the eye to remove slack.

Turn the eye a quarter-turn to the left to prepare for passing the right strand. Note that the teardrop-shaped opening created in the standing part by the passage of the first strand (the middle strand) is where the right strand will exit the standing part. Insert the marlinspike into the standing part under the strand now in front of the thumb, to the right of the strand under which the middle strand passed. Pass the right strand from right to left. Remove the marlinspike and tighten the right strand.

Now, turn the eye clockwise three-quarters of a turn to prepare for passing the left strand. Note that the small opening created by the middle strand is where the left strand will enter the standing part. Insert the marlinspike into the standing part under the strand to the left of the middle strand, still moving from right to left. Pass the left strand, remove the marlinspike, and tighten.

After the first three passes, the eye is now formed at the rope's end. You should now check for errors: all strands must exit the standing part in the same plane, and a strand of the standing part must always be between two working strands. Continuing to work from right to left, pass each working strand in turn over the next standing strand and under the following one. With each new series of passes, check that the strands exit the standing part in the same plane.

Once the required number of passes is reached, tighten the working strands well and roll the splice between your hands or on the ground under your foot to even it out. Tighten one last time and trim the excess, leaving each working strand protruding by at least 1cm. If it's a synthetic rope, melt the end of each strand carefully with a lighter flame.

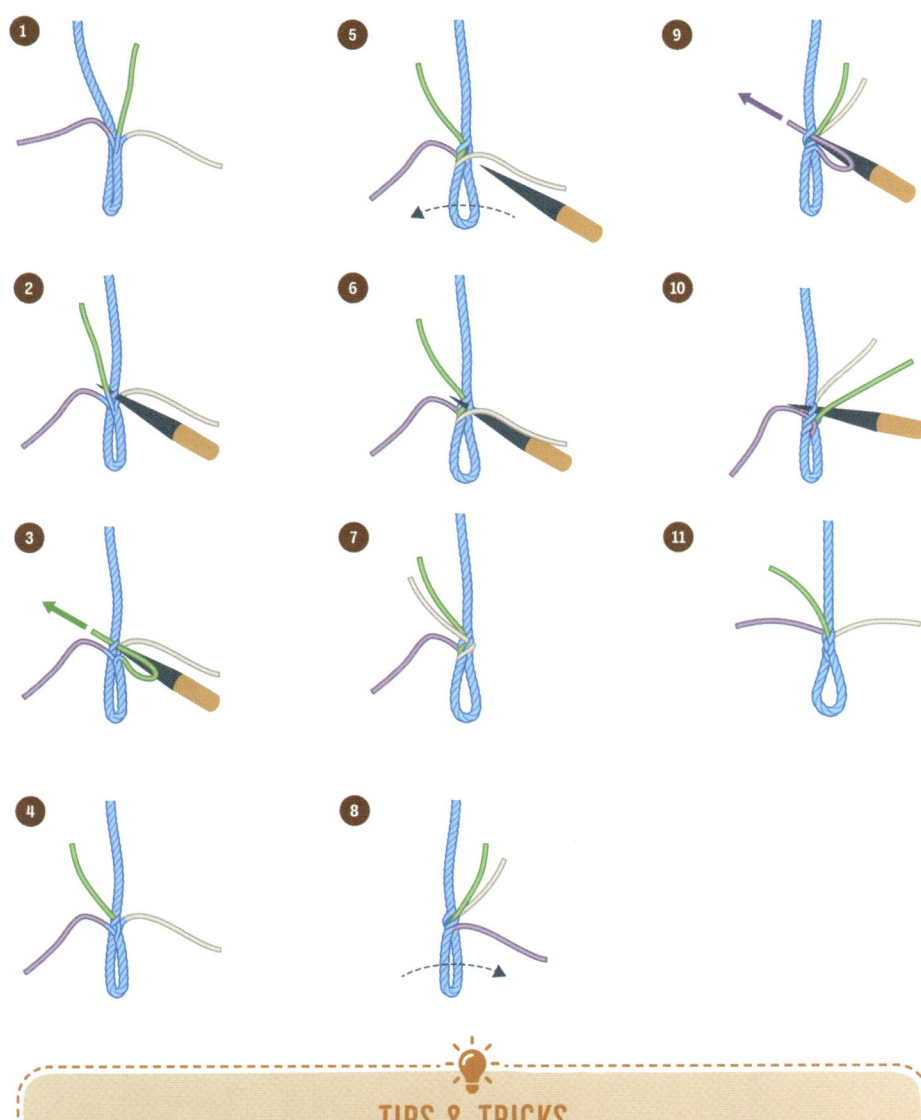

When learning this knot, use adhesive tapes of different colours to clearly distinguish the strands. To ensure the strength of the eye splice, each working strand should make a minimum of three passes for ropes made from natural fibres and five passes for synthetic ropes. To finish the splice with a tapered end, which looks better, make one extra pass with the middle strand and two more passes with the right strand. From then on, all the strands exit to the left of the standing part.

Four-strand splicing

Knot type: Loop

Method: Arrange the four strands side by side, with the first strand on the left coming from behind. Pass strand 1 under one strand of the standing part, strand 2 under the strand below it, strand 3 under the strand above it, and strand 4 under the same strand as strand 3 and under the strand directly above it (twice under). Continue the weaving following the technique described for the **three-strand splice**.

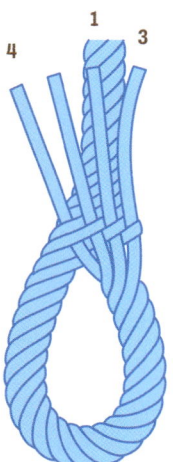

Six-strand splicing

Knot type: Loop

Method: Arrange the six strands side by side, with the first strand on the left coming from behind. Pass strand 1 under one strand of the standing part, strand 2 under the strand above it, and so on. Continue weaving following the technique described for the **three-strand splice**. A six-strand rope with a core is called a six-strand laid rope.

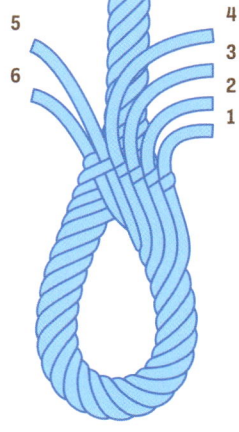

TIPS & TRICKS

Cut the core, if there is one.

Back splice

Knot type: Splicing

Use: Make a stopper knot at the end of the rope to prevent it from fraying.

Method: Unlay the rope for a suitable length and tie a **Celtic button knot** (see page 103) with the strands. Make passes following the technique described for the **three-strand splice**. This technique is useful as a substitute for whipping but unnecessarily thickens the rope's end.

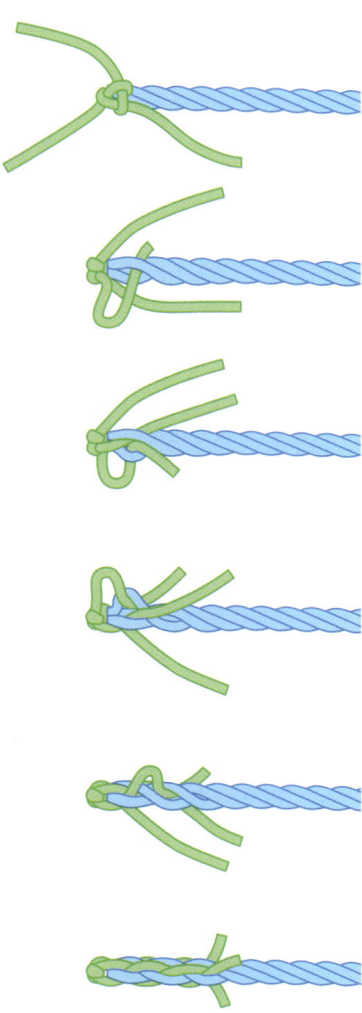

Chain splicing

Knot type: Splicing

Use: Attach a rope to a chain, for example, to create a mooring line.

Method: Unlay the rope for a suitable length. Pass strands 1 and 3 through the first chain link, for example from right to left, and strand 2 from left to right (for a four-strand rope, divide the strands into two groups, passing strands 1 and 4 one way, and strands 2 and 3 the other). Then make passes following the technique described for the **three-strand splice**.

Caution: Regularly check the rope-to-chain junction and redo the splice at the first sign of wear.

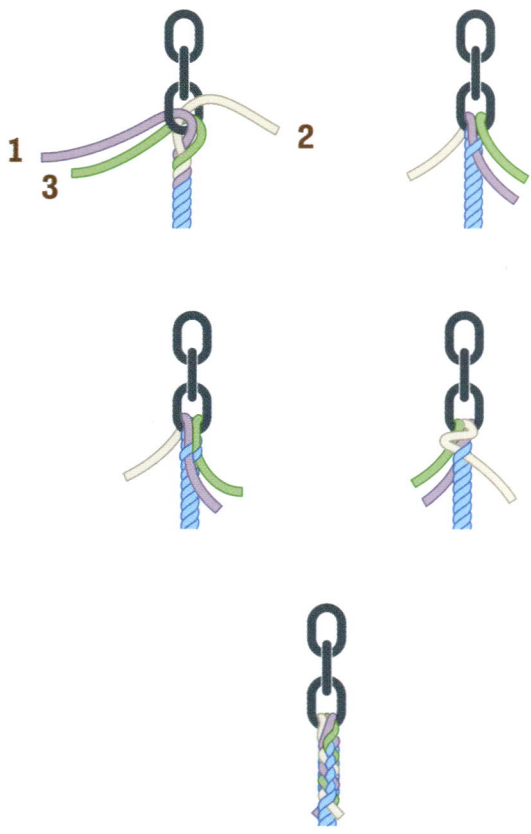

Short splice

Knot type: Splicing

Use: Join two ropes, or both ends of the same rope, permanently.

Method: Unlay each rope end for a certain length to expose the strands. Interleave the two groups of strands, so that each strand from one end lies between two strands from the other end and bring the two groups together. Temporarily hold one group of strands against the rope with a **constrictor knot**. Using the free strands, splice each strand by passing over the strand to its left and under the next strand. Make two more passes with each strand, then undo the constrictor knot and splice the remaining strands the same way. Roll the splice under your foot to make it smooth and even.

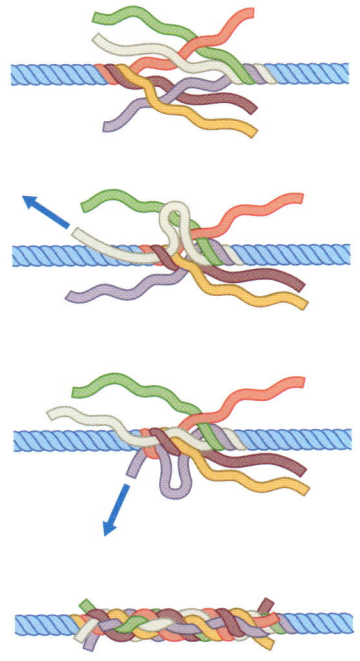

TIPS & TRICKS

With a slippery rope, make five passes on each side.

Long splice

Knot type: Splicing

Method: Interleave the ropes as if making a short splice. But this time, instead of passing the first strand over the one to its left, unlay the left strand for a certain length and fill the space with the other strand. Do the same with another pair of strands, but in the opposite direction, so the last pair of strands is evenly spaced between the first two pairs. Then tie each pair of strands with a **half-hitch** and unlay each end to flatten it and splice it under the neighbouring strand. Divide the ends in two, cut one group of strands flush, and splice the other. Roll under your foot to even out the splice along its length. This splice does not increase the rope's thickness, allowing it to still pass through a pulley or other redirecting device.

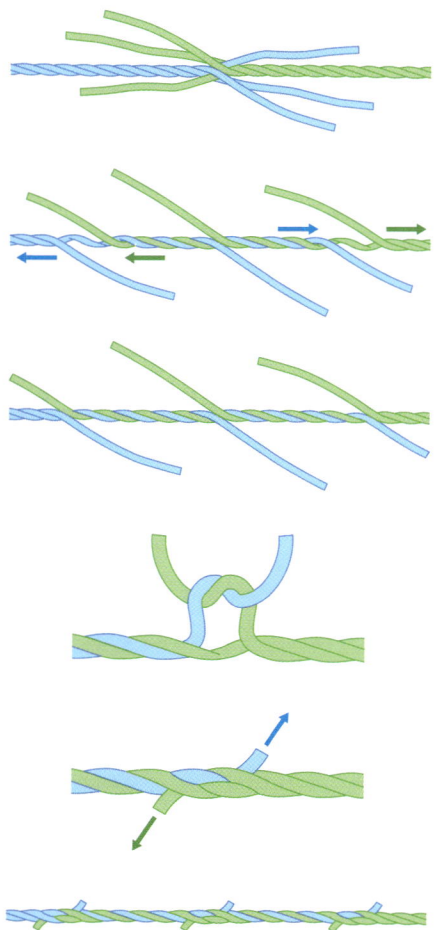

Traditional grommet splicing

Knot type: Loop

Use: Disable a pulley, make a minimalist trivet, craft a set of sailor's quoits.

Method: Using a three-strand rope, take a length equal to four times the desired circumference and separate the strands. Temporarily whip each strand with a constrictor knot and – with one strand – form the desired size of the loop. Without tightening too much, twist the strand spirally around itself in place of the second strand. Do the same to fill the space of the third strand, then go back to the start and smooth everything out. To finish, divide each strand into two smaller strands and tie one strand from each end together with an overhand knot. Pass these strands under two, over one, and under two again. Trim flush and cover with whipping.

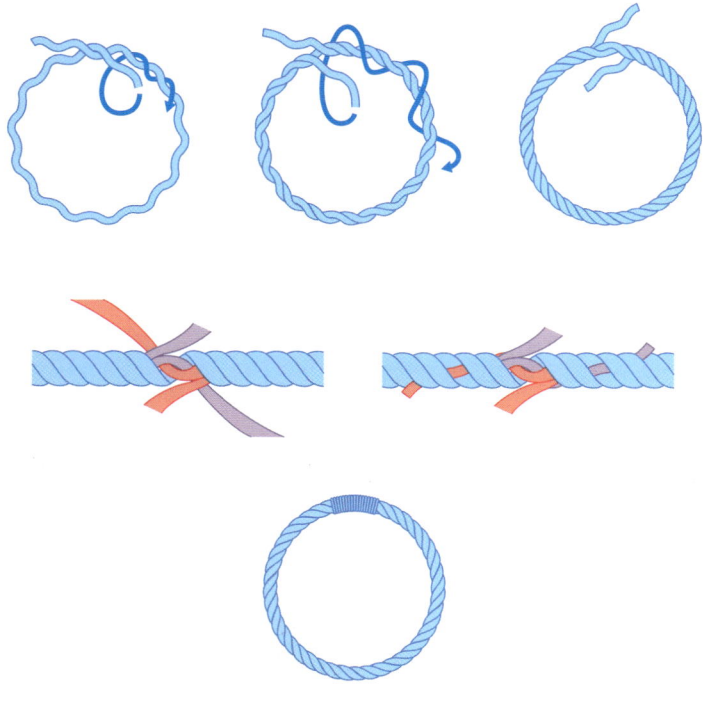

TIPS & TRICKS

Choose a fairly stiff rope to make a grommet splice, as it holds its shape more easily.

'Modern' eye splice on a single-braid rope.

Cut a piece of single-braid rope at least three times longer than the desired length of the eye splice. On the rope, mark a section corresponding to the eye splice length with markers for the start and end points. Pass one end of the rope through the braid at the furthest marker point. Then, pass the other end through the first one, right next to the crossing. Find the middle of the eye splice and insert a long-eye needle. Bring the needle out at the first crossing and pull the second end through the braid. Do the same with the other end. Expand the eye splice to its maximum size and, cutting excess if needed, bury the ends inside the braid.

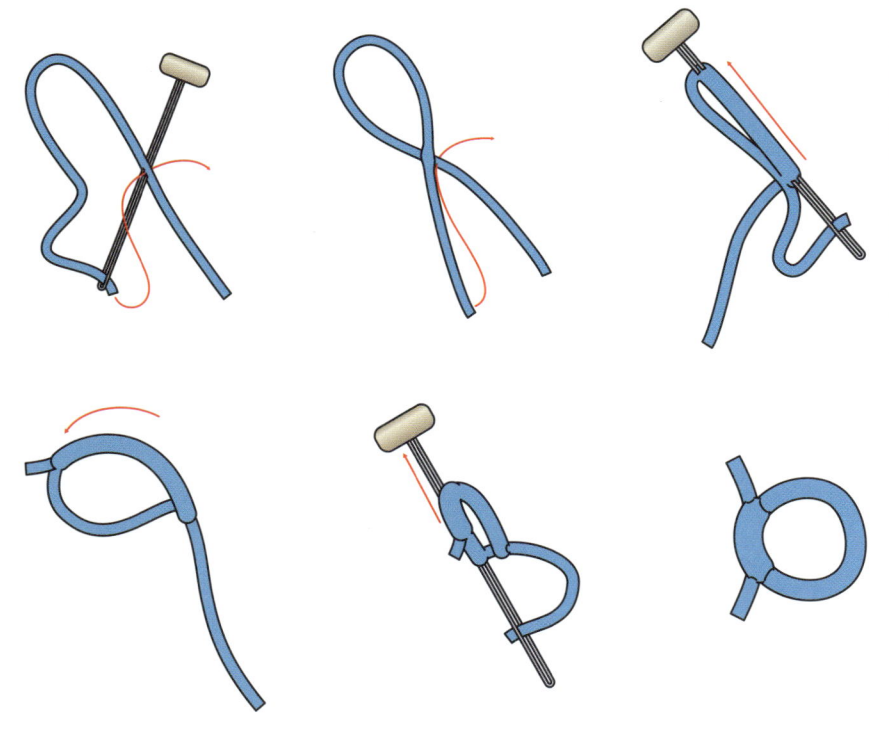

SPLICING ON MODERN CORDAGE

Long splicing

Knot type: Loop

Use: Create a permanent loop at the end of a single-braid rope.

Method: Insert the working end through the single braid at a suitable distance from the end, then pull it out at least three needle lengths further along for splicing. Trim the excess and bury the end within the braid. Add a stitch at the eye's crossing to maintain its size when the rope is not under tension.

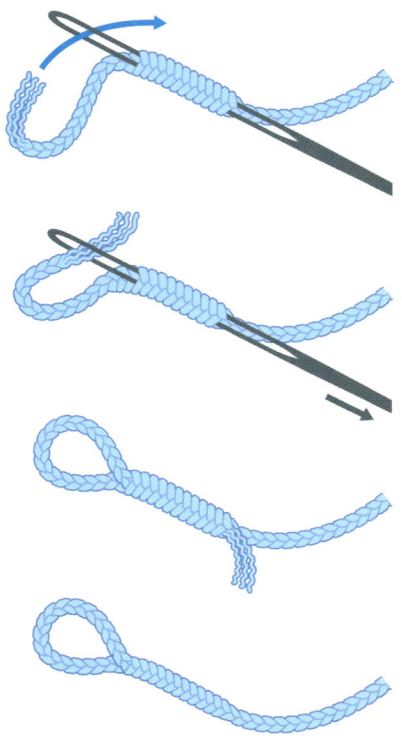

TOOLS

Here, a splicing needle or fid is used. There are several types: some are hollow so that you can insert parts of the rope inside; others are long-eyed needles, usually equipped with a small handle.

TIPS & TRICKS

This technique is suited for static operations (under constant load). For dynamic use, use the **Brummel splice** as an alternative.

Brummel splicing

Knot type: Loop

Method: Pass the working end through the braid at a suitable distance from the end, then pass the standing part through the working end about 2–3cm from the first crossing. Pull on the standing part and the loop to bring the crossings closer together.

Using a splicing needle, insert the end into the braid about 1cm from the crossing for a length equal to two or three needle lengths. Trim the excess and bury the end within the braid.

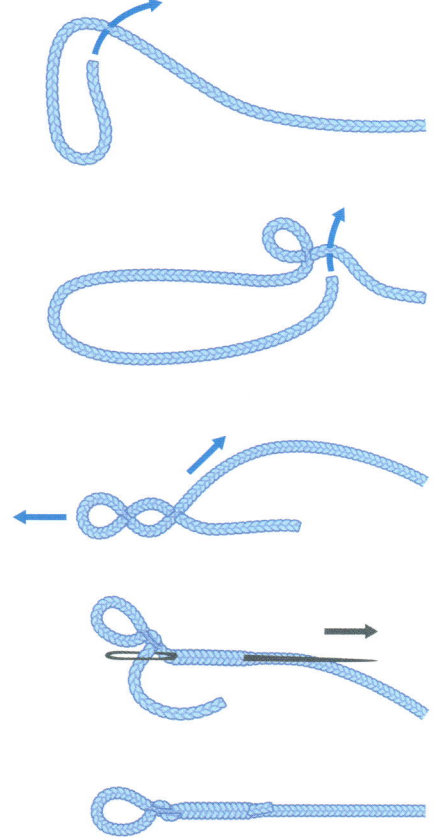

To create an eye – a permanent loop at the end of a braided rope – you can also simply make a

Stitched eye

To do this, fold the rope back on itself to form the loop and sew the end onto the standing part. Make sure to pass the needle through the centre of the rope. Use slightly angled stitches to counteract the pulling forces. Apply a tight whipping along the entire length of the sewn section.

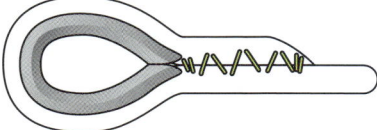
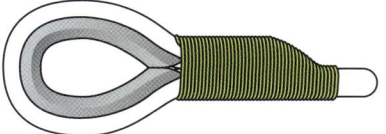

Soft shackle

Knot type: Loop

Use: Create a joining device to replace, among other things, a shackle on a sailboat.

Method: Cut a piece of single-braid rope at least three times longer than the desired length of the eye splice. Mark two points on the rope with a marker to indicate the start and end of the splice. Using a splicing needle, insert one end into the braid at the nearest marker and bring it out at the other marker. Before pulling the entire end through the braid, optionally place a piece of wood or a fid inside the loop to prevent it from closing completely. Near where the end exits the braid, pass it back through the other side to lock the splice section. With both ends, tie a stopper knot such as a **bosun's whistle knot** (see page 92). Enlarge the loop to pass the stopper knot through, then close the loop around the stopper by pulling the outer braid toward the base of the loop.

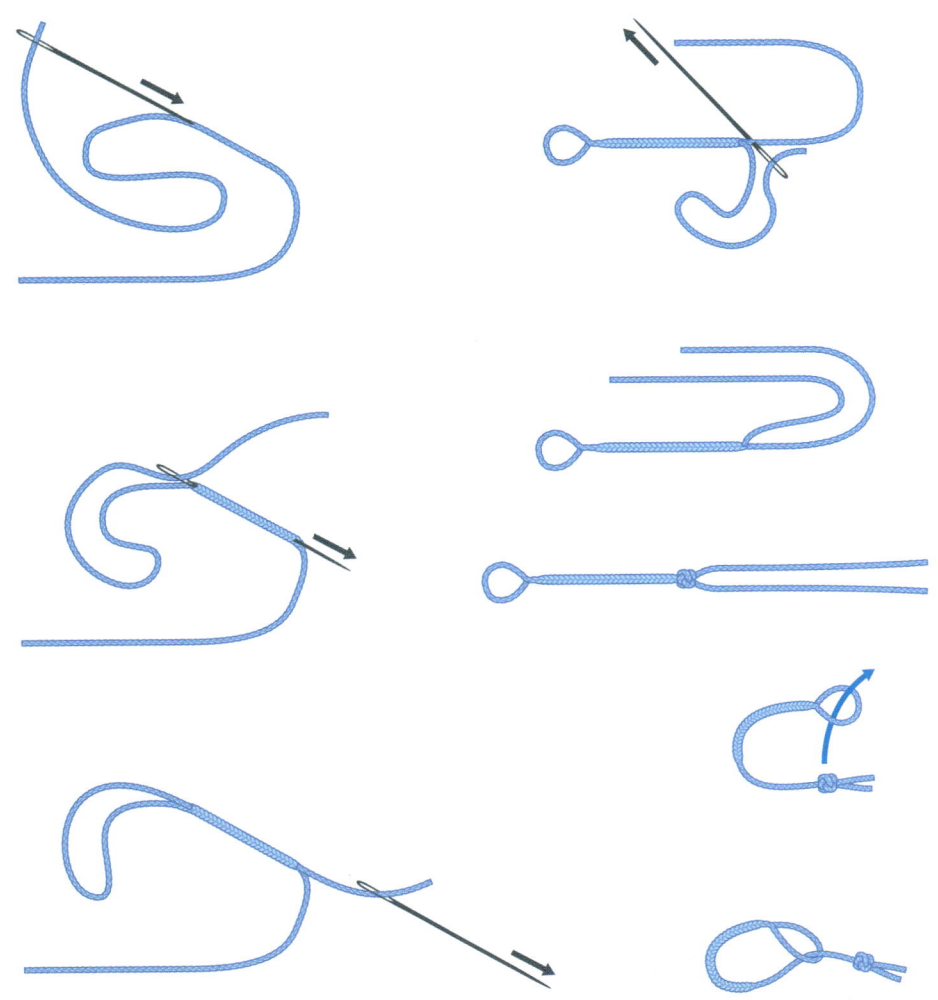

CLIMBING KNOTS

COMMON REUSABLE KNOTS

Water knot

Use: A joining knot. Avoid using as a descending knot, as it may jam in the carabiner.

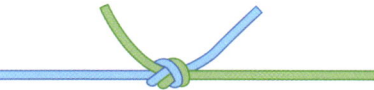

Tape knot

Use: Although it has a similar shape, the strap knot differs from the water knot by its tying method, which is adapted for flat materials.

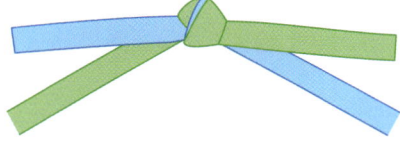

Munter mule knot

Reusable knot: Slipped running knot

Use: Used to temporarily lock a rope under tension, for example, during a self-rescue operation. It is usually paired with a **half-hitch**. Always secure the loop by tying a **safety knot** or by adding a carabiner (see page 152).

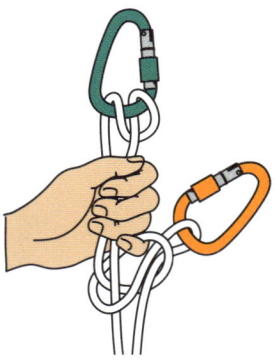

Cow tail, overhand loop

Use: Create a loop on a rope or anchor. It can be tied, if needed, without using the rope ends.

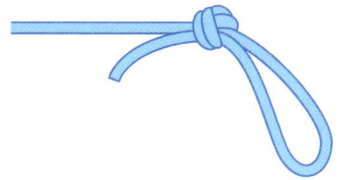

Clove hitch

Use: Intermediate knot for a handline. Never use at the end of a handline without securing it with a **safety knot or enhanced safety knot** (see page 144).

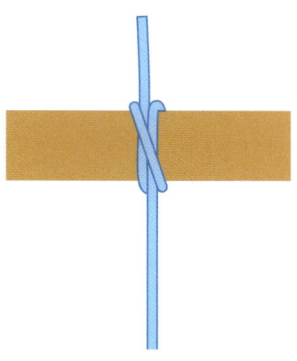

Simple descending knot

Reusable knot: Overhand bend

Use: Join two ropes together to form a descending rope. When descending, leave the ends of the knot extending about 40cm.

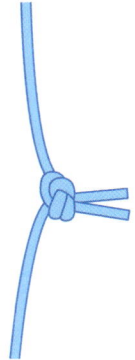

Figure eight knot

Use: Stopper knot. When descending, leave the ends of the knot extending about 40cm.

Figure eight bend

Use: Place the two ropes to be joined side by side, then tie a **figure eight knot**. When descending, leave the ends of the knot extending about 40cm.

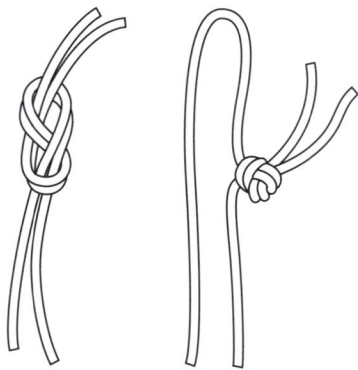

Securing knots

The safety knot or enhanced safety knot is used to secure other knots.

Caution: Regardless of the knot you tie, secured or not, always ensure the end extends at least 10cm beyond the knot to allow for any possible rope slippage. Furthermore, the knots presented in this chapter serve as a reminder or quick reference and are not a substitute for formal training. It is essential to receive supervised instruction in real conditions through a club affiliated with the British Mountaineering Council (BMC), Mountaineering Scotland, or Mountaineering Ireland before attempting to climb a vertical rock face.

Safety knot

Reusable knot: Half knot

Use: Secure any knot that might slip and come undone, especially the **clove hitch**.

Enhanced safety knot

Reusable knot: Strangle knot

Use: Secure any knot that might slip and come undone. It is more secure than the **safety knot** but also more difficult to tie.

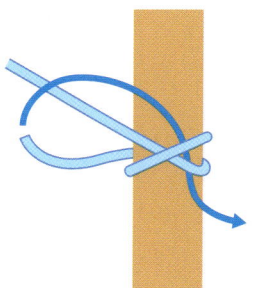

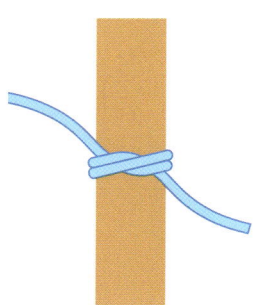

SPECIFIC CLIMBING KNOTS

Tethering knots

The bowline with a stopper turn and the figure eight on a bight, secured with a half-hitch, are known as 'tethering' knots.

Bowline with a stopper turn

Knot type: Loop

Use: Tethering knot also used to attach a rope to a fixed point – a ring, or a post, etc. – for example, at each end of a handrail.

Method for tying the knot: Pass the rope through the harness and tie a **bowline with a stopper turn**. Secure the end by attaching it to the loop using a **safety knot** or an **enhanced safety knot**, the latter being the most secure.

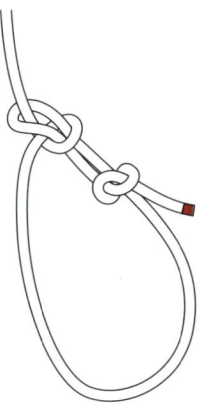 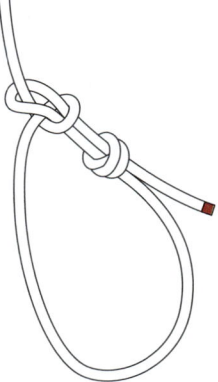

Figure eight follow-through knot

Knot type: Loop

Method for tying the knot: Make a **figure eight knot** with the end toward you. Pass the end through the harness, then follow the original knot backwards. There's no need to secure the end.

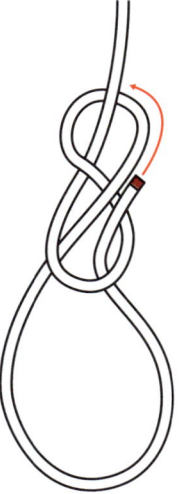

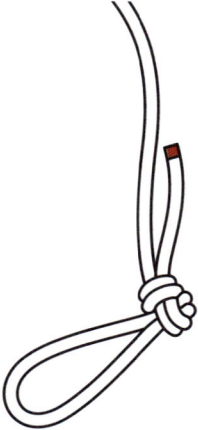

Rope loops

The loop, the figure eight follow-through knot, and the double fisherman's knot are used to join ropes – or rope ends – to form loops or slings.

Loop / cordelette

Knot type: Sling

Use: Basic component of several locking knots, as well as anchor knots.

Method for tying the knot: Tie the ends of a single rope, cord, or strap to form a textile loop of the desired size. In climbing, knots commonly used to close the loop include the **double fisherman's bend**, the **water knot** and the **Flemish bend**.

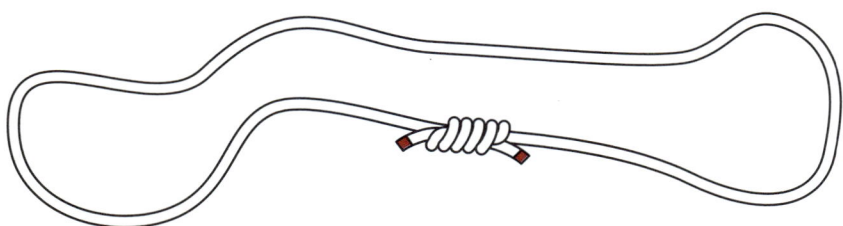

Flemish bend

Knot type: Bend

Method for tying the knot: Make a **figure eight knot** at the end of one of the ropes to be joined; then, with the end of the other rope, follow the shape of the knot in reverse. Tighten so the knot is rounded, like a button, rather than flattened.

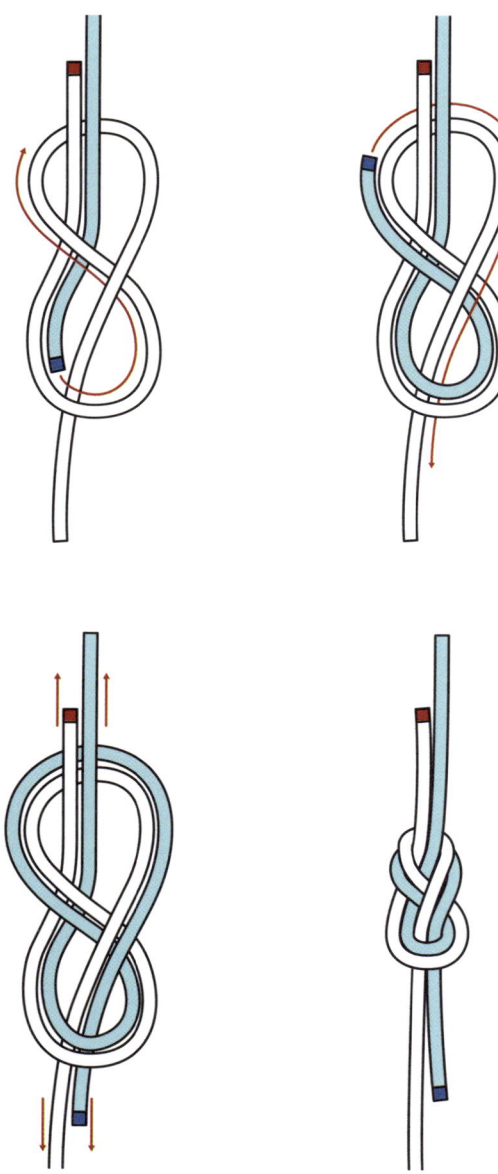

Double fisherman's bend

Knot type: Bend

Use: Probably the knot used most frequently for making a loop in a cord.

Method for tying the knot: Tie an **enhanced safety knot** loosely at one end of the ropes to be joined. Pass the end of the other rope through the knot, then make a second double fisherman's knot around the standing part of the first rope. Tighten both knots separately, then pull the standing parts in opposite directions to bring the two knots together.

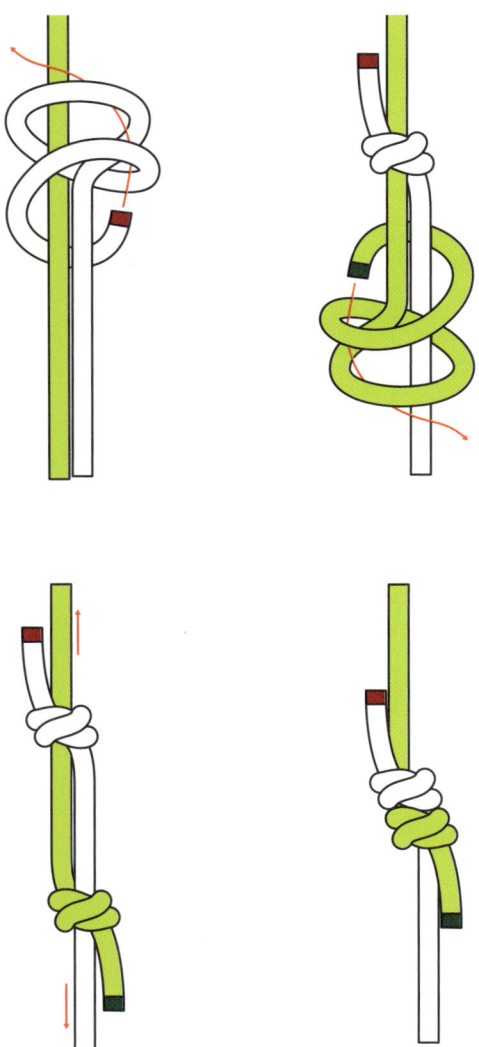

Blocking a rope

Knots used to block a rope, and thus to belay (attach) someone
or self-belay, require particular care in order to prevent accidents.

Blocking clove hitch knot

Knot type: Fastening

Use: Self-belay at the anchor point.

Method for tying the knot: See **open-ended clove hitch** in the basic knots section. This knot
is easy to tie and adjust. It works on either strand. You can adjust the length of the strands
without untying the knot.

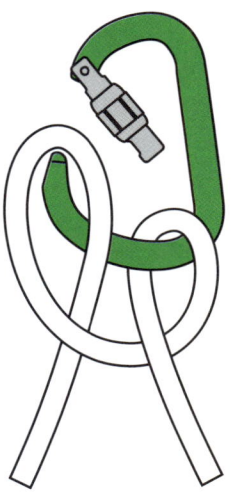 

TIPS & TRICKS

You can also tie a **one-handed blocking clove hitch**. To do this, make a **half-hitch**
on the carabiner with the right descending strand in front, then make a second
half-hitch with the left descending strand behind the horizontal part of the knot.

Munter hitch

Knot type: Locking

Use: Belay a climbing partner or set up an improvised descent.

Method for tying the knot: Make a **half-hitch** on the carabiner with the right descending strand in front, then pass the rope again but in the opposite direction. The belayer attaches to the left strand.

Caution: Although this knot is simple and effective, it causes wear and heat on the carabiner.

 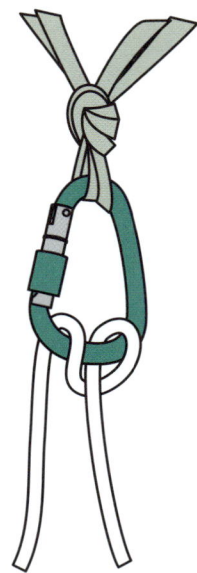

Munter mule knot

See also page 142 in the common reusable knots.

Knot type: Loop

Use: Temporarily lock a rope under tension.

Method for tying the knot: Hold the tensioned rope and the free end in one hand. Make a **half-hitch** with the free end around the little finger of the hand holding both strands. Double the rope and pass it around and through the half-hitch. Remove the finger and tighten the half-hitch around the loop. From now on, the mule knot will lock the tension by pressing against the carabiner.

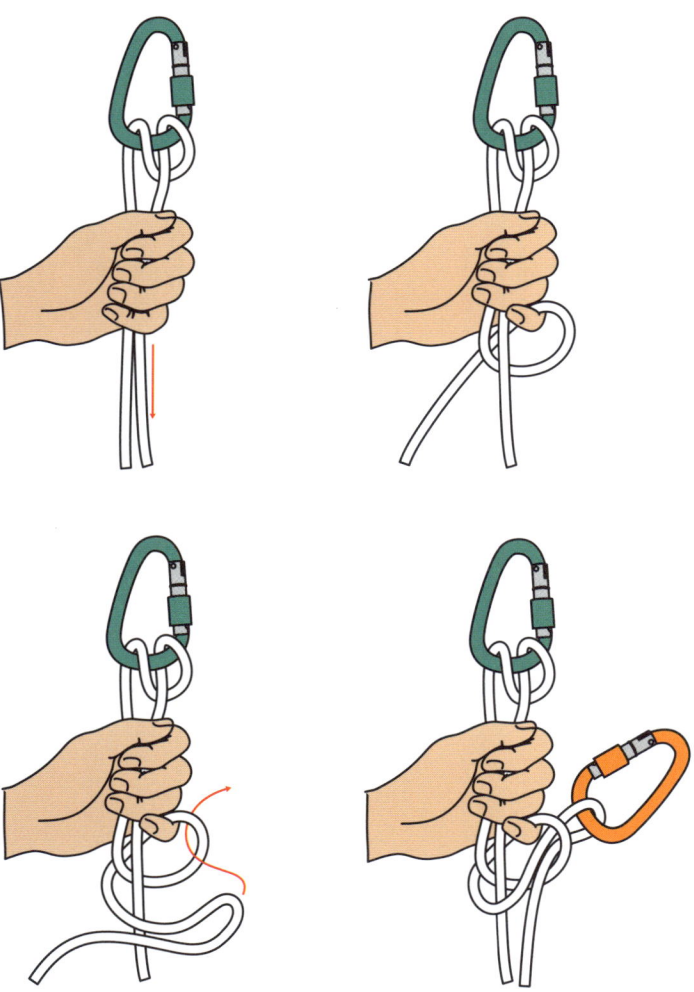

Self-locking knots

On a rope or on a carabiner, self-locking knots are used for rappelling, ascending a rope, or creating a hauling system. Always test the number of wraps needed for a secure hold before use.

Machard knot

Knot type: Self-locking

Use: Belay a descent, climb a rope, or set up a hauling system. Always test the number of wraps needed for a secure lock before use.

Method for tying the knot: Wrap the cord **loop** around the fixed rope at least three times, then stack the loops to hold the carabiner. This knot was invented by Serge Machard.

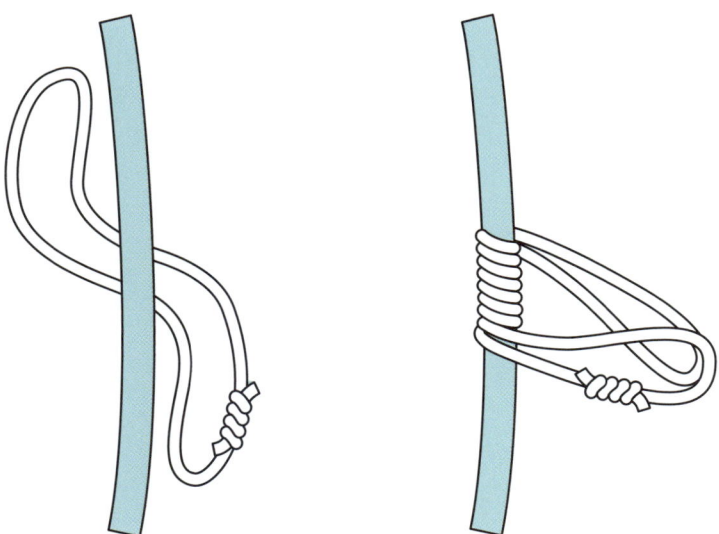

Braided Klemheist knot

Knot type: Self-locking friction knot

This knot is uni-directional.

Method for tying the knot: Wrap the **loop** of cord around the fixed rope at least three times, then bring the upper loop down toward the lower loop in spirals. Cross the two loops around the fixed rope, one passing over and the other under. Bring the upper loop back to the front, wrapping it around the fixed rope. Stack the loops to receive the carabiner.

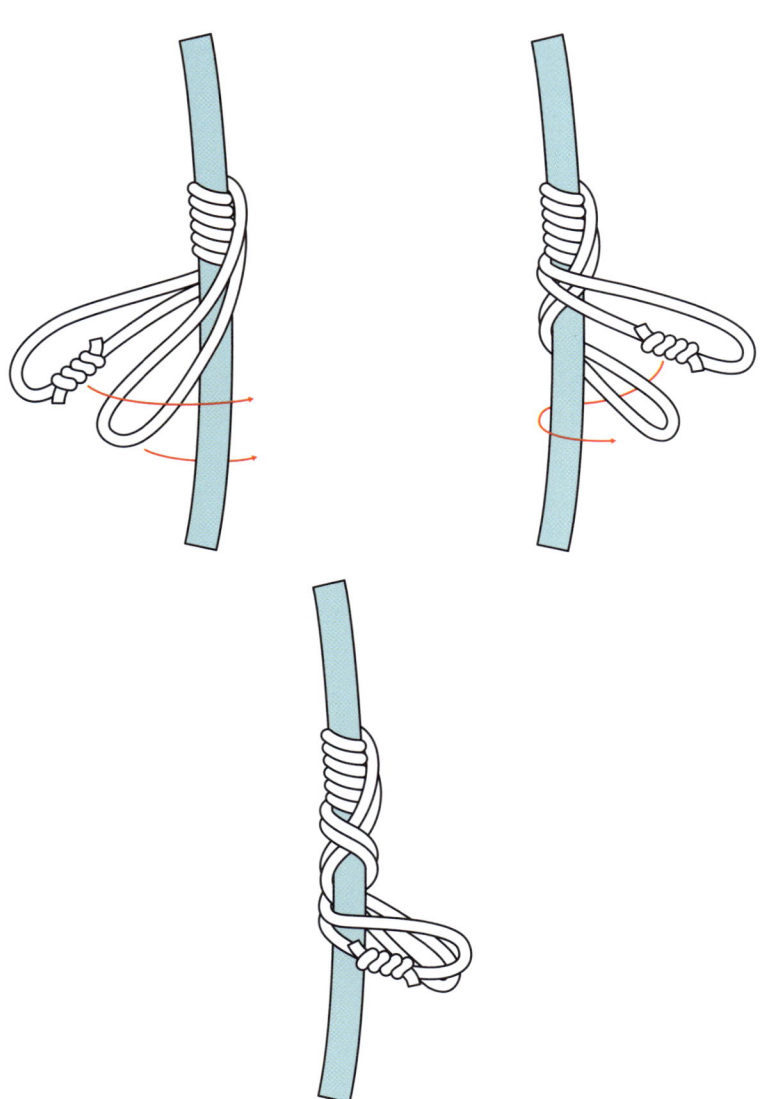

Klemheist knot

Knot type: Self-locking friction knot

This knot is uni-directional.

Method for tying the knot: Wrap the **loop** of cord around the fixed rope at least three times, then pass the lower loop through the upper one to form the loop that will hold the carabiner.

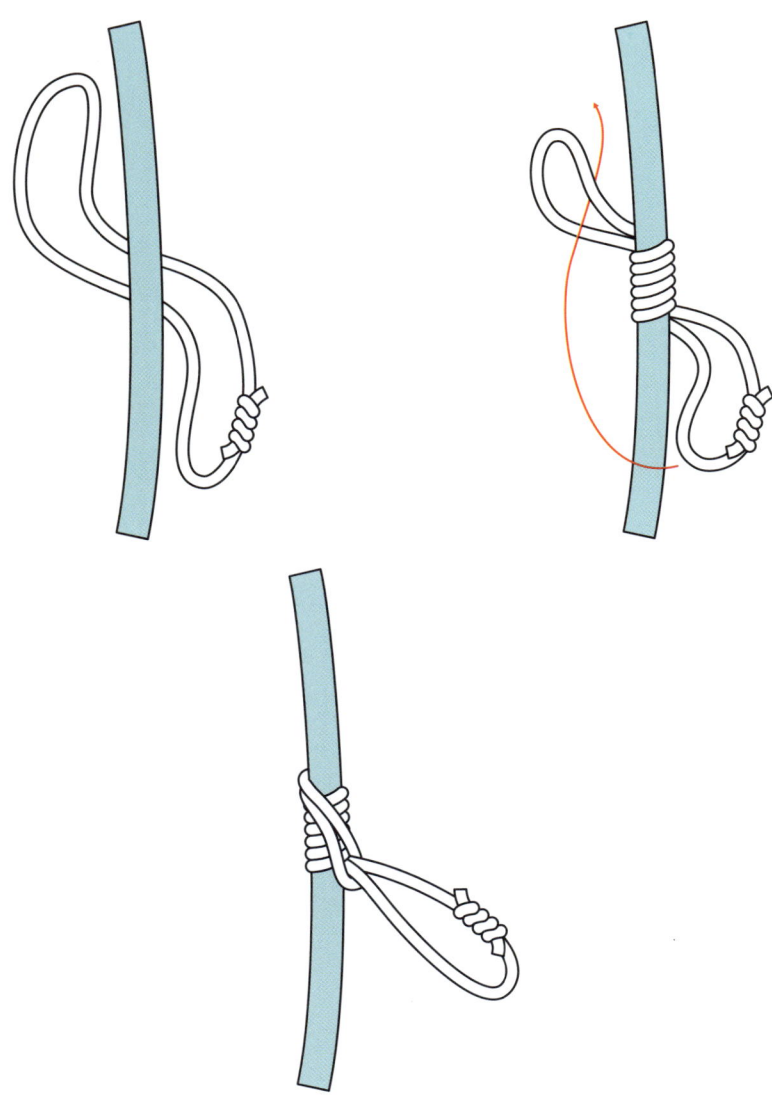

Prusik knot

Knot type: Self-locking friction knot

Method for tying the knot: Wrap the **loop** of cord around the fixed rope, passing one loop through the other at least three times. This knot was invented by Karl Prusik.

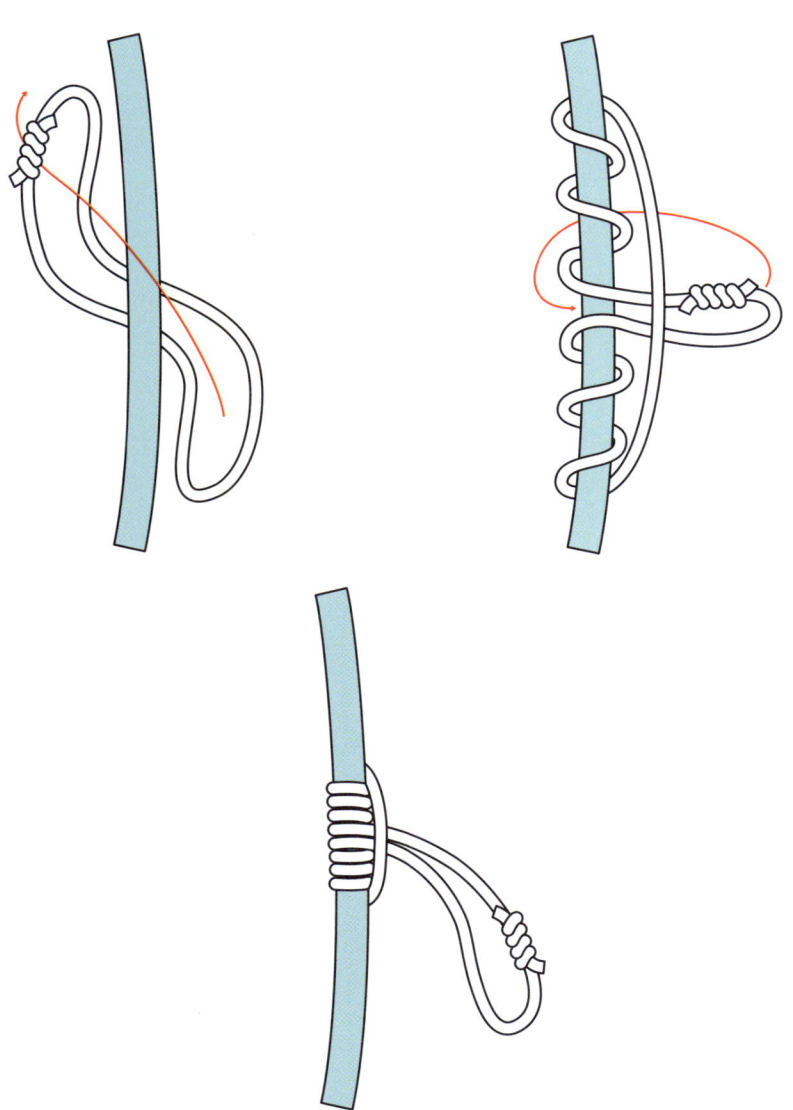

Valdotain tresse

Knot type: Self-locking friction knot

Method for tying the knot: Wrap the moving rope around the fixed rope like an **Machard knot** (see page 153). Connect the two ends using a **bowline knot**, then secure the end with a **safety knot or enhanced safety knot**. This knot is made with a single strand. It minimises the number of ropes needed to create a pulley system and works in both directions.

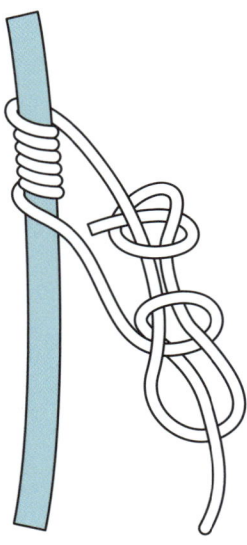

Blake's hitch

Knot type: Self-locking friction knot

Method for tying the knot: Wrap the moving rope upward around the fixed rope; then – with the end – pass underneath the standing part, go back up, and pass under the second-to-last turn. Secure with a **figure eight knot**.

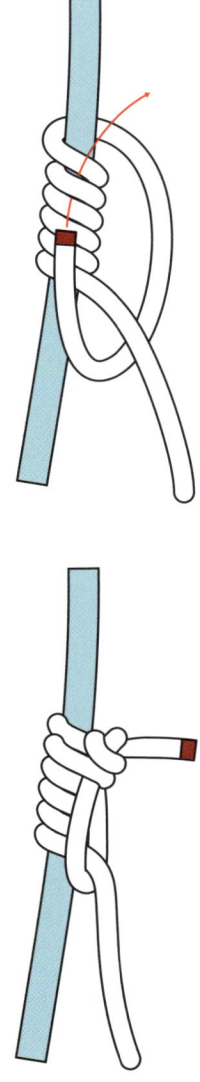

Garda hitch

Knot type: Self-locking

Use: Secure a climbing partner or create an ascent on a fixed rope.

Method for tying the knot: Pass the rope over both carabiners. Then, wrap it again over the left carabiner, moving clockwise. The knot locks as soon as the left strand is under tension.

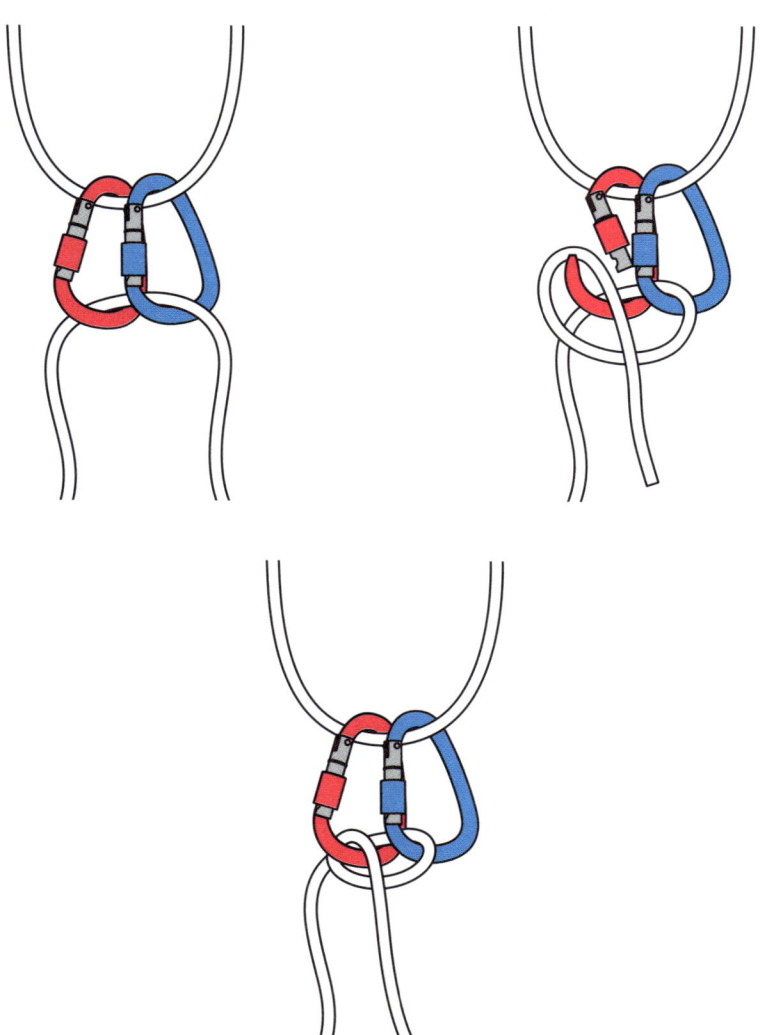

Self-locking half-hitch

Knot type: Self-locking

Use: Secure a climbing partner.

Method for tying the knot: Make a **half-hitch**, then add a second carabiner on the initial half-hitch. The belayer attaches to the left strand.

Caution: It is difficult, or even impossible, to give slack if the knot is under tension.

It is also called the running knot.

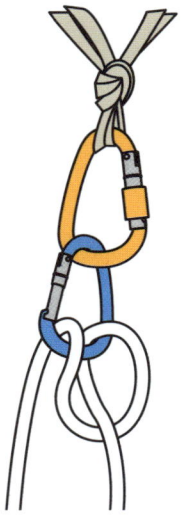
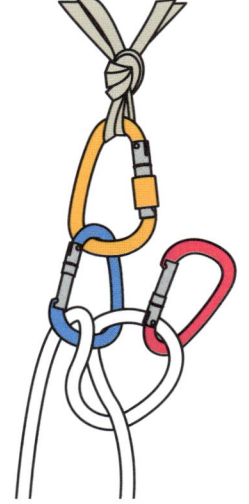

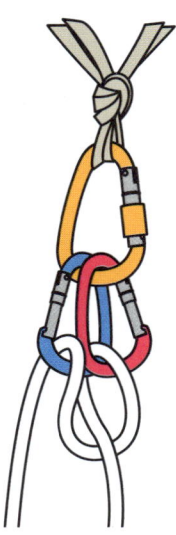

Lorenzi's hitch

Knot type: Self-locking

Use: Secure a climbing partner.

Method for tying the knot: Make a wrap (turn) around the carabiner, then slide it upwards. Attach a second carabiner under the knot's crossing and be sure to pass both strands through it. The climber ties onto the left strand (the one on top).

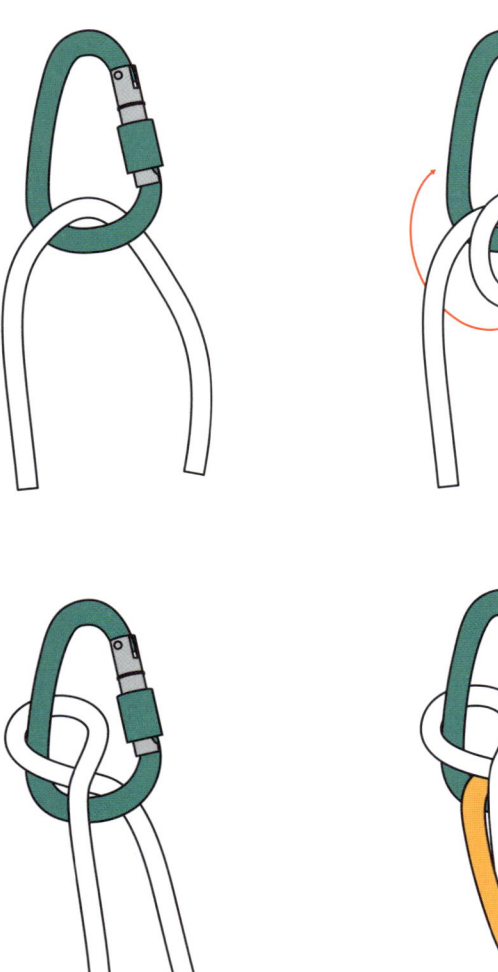

Anchorage points

For anchor knots, it's generally important to always use very solid anchor points to prevent falls and accidents.

Figure eight loop on a bight

Knot type: Loop

Use: Create a loop on a rope or anchor.

Method for tying the knot: Fold the rope and tie a **figure eight knot** with the bight.

TIPS & TRICKS

Can be tied, if needed, without using the rope ends. Its final shape is identical to the **figure eight follow-through knot**.

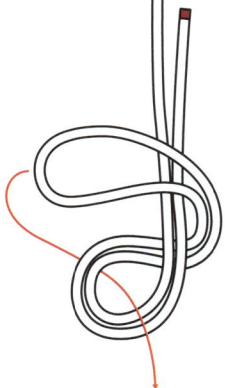

Bale sling hitch

Knot type: Fastening

Use: Attach a loop of rope or webbing to a support such as a tree, post, or beam.

Method for tying the knot: See the **bale sling** in the basic knots. This knot will move less on the support than a simple anchor (without a turn). It also takes up less space on the carabiner.

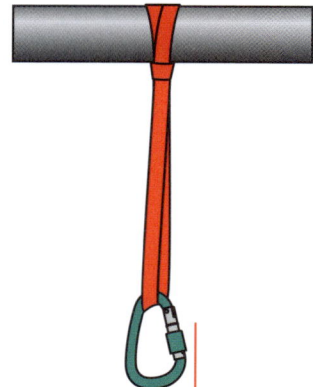

Uni-directional two-point anchor with a loop

Knot type: Sling

Use: Set up a fixed rope, a descent, a hauling system, etc.

Method for tying the knot: Double the loop, then tie the attachment loop with a **figure eight knot** or a **cow tail knot**. Anchor points are secured with carabiners. This uni-directional knot is safe even if one of the points tears off or the loop breaks on one of the anchor points.

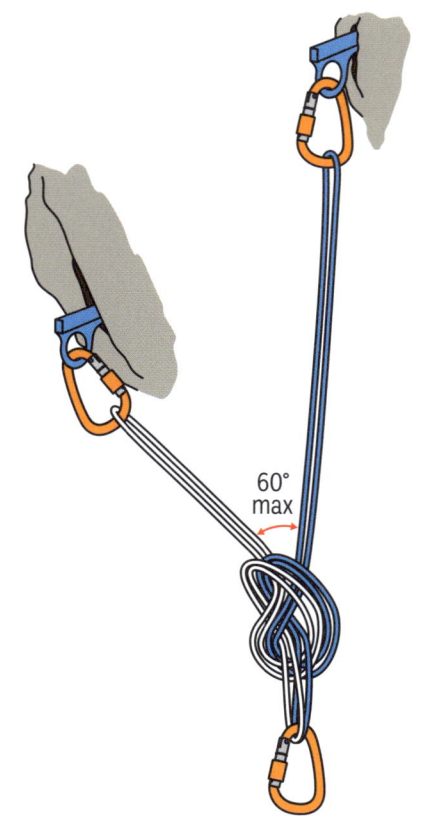

60°
max

Multi-directional two-point anchor

Knot type: Sling

Use: Set up a fixed rope, a descent, a hauling system, etc.

Method for tying the knot: Attach the **loop** to the two anchor points, then make a loop on the upper strand. The attachment carabiner hooks around the lower strand and through the loop. This multi-directional knot is secure even if one of the points fails.

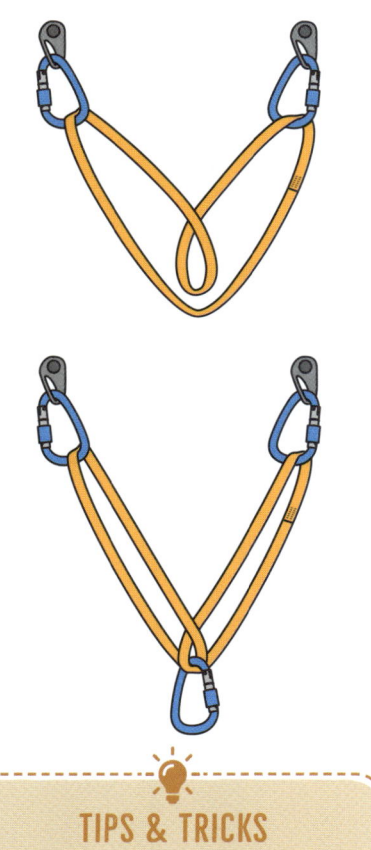

TIPS & TRICKS

Use with very strong anchor points because in case of failure, the remaining point is subjected to intense stress.

Three-point uni-directional anchor

Knot type: Sling

Use: Set up a fixed rope, a descent, a hauling system, etc.

Method for tying the knot: Make a **multi-directional three-point anchor** (see page 164) and tie the two half hitches and the lower turn with a cow hitch or a **figure eight knot**. This uni-directional knot is secure even if one of the points tears out or the **loop** breaks at one of the anchor points.

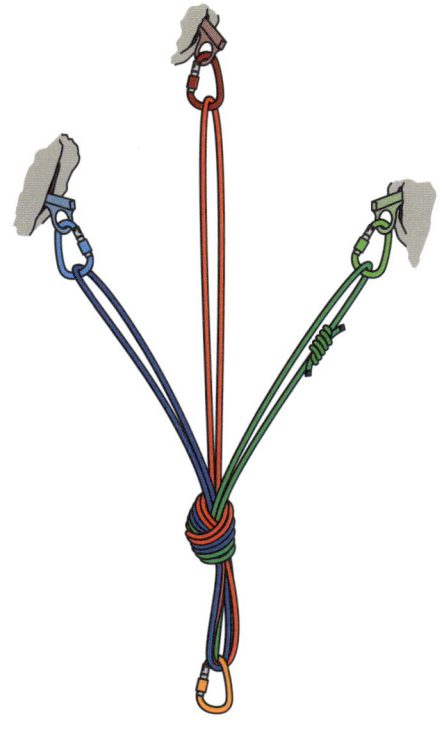

Multi-directional three-point anchor

Knot type: Sling

Use: Set up a fixed rope, a descent, a hauling system, etc.

Method for tying the knot: Hang the top of the ring on the three anchor points so that one strand hangs between the right and left points without passing through the middle one. Twist the strand between the left and middle points to the left to form a loop, then do the same with the strand between the middle and right points. Overlap the two loops and attach the carabiner around the lower strand and through the loops. This multi-directional knot is secure even if one of the points fails.

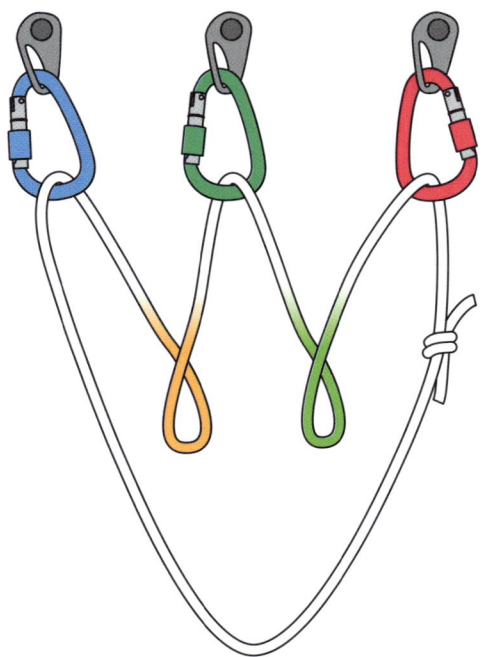
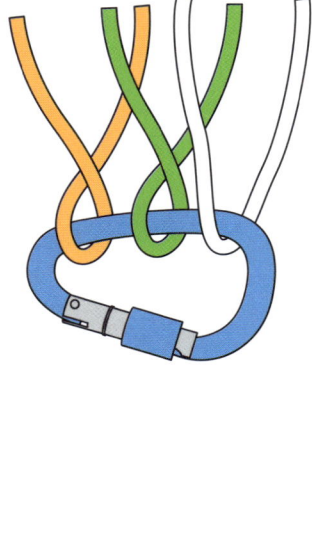

Uni-directional two-point anchor on a single strand

Knot type: Sling

Use: Set up a fixed rope, a descent, a hauling system, etc.

Method for tying the knot: Tie a **figure eight knot on the bight** or as a **follow-through knot**. The attachment loop can be made with a **cow hitch** instead of a figure eight knot. This one-way knot is secure even if one of the points pulls out or the ring at an anchor point breaks.

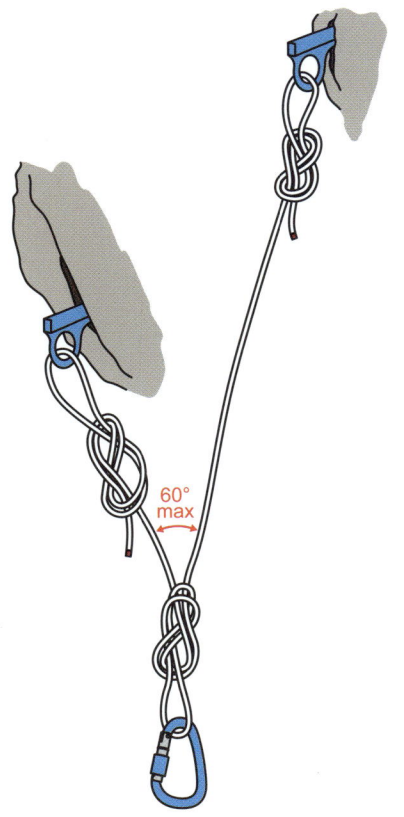

60°
max

Simple anchor

Knot type: Sling

Use: Set up a fixed rope, a descent, a hauling system, etc.

Method for tying the knot: Make two turns around the anchor point (rock, tree, post) and join the two ends with a double **fisherman's bend** or a **figure eight follow-through knot**.

Caution: It is better to use a multi-point anchor to reduce the risk of failure or pulling out.

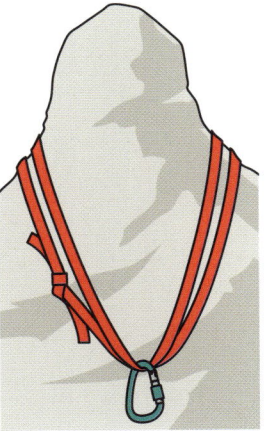

Alpine butterfly loop

Knot type: Loop

Use: Intermediate knot for a handline or used to tie in a second climber on a belay loop.

Method for tying the knot: Fold the rope to make a loop, then twist twice to the right. Bring the loop down while keeping a hole in the middle of the knot. Pass the loop through the hole from behind to complete the loop. Finish tightening by pulling the strands on each side of the knot in opposite directions.

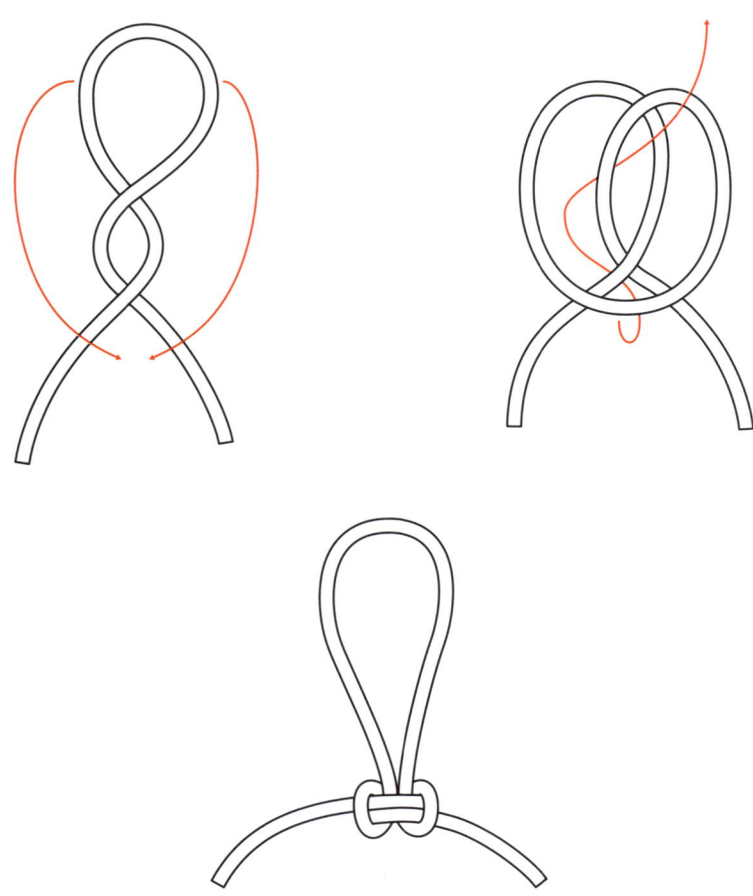

Setting up a hauling system

A hauling system is a setup that allows you to lift or raise a heavy object and can also be used to rescue someone who has fallen into a crevasse.

Simple hauling system

Knot type: Assembly

Use: Hoist a heavy load or haul someone out of a crevasse.

Method for tying the knot: Make a **friction knot** on the rope and attach it to the anchor's caribiner. Pass the standing part of the rope through the anchor's carabiner. Tie a second friction knot lower on the rope and attach a carabiner to it. Pass the rope's end through this carabiner. Pull on the rope's end to set the hauling system in motion. When the lower friction knot reaches the anchor, clip its carabiner to the anchor, then redo the upper friction knot around the standing part to keep the length of rope hauled in. Repeat this procedure as many times as necessary. Requires an immovable anchor point. In theory, it multiplies the effort by about three times, but in practice, friction around the carabiner significantly reduces this advantage. Be careful about the standing part rubbing against the rock face.

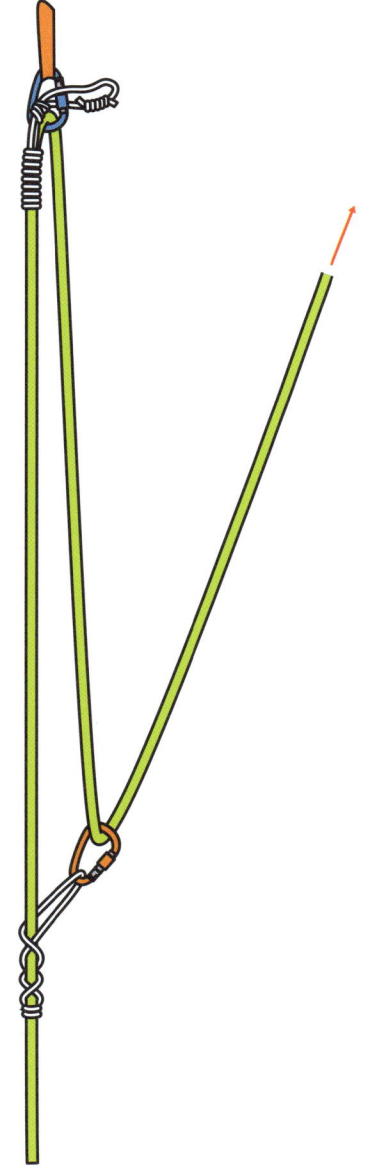

Enhanced hauling system

Knot type: Assembly

Use: Hoist a heavy load or haul someone out of a crevasse.

Method for tying the knot: Set up a simple hauling system but add an intermediate strand that passes through the lower carabiner and is attached to the rope's end (next to the anchor) using a **friction knot**. Pass the rope's end through the intermediate strand's carabiner and pull to engage the hauling system. This time, points B and C will move closer together. Redistribute the friction hitches on the rope to repeat the process. This setup offers better efficiency than a simple hauling system, with a theoretical mechanical advantage of about five times. It requires an unbreakable anchor point. Be careful of friction between the rope's standing part and the rock face.

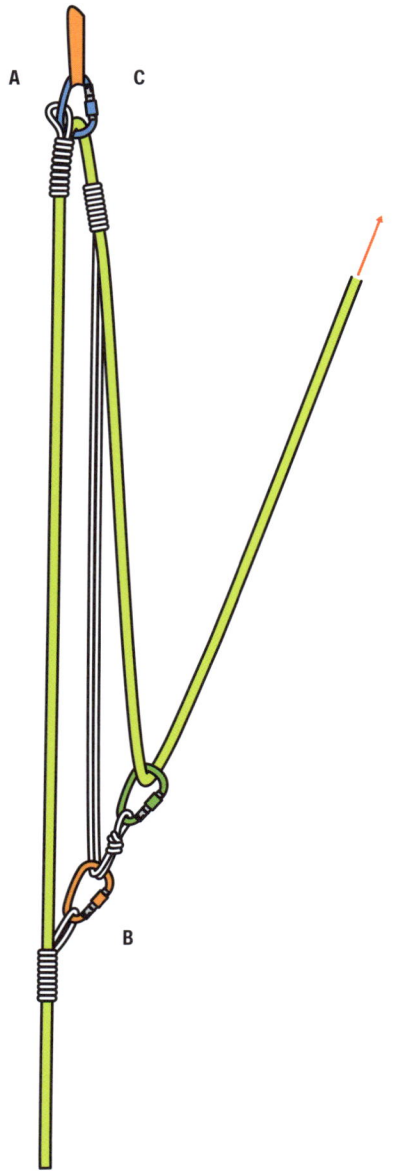

Coiling techniques

Coiling a rope makes it easier to store or carry.

Alpine coil

Knot type: Coil

Use: Carry a rope slung over the shoulder.

Method for tying the knot: Coil the rope and double the end to create a bight. Wrap the starting end around the rope and over the looped part. Pass the starting end through the bight, then pull on the loop's end to close it. Tie the two ends together with a **reef knot**.

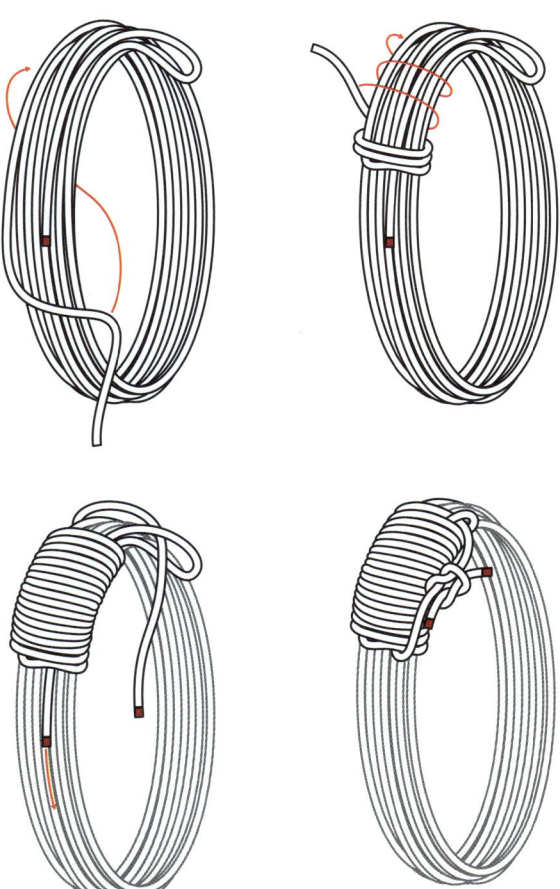

Backpack coil

Knot type: Coil

Use: Carry a rope on your back.

Method for tying the knot: Coil the rope and fold it in half. Unravel each end for one or two turns, then wrap them around the coiled rope (several wraps from top to bottom). Double the ends to form a loop, then pass it through the coiled rope. Thread the ends through the loop to lock everything in place. To wear it as a 'backpack', pass the ends over your shoulders and behind your back, then tie them at your waist with a **reef knot**.

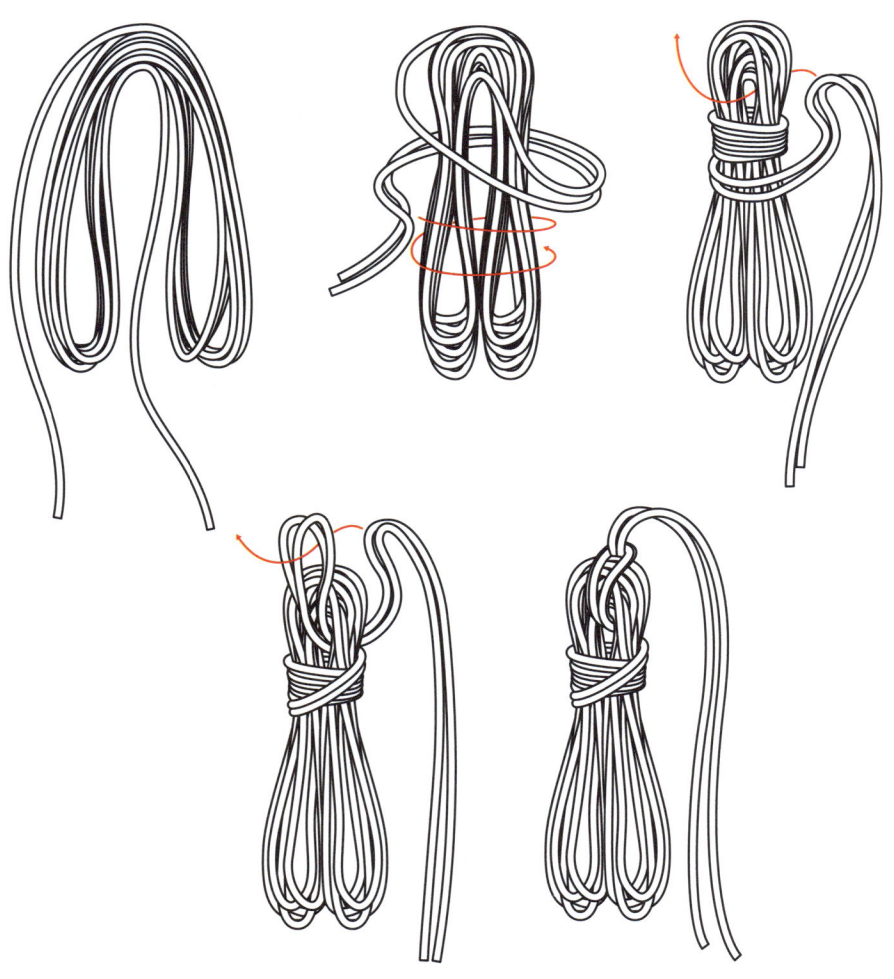

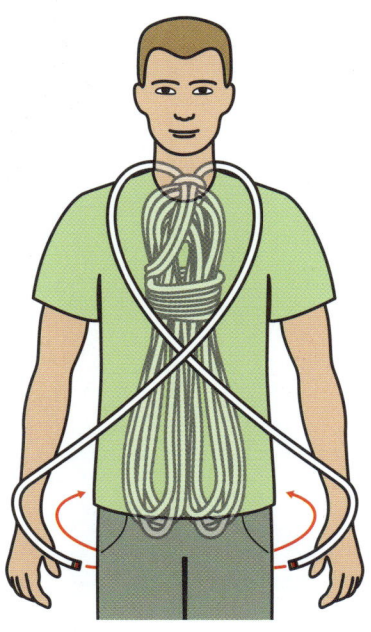

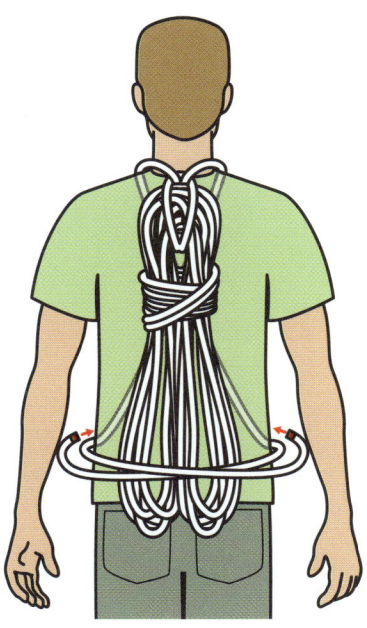

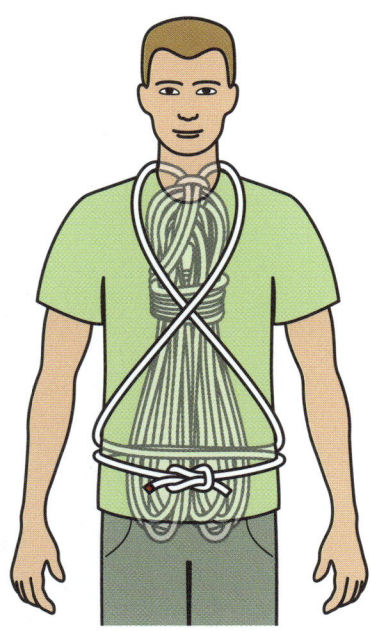

FARM KNOTS

COMMON REUSABLE KNOTS

Farm knots

When it comes to farm life, knowing your way around a few knots is an absolute must: whether you're catching or tying up animals, tidying tools, or bundling hay into neat little stacks, they're indispensible.

Military halter knot

Knot to use: Groundline hitch

Use: Securely tie a halter, lead, leash, or any other rope to a fixed support like a fence or a taut line. Avoid using a vertical post, as the animal might spin around and undo the knot (better to use the **long knot** in this situation, see page 176). For a temporary tie, make a bight at the end so that you can easily untie.

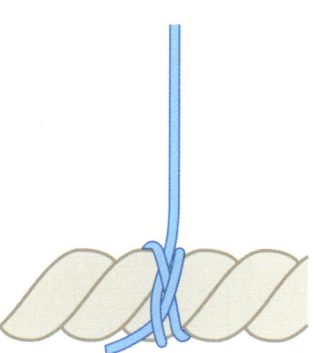

Cormick-type bottle knot

Knot to use: Overhand loop

Use: Tie up a bale of straw or hay. This knot is more of theoretical interest, as it's the one made by mechanical binders. When tying by hand, the **packing knot** (see page 64) is better suited to the task.

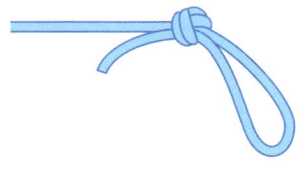

Deering-type binding knot

Knot to use: Overhand bend

Use: Tie up a bale of straw or hay. This knot is more of theoretical interest, as it's the one made by mechanical binders. When tying by hand, the **packing knot** is better suited to the task.

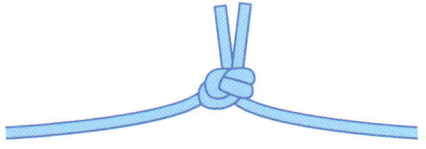

Square knot

Knot to use: Reef knot

Use: Join two lengths of agricultural twine. The 'square knot' is the country name for this knot. People say never to use this knot to join two ropes, but it actually holds very well with agricultural twine.

ANOTHER KNOT TO REUSE:
the alpine butterfly loop (see page 166)

Use: The alpine butterfly knot is used to create a tie line that allows horses to be tied while keeping them spaced apart. Use a **halter knot** to attach the horses' lead ropes to the loops formed by the knots along the tie line.

SPECIFIC TYPES OF FARM KNOTS

Hitching animals

Long knots, manger knots, halter knots, hobble knots, military halter knots, and tie lines (see reusable common knots) are all used for securing animals.

Long knot

Knot type: Fastening

Use: Tie an animal to a post or stake so it can graze.

Method for tying the knot: Tie the end of the lead rope to the post using a **cow hitch**. Unlike other fastening knots, such as the **clove hitch**, the lead rope knot resists twisting, allowing the animal to turn around its post without untying the knot.

Manger hitch

Knot type: Fastening

Use: Tie an animal to a ring.

Method for tying the knot: Pass the rope around the support, creating a long loop. Then, wrap the end twice around both sides of the loop. To finish, make a binding and pass the end over the wraps and through the **half-hitch** formed by the wraps. If the animal drools (as a cow might do, for example) on a natural fibre lead rope, the fibres can swell and make most knots hard to undo, which is why the wraps in this knot are particularly useful.

 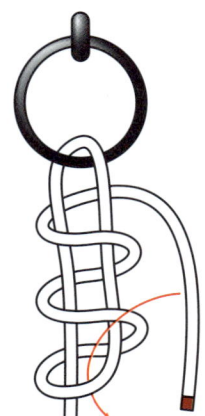 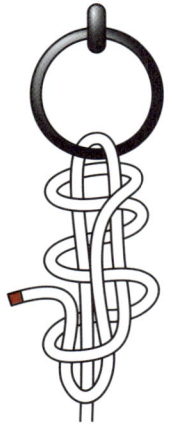

Halter knot

Knot type: Bend

Method for tying the knot: Pass the halter through the ring, then make a loop around the standing part with the crossing on top. Double the end and pass the loop through the loop, forming a **overhand loop** around the standing part. Secure the knot by passing the end through the loop.

TIPS & TRICKS

Tying the overhand loop allows for the quick release of the halter, but a clever animal might free itself by pulling on the end with its teeth. The solution is to pass the end through the loop.

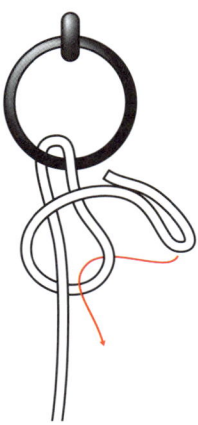

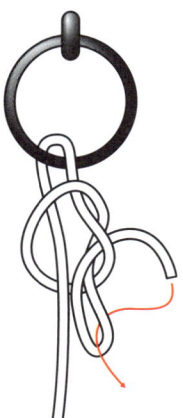

Highwayman's hitch

Knot type: Fastening

Use: Attach an animal to a railing or fence.

Method for tying the knot: Fold the lead rope back onto itself to form a loop and pass this loop underneath the attachment point. Form a second loop in the standing part and pass it over the attachment point and through the first loop. Finally, make a third loop in the running end that will pass through the second loop. Pull on the standing part to tighten and on the running end to undo the knot.

Caution: If the animal is clever, pass the end through the loop as with the halter knot. This is also called the escapee knot.

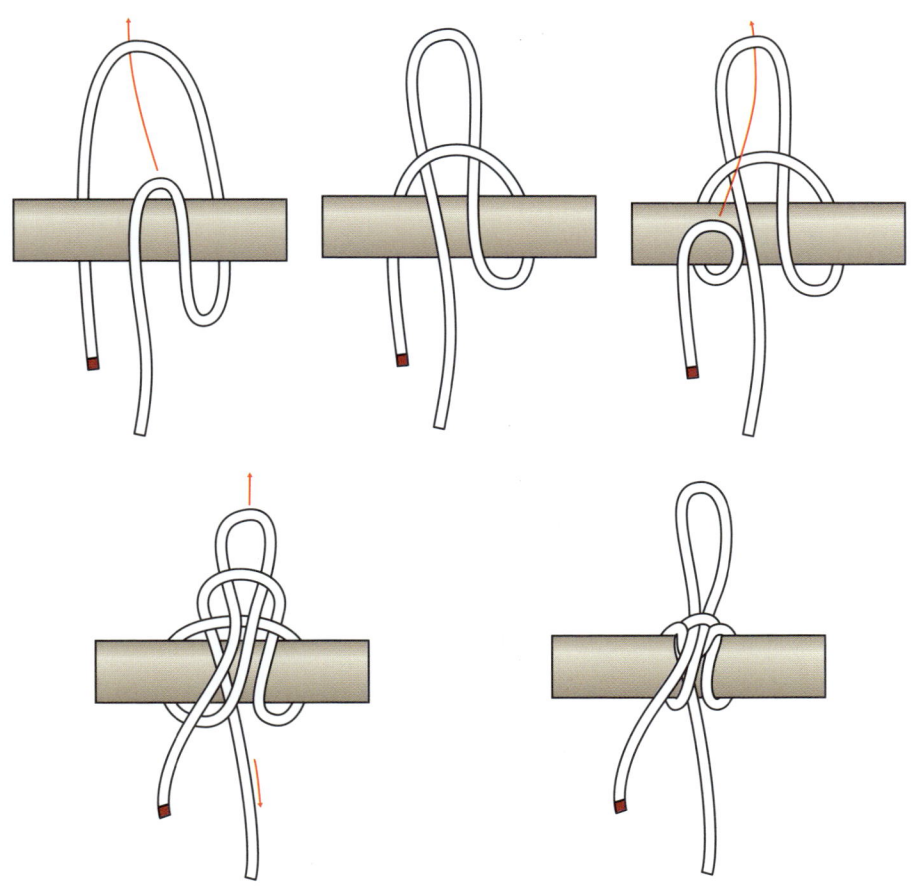

Hobble knot

Knot type: Fastening

Use: Restrict the movement of a horse, pony, donkey, or other animal to prevent it from running away, without tying it to a post.

Method for tying the knot: Fold the rope to find its midpoint, then make a **square knot** around one of the animal's front legs. Tie a second square knot, then pass the working ends around the other front leg and finish with a third square knot.

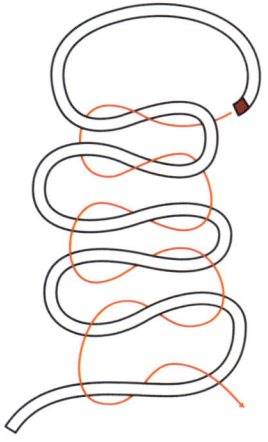

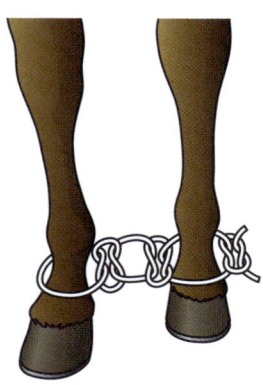

Leads, lassos, and halters

Halters, lead ropes, grass knots, and lassos, as well as emergency bridles, are very useful for handling animals.

Farm halter knot

Knot type: Loop

Use: Create a loop for a lead rope suitable for any animal.

Method for tying the knot: Make a loose overhand knot at a suitable distance from the end of the lead rope. Tie a second one at the other end, then pass the end through the first overhand knot. The second knot will stop against the first, preventing the lead rope from tightening around the animal's neck. This is also known as a **honda knot** (page 22).

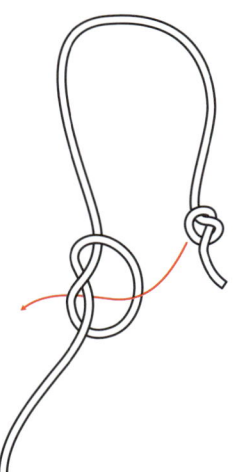
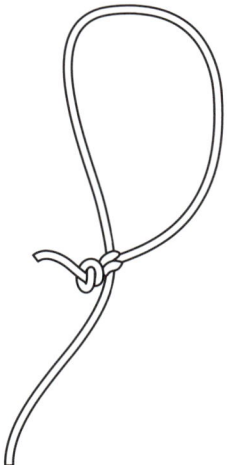

Enhanced halter knot

Knot type: Assembly

Use: Create a rope halter for a horse, pony, or donkey (see opening photo on page 172).

Method for tying the knot: Start by making two **overhand knots** (1) in the centre of the rope, spaced about one-and-a-half times the width of the muzzle apart; these will later guide one end towards the other.

Bring the two ends together under the muzzle and tie a **fiador knot** (2) (see page 184).

Next, behind the jaw, join the two ends with a **overhand bend** (3).

Set one end aside, fold the other back on itself, and make a **overhand loop** (4) about 10cm below the ear. Then, weave this end through the two initial overhand knots so that it passes to the other side of the horse's head (5).

Bring the two ends together about 10cm below the other ear, tying a **overhand bend** (6).

Finally, pass the ends over the neck, behind the ears, and through the slip knot. Close the halter with a sheet bend knot.

TIPS & TRICKS

This method allows you to make a unique halter perfectly adapted to the shape of each horse. To ensure the animal's comfort, avoid using rough ropes.

The simple halter knot

This is a joining knot that lets you create an emergency halter for a horse, pony, or donkey. Make a fixed loop at the end of the rope, for example, with a overhand loop. Double the standing part and pass the bight through the fixed loop. Then, slip this loop over the animal's muzzle. Make sure you hold the halter close enough to the head.

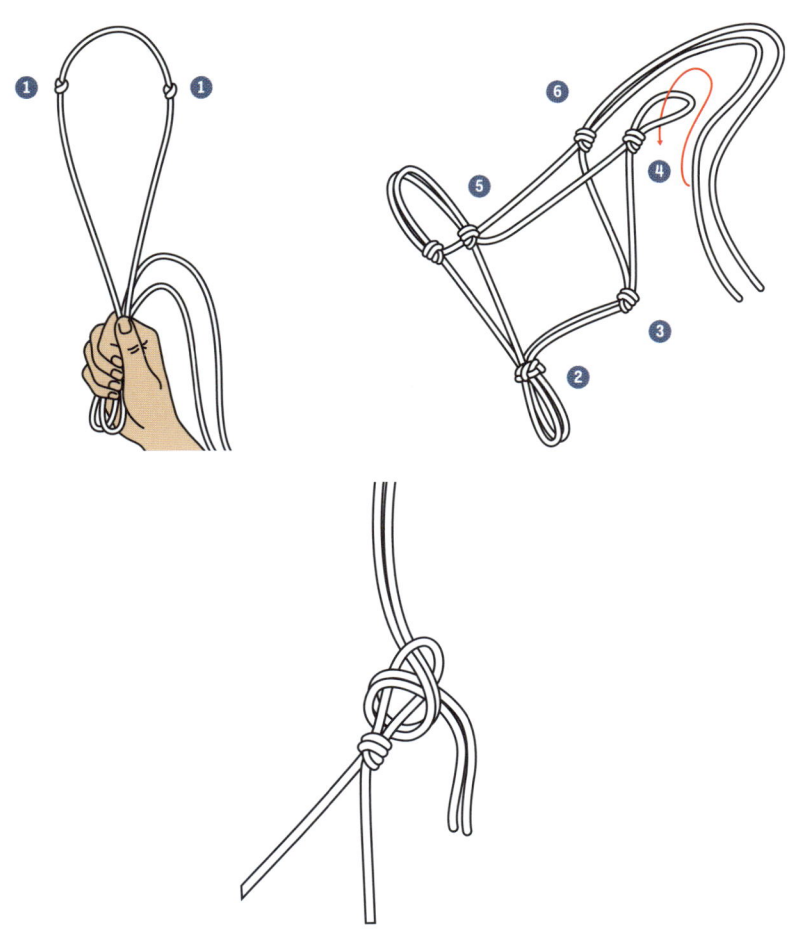

Fiador knot

Knot type: Loop

Use: Create a tie loop for the enhanced halter.

Method for tying the knot: Fold the rope in half, then fold it twice more to form a flattened Z shape. Temporarily whip it in two places: at the top, a whipping that binds one loop and the ends (three groups of two strands); at the bottom, a whipping around a single loop (two groups of two strands). Lift the starting loop and twist it so that the strands of the loop are arranged vertically. Pass the ends through the loop (one from left to right, the other from right to left). Next, pass the ends through the two loops formed by the top whipping, following the weaving pattern shown in the illustration. Remove the top whipping and tighten the knot. To finish, remove the bottom whipping.

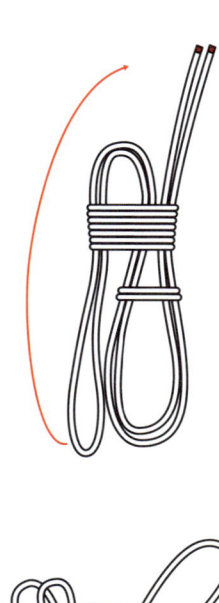

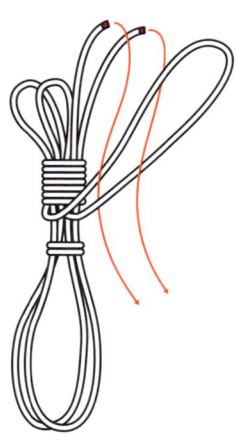

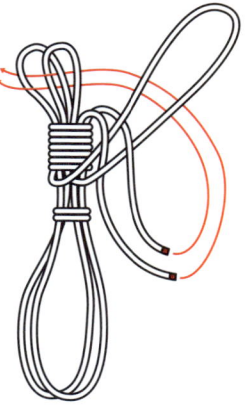

Emergency halter

Knot type: Fastening

Use: Create a halter for a horse, pony, or donkey.

Method for tying the knot: Make **two clove hitches** around the lower jaw, with the crossings at the bottom.

Caution: This kind of halter is quite rudimentary and should only be used in extreme necessity.

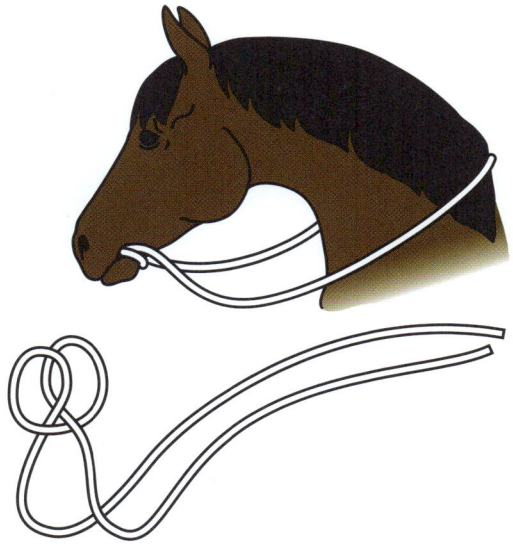

Grass-binding knot

Knot type: Bend

Use: Repair a piece of leather halter or any other flat material.

Method for tying the knot: Make a **half-hitch** on one of the ends to be joined, then pass the other through and make a second half-hitch around the standing part. As its name suggests, this knot can be used to join two long, flat strips, as well as stalks of straw.

Lasso knot

Knot type: Loop

Use: Add a slip loop to a long rope in order to catch stubborn or wild cattle.

Method for tying the knot: Make a **honda knot** at the end of the rope, then pull the standing part through the loop.

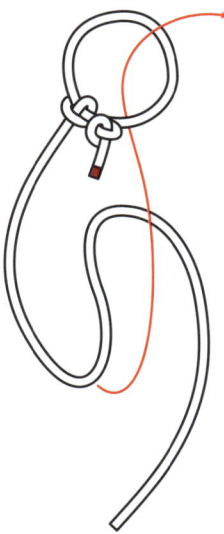

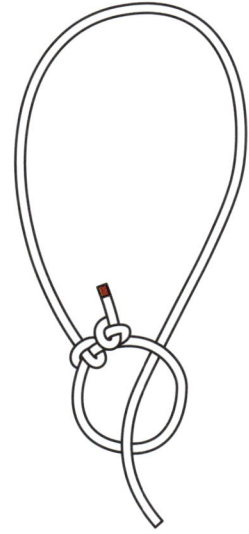

Knots for bundling

Bundling means 'tying into a bundle'. The sheaf knot and the baling-twine bend, along with the Cormick bundling knot, the Deering bundling knot, and the square knot (see the reusable common knots), are all useful for bundling.

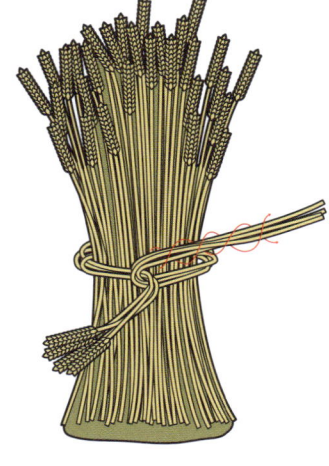

Sheaf knot

Knot type: Binding

Use: Tie a sheaf of grain or a bouquet of flowers.

Method for tying the knot: Gather the stems to be tied into a sheaf. Twist a few strands together to make a coarse cord. Wrap it around the sheaf, then twist the ends together. Once the binding is tight enough, double the end and slip the loop between the tie and the sheaf.

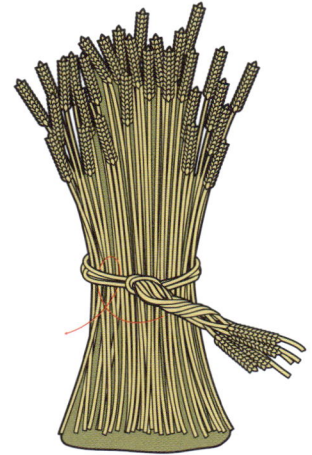

TIPS & TRICKS

This is an old technique, from before the invention of the straw and hay baler. For a wildflower bouquet, twist a blade of grass several times around the stems before bringing the ends together and tying the knot.

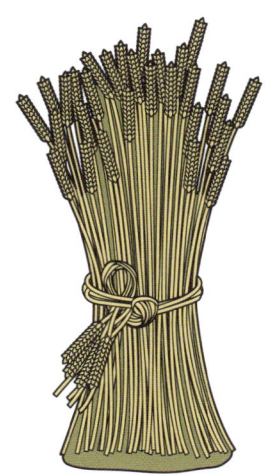

Baling-twine bend

Knot type: Bend

Use: Repair a broken agricultural twine or join the end of a spool to the beginning of a new one.

Method for tying the knot: Make a **sheet bend**, then fold and pass the working end under itself to complete the **figure eight knot** around the initial loop. With both ends coming out on the same side, the knot can pass through the baler machine without catching.

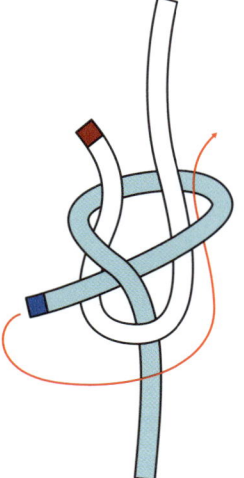 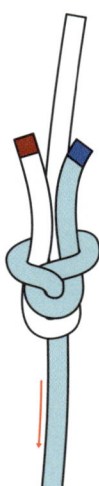

Carpet beater knots

Before the invention of the vacuum cleaner, people had to take their rugs outside and beat them with a carpet beater to get rid of dust and bugs. Today, the carpet beater remains a great way to freshen up a horse blanket or a picnic cover. For the next three carpet beaters, the method is the same: use three long rods of rattan or willow. Draw the pattern on a board and mark the intersections with nails. Start the pattern at the centre of the rods. If the rods aren't long enough to form the handle, attach the flail to a broomstick using a whipping knot.

Simple carpet beater

Knot type: Mat-style

Method for tying the knot: The figure starts at the loop touching the handle.

Round carpet beater

Knot type: Mat-style

Method for tying the knot: The figure starts at the loop farthest from the handle. (This is the most common style and it's still being sold.)

Triangular carpet beater

Knot type: Mat-style

Method to tie the knot: The pattern starts at the loop farthest from the handle.

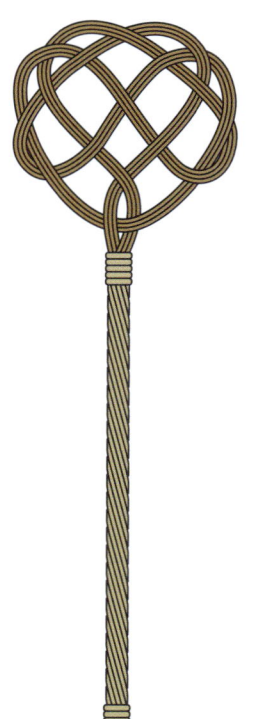

Storage knots

The miller's knot, the haynet knot, the rope coil, and the mud
knot help to keep your workspace tidy and organised.

....

Miller's knot

Knot type: Binding

Use: Securely close a sack of flour, fertiliser, potatoes, etc.

Method for tying the knot: Make a **half-hitch** around the sack opening with the working end on
top. Make an additional **turn** to lock the standing part again, then pass the end over the extra
turn and between the sack and the starting half-hitch. Pull both ends to tighten the knot.
This is a variation of the **constrictor knot**.

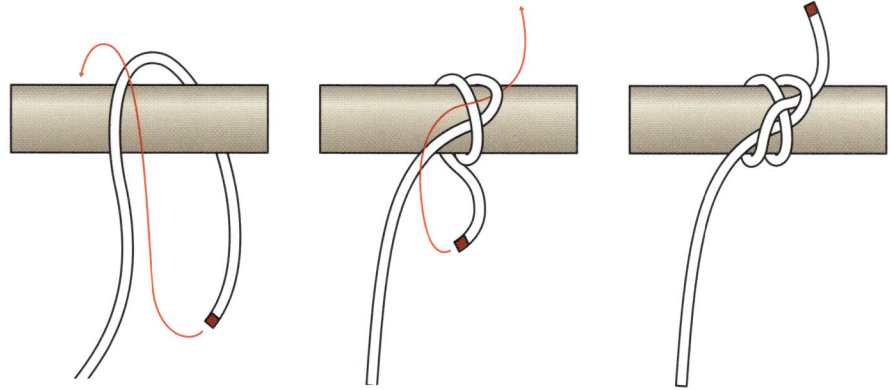

Haynet knot

Knot type: Coil

Method for tying the knot: See the **cylindrical net** (page 199). When making the first row, create larger meshes to make it easier to open and hang the net. Close the bottom of the net by **reducing the mesh size**. See mesh reduction (page 198), over two or three rows, depending on the net's diameter. Finish with a lacing. The meshes should be open enough to allow animals to access the hay.

Rope coil

Knot type: Coil

Use: Wrap and store a rope on a hook or a nail.

Method for tying the knot: Coil the rope, then double the end to form a loop. The working end should split the coil's opening in two. Pass the loop around the coil, behind it, and through the opening.

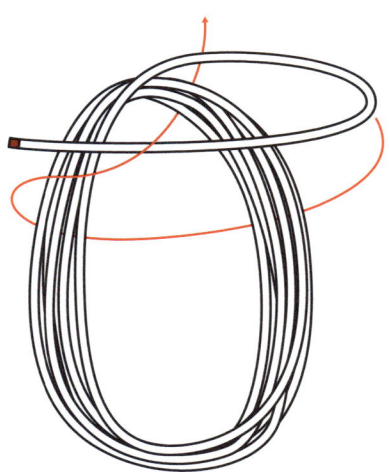

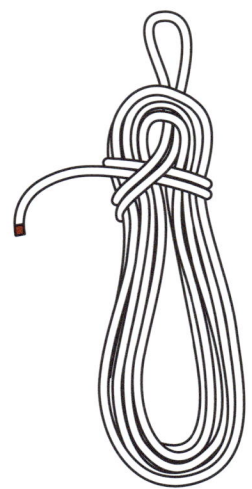

Mud knot

Knot type: Stopper

Use: Shorten a ponytail so it doesn't drag in the mud.

Method for tying the knot: Divide the ponytail into two strands and tie an overhand knot. Wrap one of the strands around the part of the ponytail above the **simple knot**. Then, do the same with the other strand, but in the opposite direction. Finally, join the two ends together with a **reef knot**.

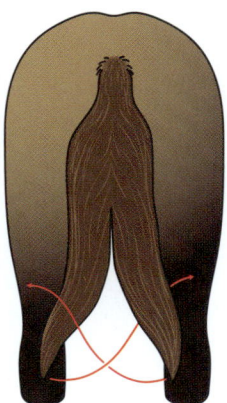 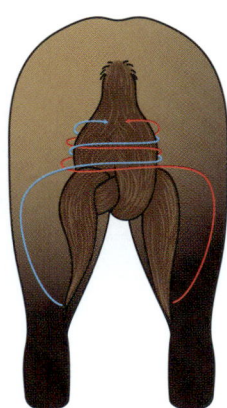 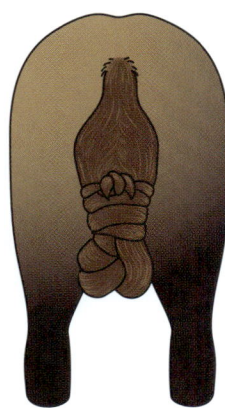

NETS

KNOTS AND ASSEMBLIES FOR NET-MAKING

Headline knot (tied like a clove hitch)

Knot type: Fastening

Use: Attach the first row of mesh to a rope or another support (stick, ring, etc.).

Method for tying the knot: Make a **clove hitch knot** around the support.

Headline knot (tied like a cow hitch)

Knot type: Fastening

Use: Attach the first row of mesh to a rope or another support (stick, ring, etc.).

Method for tying the knot: Make a **cow hitch** around the support.

Mesh knot

This is the basic knot of the net, similar
to the **sheet bend**. When setting up a net,
you can use a gauge – a support made of
wood or other material – sized to form the
meshes (see the diagrams for 'reducing the
mesh'). Wrap the twine around the gauge
before tying mesh knots on the top row or on
the support.

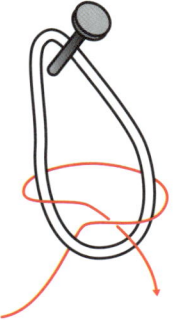

TOOLS

For making nets, you can use a gauge that helps keep the meshes the right size
(see page 198). The tool used to pass the threads through is called a **netting needle**.

Double mesh knots

Knot type: Bend

Use: Make a square net.

Method for tying the knot: Pass the twine through the mesh once, then make a **mesh knot**.
With a double mesh knot, you get a mesh and a loop.

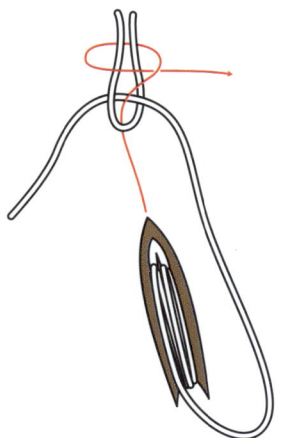

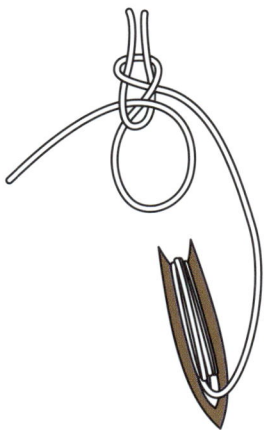

Reducing the mesh

Knot type: Bend

Use: Reduce the width of a row to finish a pointed net or to close the bottom of a circular net.

Method for tying the knot: Pass the twine through two meshes, then make a **mesh knot** around these two meshes.

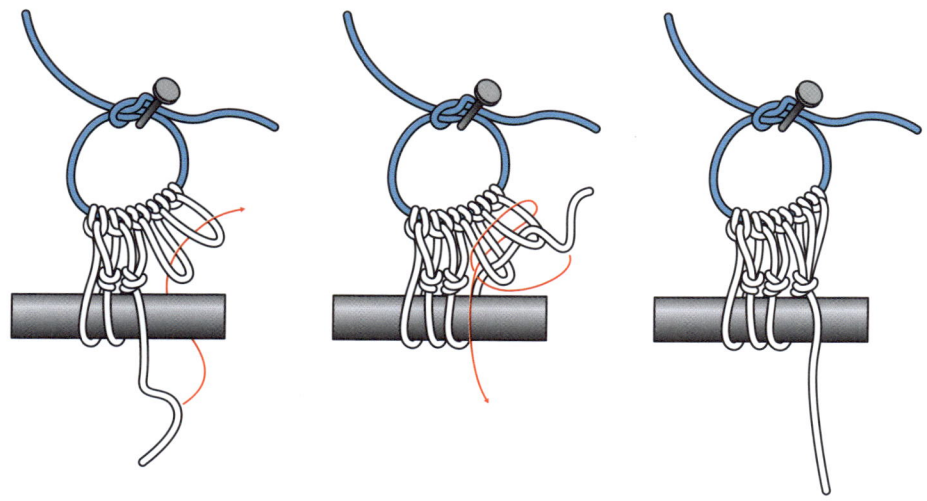

Diamond net assembly

Knot type: Assembly

Method for tying the knot: Attach the first row of meshes to the support using close-set **headline hitches**. A gauge can be used to ensure uniform mesh size. At the end of the row, turn the net over and make the next row with **mesh knots**. Space the lacing hitches apart by one mesh width to 'open' the net. This is the classic net used by fishermen and hammock-makers.

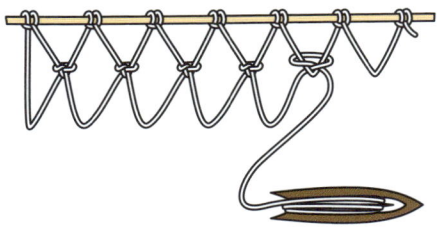

Cylindrical net assembly

Knot type: Assembly

Method for tying the knot: On a cylindrical support, tie the first **headline hitch**, leaving a tail slightly longer than the total desired length of the net. Continue making lacing hitches all around; then, upon reaching the start, form the last mesh of the row on the tail with a **simple sheet bend**. Make the next row with **mesh knots**, then close the row again with a simple sheet bend.

TIPS AND TRICKS

This is the technique for making a basketball net or a lampshade. For butterfly nets and other similar nets, reduce the mesh size to close the bottom of the net.

Square net assembly

Knot type: Assembly

Method for tying the knot: Create a loop of twine to hang on a high nail. Tie two meshes with **mesh knots** (see page 197), then flip the whole piece to place these two meshes on the right.

Start the next row with a **mesh knot**. Then make a **double mesh knot** (see page 197), creating a row of three meshes. Flip the piece again as before, then make the next row with mesh knots, finishing with a double mesh knot on the last one.

Continue this way, always making a double mesh knot at the end of the row, and flipping the net before starting each row. When you reach roughly the desired length, at the end of the last row, tie the last two meshes together (see '**reducing the mesh**' page 198).

The following row will end with a double mesh knot. The last row consists of two meshes, which are tied together.

Used for tennis and badminton nets, the square net is also used to make handball and football goals.

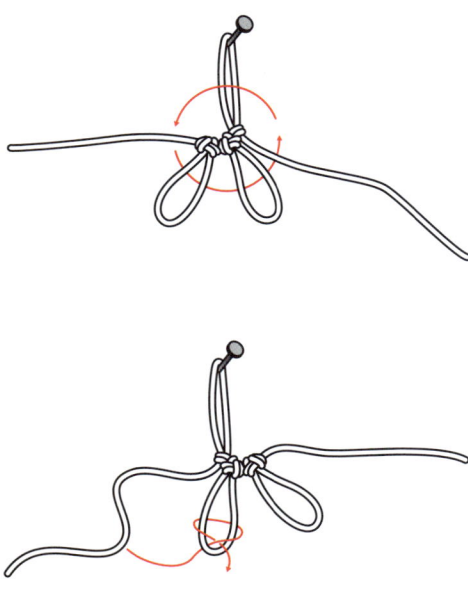

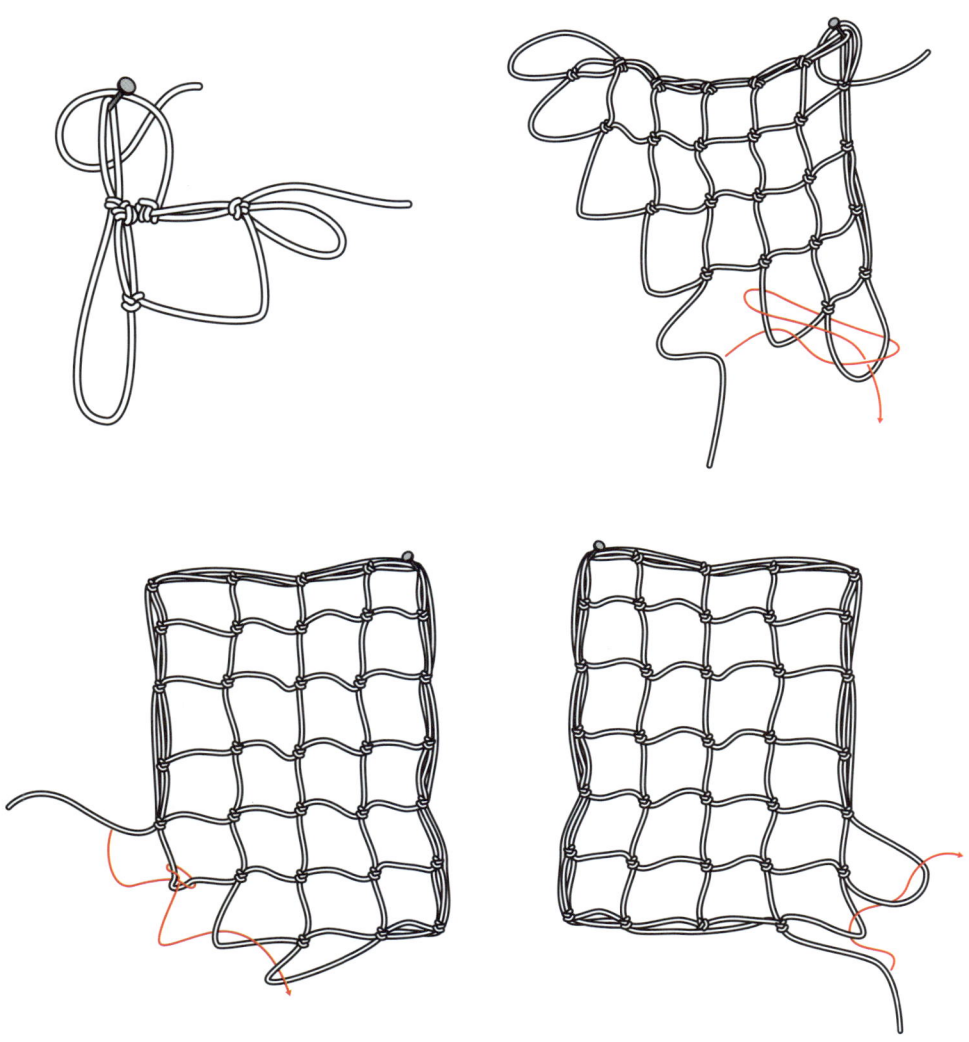

Decorative net assembly

Knot type: Assembly

Method for tying the knot: Attach several lengths of twine to the support using **clove hitch knots** or **cow hitches**. Form the meshes by tying each right twine of a pair to the left twine of its neighbour. Use decorative knots such as the **love knot** (see page 90), the **carrick bend** (see page 257), the **reef knot**, the **cow hitch** ... or any other from the repertoire.

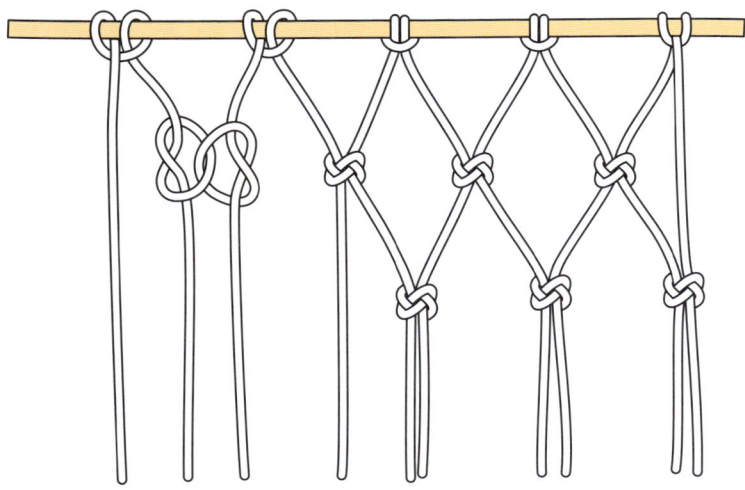

Fringe knot

Knot type: Stopper

Method for tying the knot: Finish the last row of a decorative net with simple joining knots.

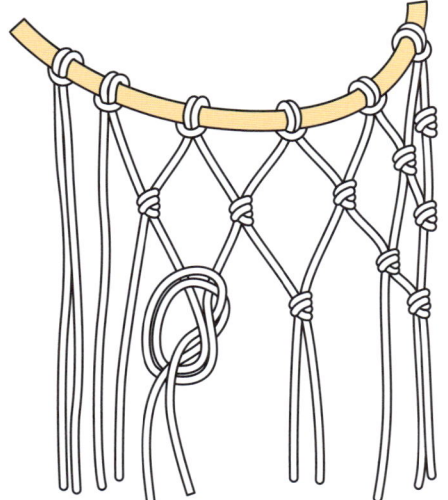

Hammock netting pattern

Knot type: Assembly

Use: Connect each hammock mesh loop to a fastening ring.

Method for tying the knot: Attach to the ring, using **cow hitches** and a sufficient number of cords to secure each mesh of the hammock. Starting from the outside, alternate weaving each cord through its neighbours. Tie the last two cords together with a **half-hitch**. Once the weaving is complete, simply thread each cord through its hole in the wooden spreader bar of the hammock before attaching it to a hammock mesh with a **double sheet bend**.

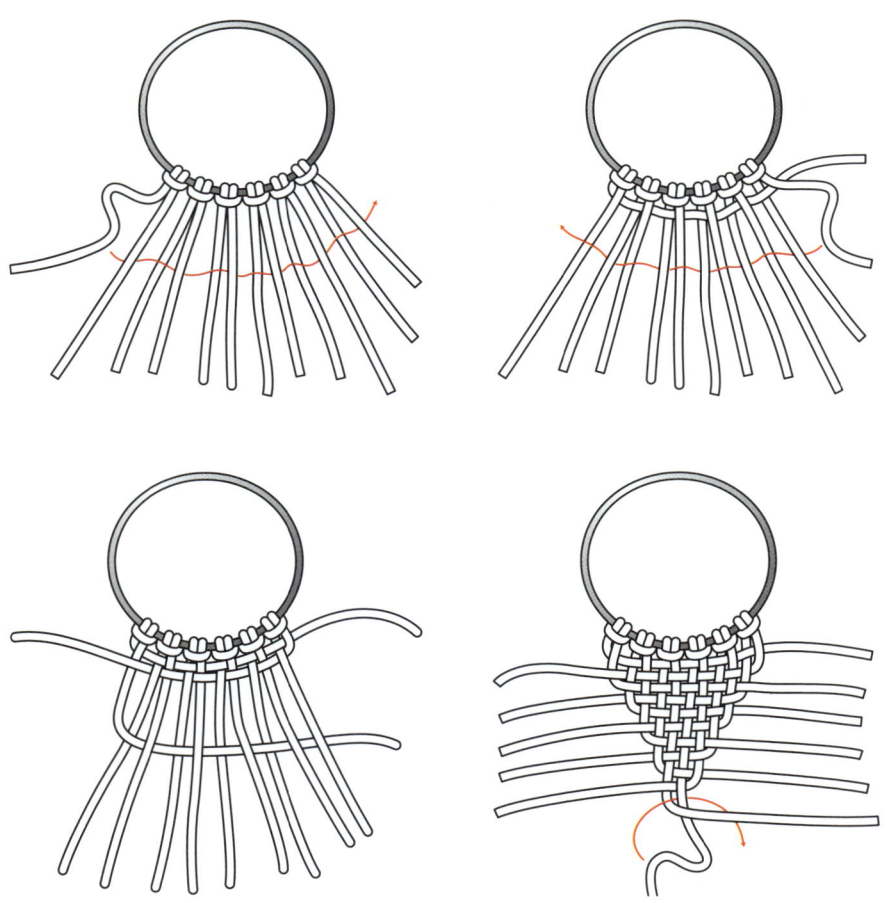

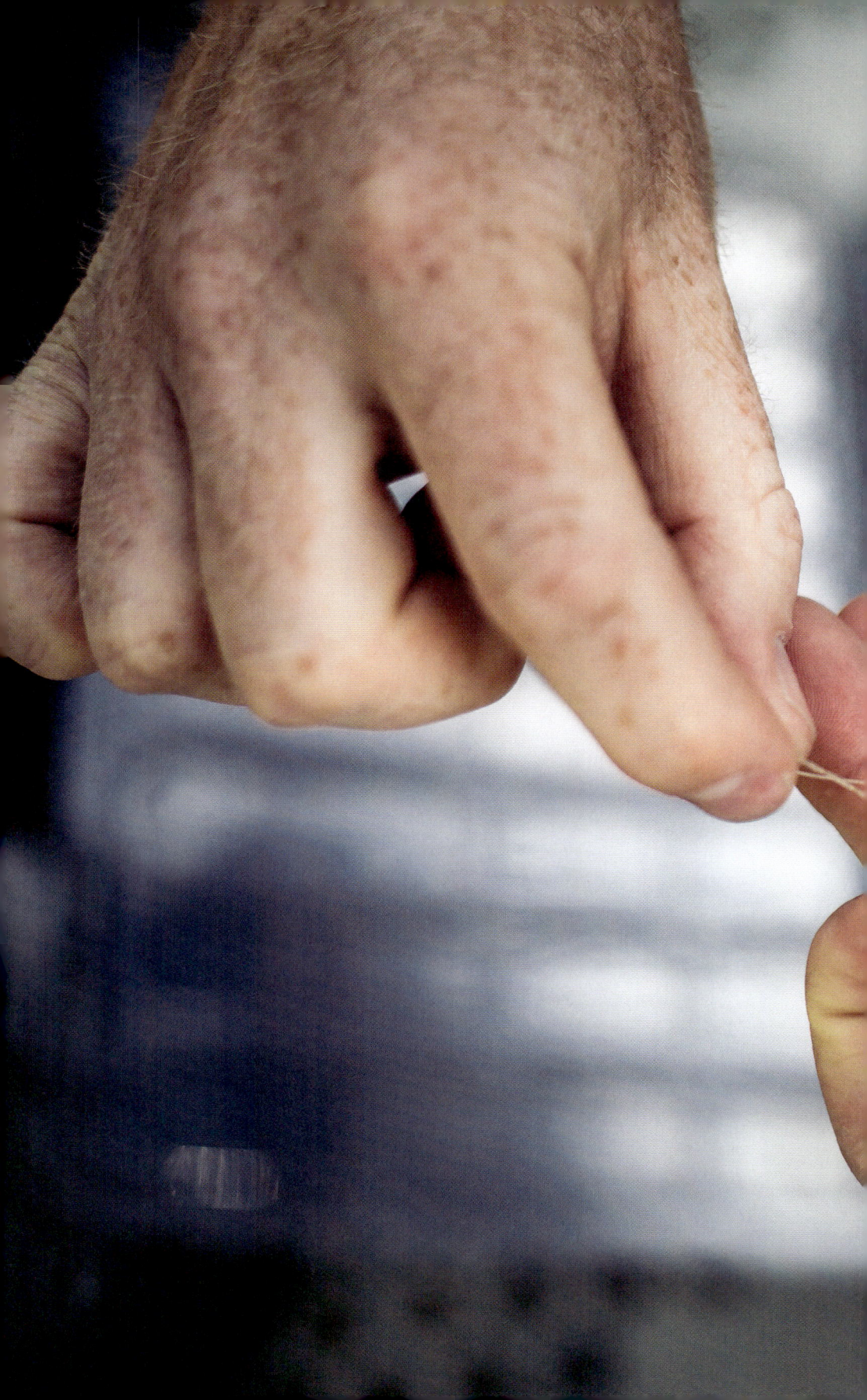

FISHING KNOTS

SPECIFIC FISHING KNOTS

Anchoring the line to the reel timber hitch knot

Knot type: Fastening

Use: Tie the fishing line to the reel spool.

Method for tying the knot: Pass the line around the reel spool and tie the end to the standing part using a **half-hitch**. Add a simple knot to prevent the end from slipping. A simple and effective solution, the reel spool knot can also be replaced by any slip knot, such as the **hangman's knot** (see page 220).

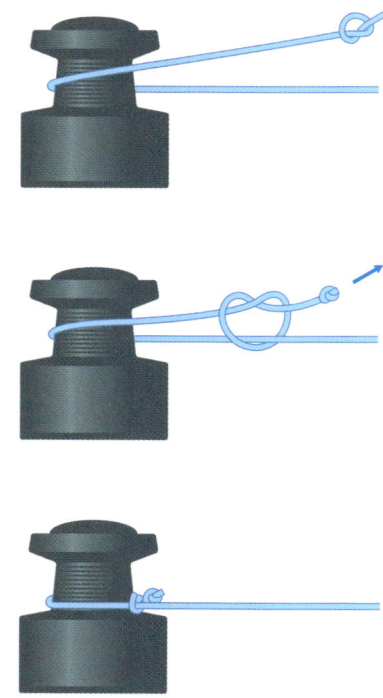

Joining two lines

Some knots allow the joining of two different lines. Some simply belong to the family of bend knots, while others are capable of joining two lines of different diameters. Finally, some knots can create loops.

The simplest bend knot is the fisherman's bend, which consists of overlapping the two lines over about 10cm, then tying each end around the standing part of the other with an overhand. The double fisherman's bend is a joining knot whose method is detailed in the climbing chapter (see page 149).

Finally, the water knot (see basic knots) is an excellent bend knot for natural fibres. However, it is less reliable when it comes to synthetic lines.

Barrel knot

Knot type: Bend

Method for tying the knot: Overlap the lines for about 20cm. Make a **turn** around with one of the lines around the standing part of the other. Then, pass its end through the gap created by its standing part and the other line. Do the same with the other line, making sure its end comes out of the central gap on the same side as the first line.

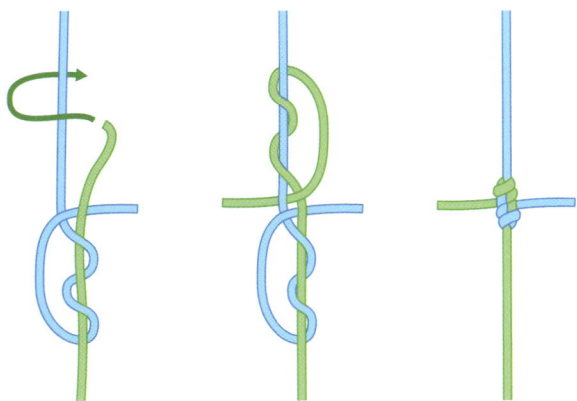

Peixet knot

Knot type: Bend

Method for tying the knot: Overlap the lines over about 20cm and make a **half-hitch** with one line (the lower side of the line) around the standing part of the other. Wrap the line that passes through the half-hitch around the standing part for at least six tight turns. Then, tuck the end under itself and make turns in the opposite direction, back to the initial half-hitch. Tighten the half-hitch moderately, then pull both ends of the turns to butt them against the half-hitch. Finally, tighten the half-hitch firmly, then the turns. Cut off the excess.

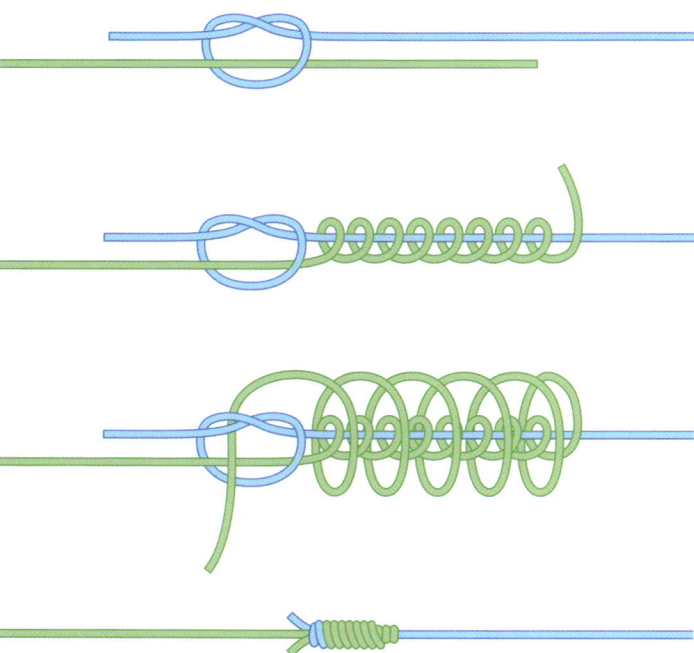

TIPS AND TRICKS

Some use a **figure eight knot** instead of the half-hitch.

Surgeon's knot

Knot type: Bend

Method for tying the knot: Overlap the lines by about 20cm. Using the end of the longer line and the standing part of the shorter line, make a **double overhand knot**. Tighten by pulling simultaneously on both pairs of strands and trim the excess.

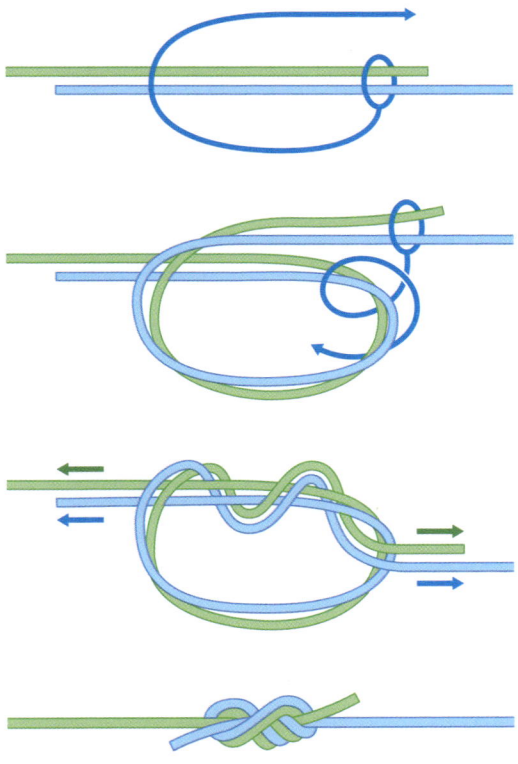

💡

TIPS AND TRICKS
....

If the two lines are very long, or the ends are inaccessible, tie using a **water knot**.

Nail knot

Knot type: Joining

Method for tying the knot: This knot is for joining lines of different diameters. Place the nail (or needle or straw) next to the thicker end. Wrap the other end around both at least six times, making sure that the standing part of the thinner end is tucked under these wraps. Remove the nail and pull the thinner end into its place. Using a needle, pass the thinner end through the eye and out from the wraps. Tighten by pulling firmly on both ends of the thinner line.

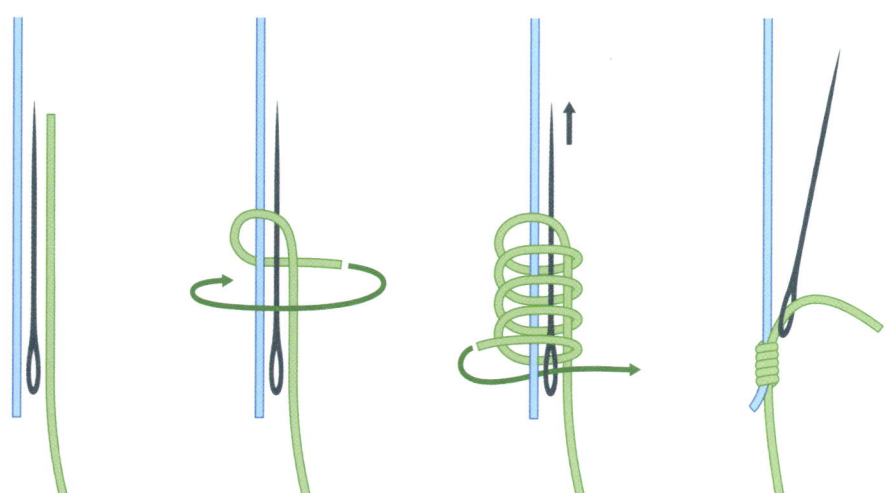

Needle knot

Knot type: Joining

Method for tying the knot: This knot is for joining ropes of different diameters. Insert a fine needle into the body of the line and bring it out about 1cm from the end. Using the needle and pliers if needed, wrap the entire length of the lower line, leaving only 15mm of line protruding. Use the needle to tie the **needle knot**. This solid assembly is smooth enough to pass through seaweed and debris without snagging.

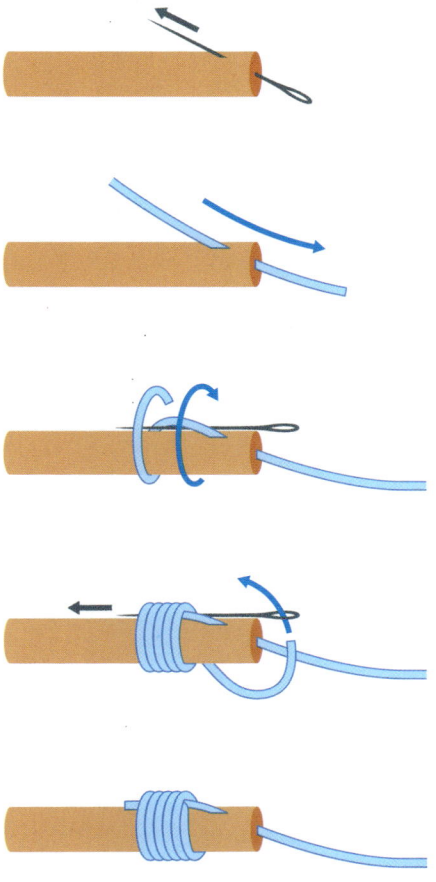

Albright knot

Knot type: Joining

Method for tying the knot: This knot is for joining ropes of different diameters. Form a loop with the thicker line. Pass the end of the other line through this loop. Wrap the end around the loop while ensuring that the standing part of the end is trapped under the wrapping. After about ten turns, pass the end through the loop in the direction of its standing part. Pull on the loop's end to close the knot.

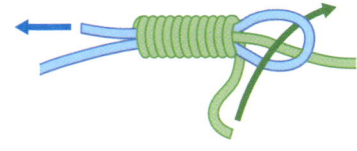

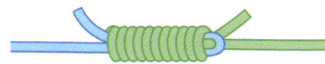

Surgeon's loop

Knot type: Bend

Use: Make a simple, fixed loop at the end of a line.

Method for tying the knot: Make an **overhand loop**, then pass the line once more through the initial simple knot. When tightening, ensure that the loop of the initial simple knot is centred within the crossings. This is also called a simple loop.

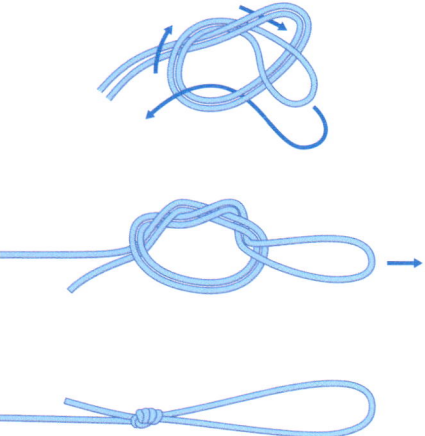

Loop on loop

Knot type: Bend

Use: Attach a leader with the hook already tied on.

Method for tying the knot: Tie a **surgeon's loop** at the end of each line to be joined. Pass the lower leader's loop over the other and thread the hook end through the leader's loop. While this may not be the strongest knot, it has the advantage of being easy to tie.

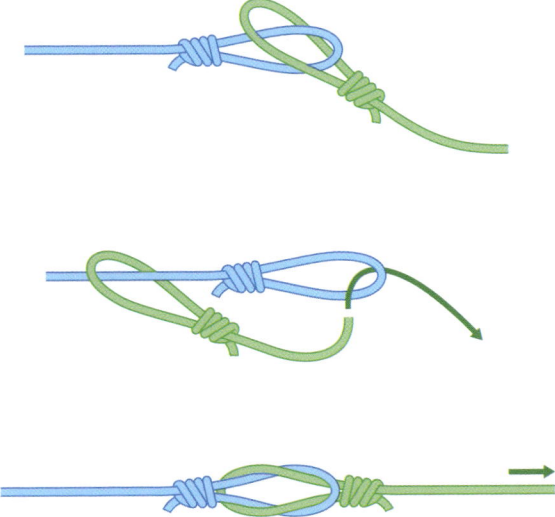

Paternoster loop

Knot type: Loop

Use: Create a hanger loop on a fishing line.

Method for tying the knot: Make a **turn** with the working end underneath, then lay it over the standing part. Twist the working end and standing part for two or three **turns**. Pass the large loop through the gap formed by the twists. Pull the ends to tighten the knot. Make sure the wraps on each side of the loop form a **capuchin knot** (see page 109). The paternoster loop is asymmetrical with a different number of wraps on each side of the loop.

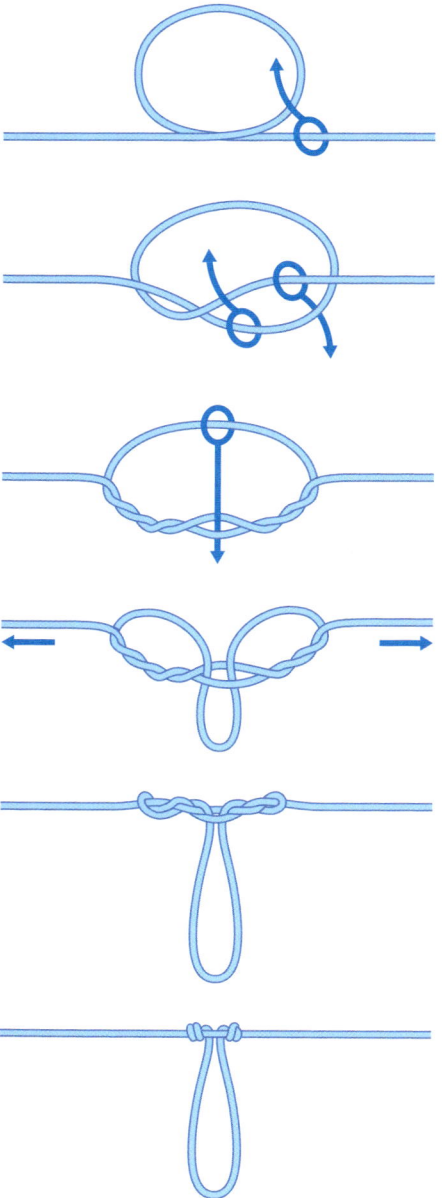

Joining two lines

The following knots are used to attach hooks or swivels for fishing lines. Some are hitch knots, others are slip loops.

Half-barrel

Knot type: Fastening

Method for tying the knot: Pass the end through the eye of the hook. Make several turns around the standing part, then pass the end through the loop formed by the first turn. Tighten and trim the excess. This knot is quite similar to the barrel knot.

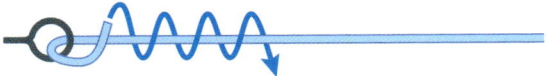

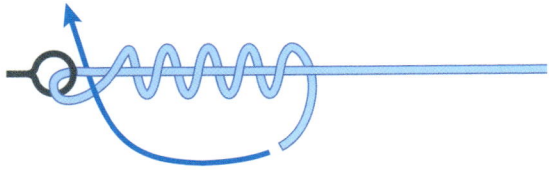

Palomar knot

Knot type: Fastening

Method for tying the knot: Fold the line back on itself to form a bight and pass this bight through the eye of the hook. Make a **half-hitch** with the bight. Pass the hook through the bight and tighten the knot. This knot is suitable for hooks with a relatively large eye.

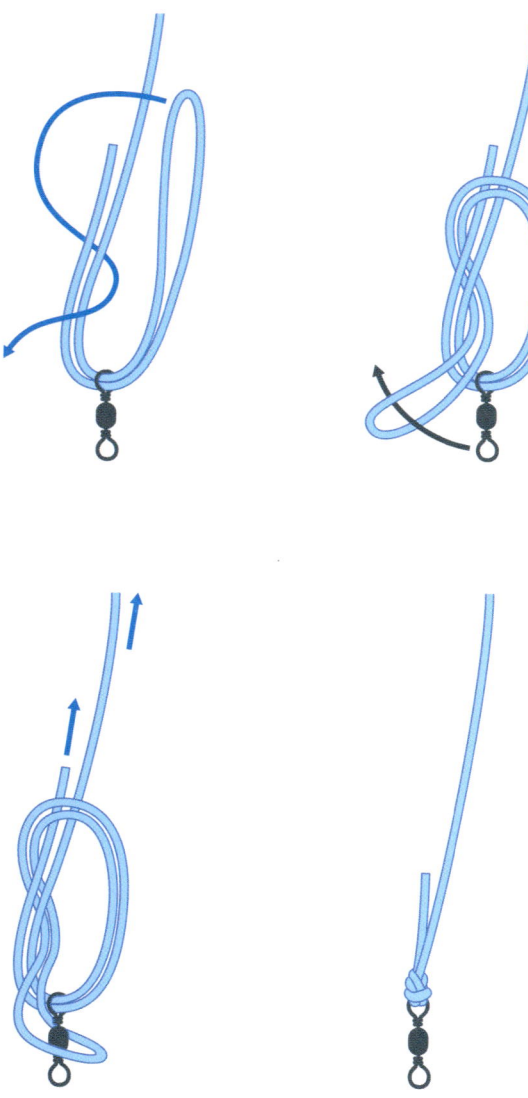

Turle knot

Knot type: Fastening

Method for tying the knot: Fold the line back on itself and tie the end around the standing part with a **half-hitch**. Pass the curved part of the hook through the loop, then tighten the knot around its shank. Slide the knot up until it rests against the standing part passing through the hook's eye. Tighten firmly and trim the excess. This knot is also called the turtle knot.

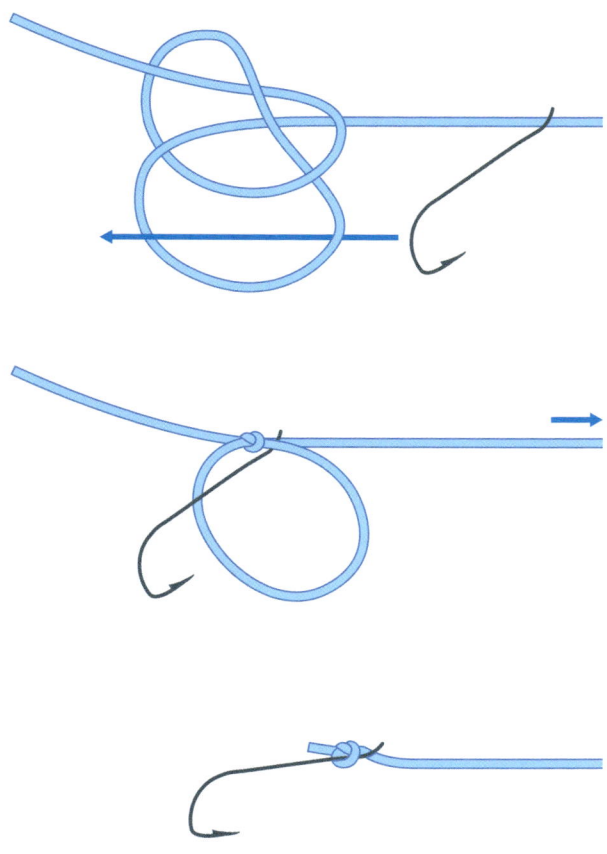

Double turle knot

Knot type: Fastening

Method for tying the knot: Make a **turn** (round turn) at the end of the line and tie the end around the two strands of this turn using a **half-hitch**. Finish the knot following the instructions for the **turtle knot**.

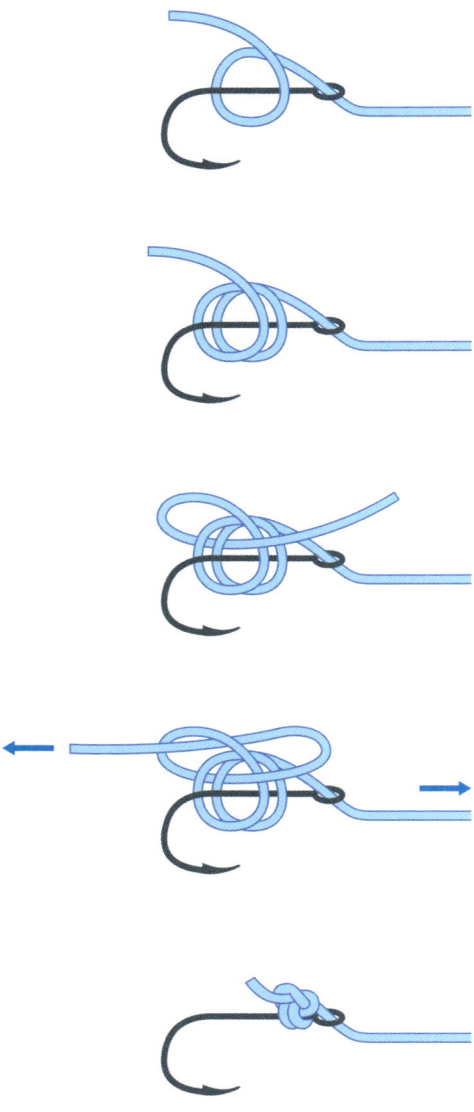

Pitzen knot

Knot type: Loop

Method for tying the knot: Pass the end through the eye of the hook and fold it back on itself to form a loop. Make several **round turns** around both strands of the loop, then pass the end through the first **turn** of the wraps. Tighten the round turns well before pulling firmly on the end. The pitzen knot tends to deform if the round turns are not tightened enough.

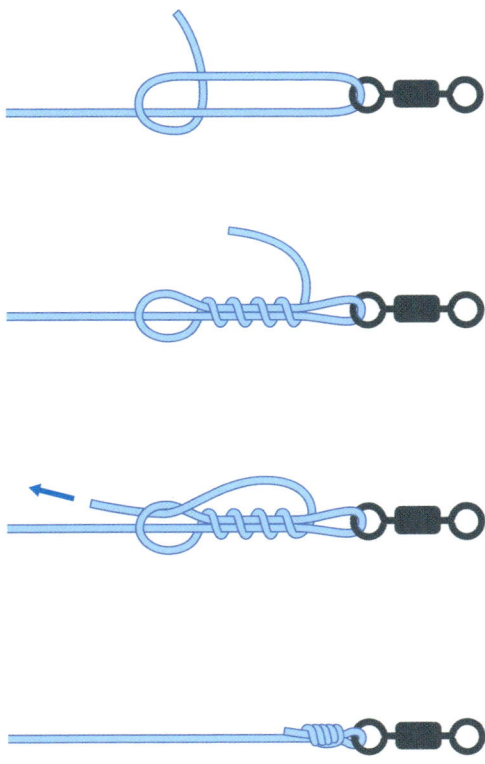

Hangman's knot

Knot type: Loop

Method for tying the knot: Pass the end through the eyelet of the hook and fold it back on itself twice to form a second loop. Wrap the end around the two loops with three or four **tight turns**. Thread the end through the second loop. Pull on the first loop to tighten the second loop around the end. Cut off the excess.

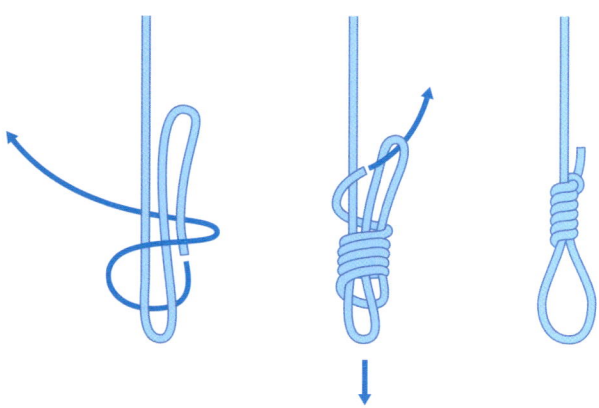

Universal loop knot

Knot type: Loop

Method for tying the knot: Pass the end through the hook eye and fold it back to form a bight. Wrap the end around both bights several times without tightening. Pass the end through the wraps to form a **half-hitch**. Tighten and trim the excess. This is the slip version of the capuchin knot, also known by other names, such as the scaffold knot and the gallows knot.

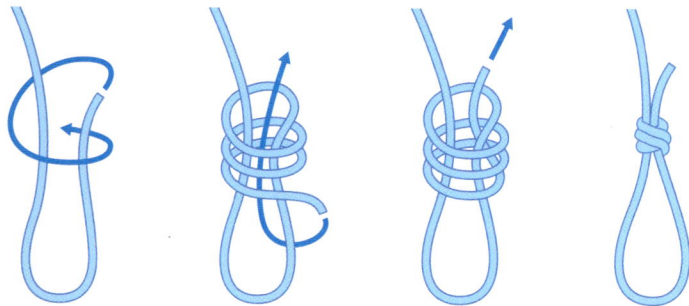

Snell knots

A snelled hook is a hook that features a slightly curved part on the top of the shank. Snelled hooks are recommended, for example, for when using certain baits.

Snelled hook knot

Knot type: Fastening

Method for tying the knot: Place the hook next to the line about 10cm from the end. Fold the line to form a bight and wrap the end around the standing part and the hook shank for two or three **turns**, moving from the blade towards the hook bend. Fold the line again and pass the end through the bight. Tighten the wraps well before pulling on the standing part to finish the knot. Trim the excess.

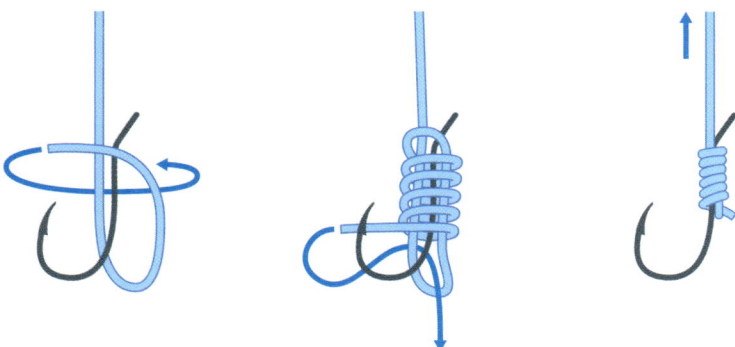

Enhanced snelled hook knot

Fastening

Method for tying the knot: Place the hook next to the line about 10cm from the end. Fold the line to form a bight and wrap the end around the standing part and the hook shank for two or three **turns**, moving from the pallet towards the hook bend. Fold the line again and pass the end through the bight. Tighten the wraps well before pulling on the standing part to finish the knot. Trim the excess.

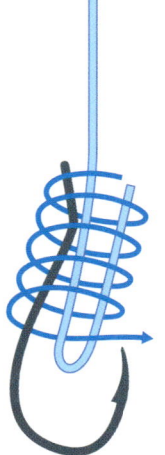 

Traditional longline

A mainline is a fishing line – usually equipped with several hooks, sometimes weighted – that is submerged for fishing.

Killick hitch

Knot type: Fastening

Use: Attach a rope to a weight, such as a rock, in order to ballast a bottom fishing line.

Method for tying the knot: Wrap the weight with a **timber hitch**, then add a **half-hitch** to form a **killick hitch**.

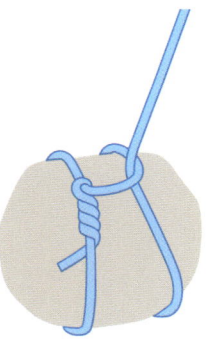

Bottom line knot

Knot type: Fastening

Use: Attach the gangions to the main line or longline.

Method for tying the knot: See the **groundline hitch** (page 22) in the basic knots section.

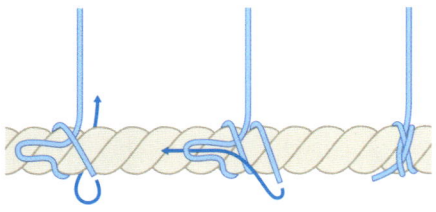

TIPS & TRICKS

Choose a rock with a shape suitable for the task (such as one that's slightly elongated).

Fisherman's loop on the line

Knot type: Loop

Use: Create a loop on the gangion to hold a hook or to form a loop at the end of a bottom line.

Method for tying the knot: Make a loop. Wrap the working end twice around the base of the loop, creating a bight. Pass the bight over the end and through the loop.

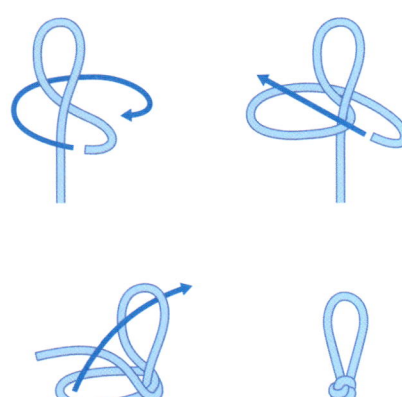

Fisherman's loop

Knot type: Loop

Use: Create a loop at the end of a bottom line.

Method for tying the knot: Fold the rope to form a bight, then fold this bight onto itself to create two **half-hitches**. Place the right half-hitch over the left one, then pass the first loop through the standing parts and the gap formed by the half-hitches. Pull on the right half-hitch to create two **half-knots**, one of which must pass over the other before tightening.

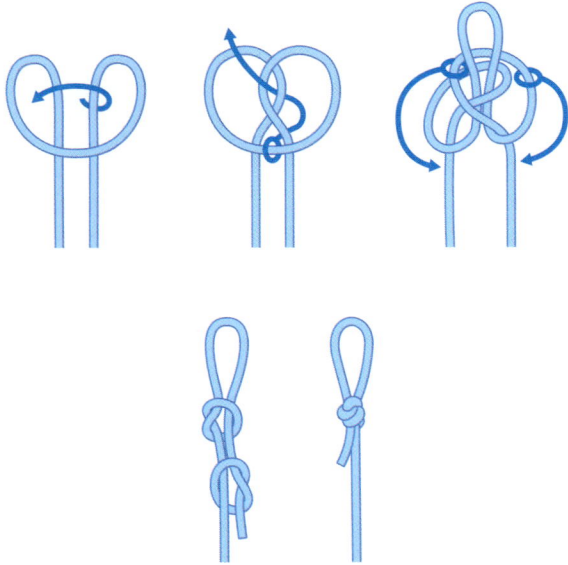

KNOTS FOR CLOTHING

KNOTS FOR CLOTHING

Tie knots

A sharp tie instantly ups your style game, if you know how to tie it right!

Simple tie knot

Knot type: Binding

Method for tying the knot: Wrap the wide end around the narrow end. Bring the wide end up from underneath the collar and tuck it under itself. Tighten it. This classic necktie knot is also known as the four in hand.

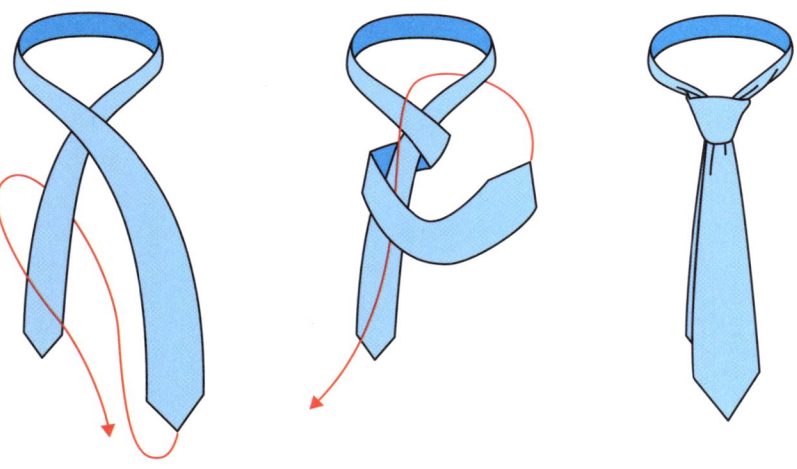

Enhanced tie knot

To add more volume to the classic tie knot, wrap the wide end around the narrow end two or more times. Bring the wide end up from underneath the collar and tuck it under itself. Tighten.

Windsor tie knot

Knot type: Binding

Method for tying the knot: Cross the tie ends, with the wide end passing over the narrow one. Bring the wide end up under the collar and fold it down on the same side. Pass it under the narrow end and repeat the previous step. Finish as you would with the classic tie knot. This knot is said to have been invented by an English king whose main residence was at Windsor.

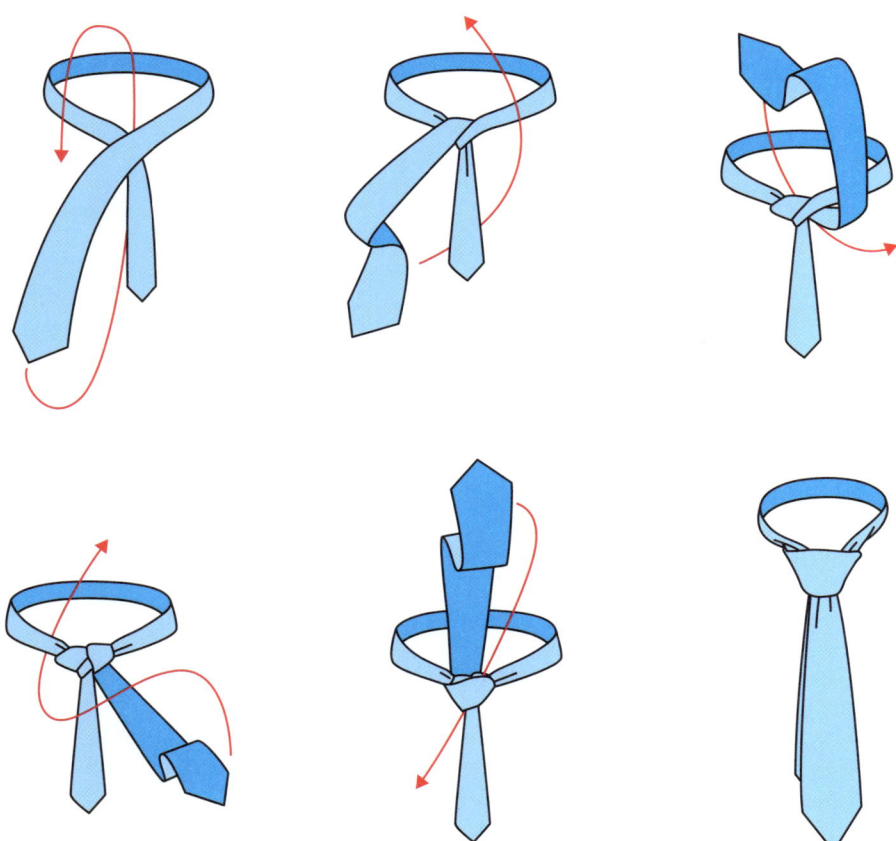

Eldredge tie knot

Knot type: Binding

Method for tying the knot: Cross the narrow end over the wide end. Pass the narrow end under the wide end and bring it up over the collar. Fold it behind the collar and to the opposite side. Now, pass the narrow end in front of the wide end and under the collar. Fold it in front of the collar and to the opposite side. Pass the narrow end behind the wide end and under itself. Fold the narrow end behind the collar on the same side of the knot, then to the other side. Bring the narrow end up under itself and tuck the tip inside the collar. A fairly recent knot, this one was invented by Jeffrey Eldredge in 2007.

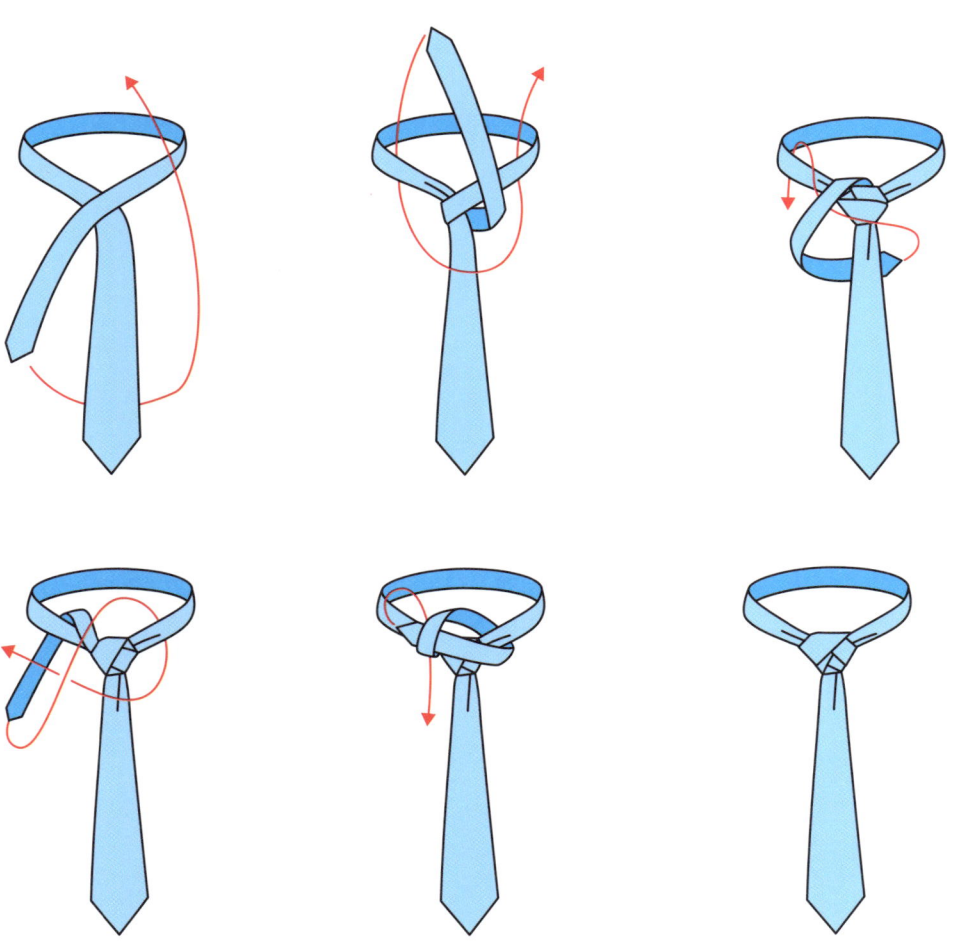

Ascot tie knot

Knot type: Binding

Method for tying the knot: Cross the ends, then bring the front one up under the collar and fold it down in front. Fold the second end over itself and behind the first. Bring the front end up through the loop formed by the back end. Tighten the knot and cross the ends again. To tie the Ascot, you need a tie with ends of the same width. This knot dates back to the 19th century, originating from the Royal Ascot horse racing event in England.

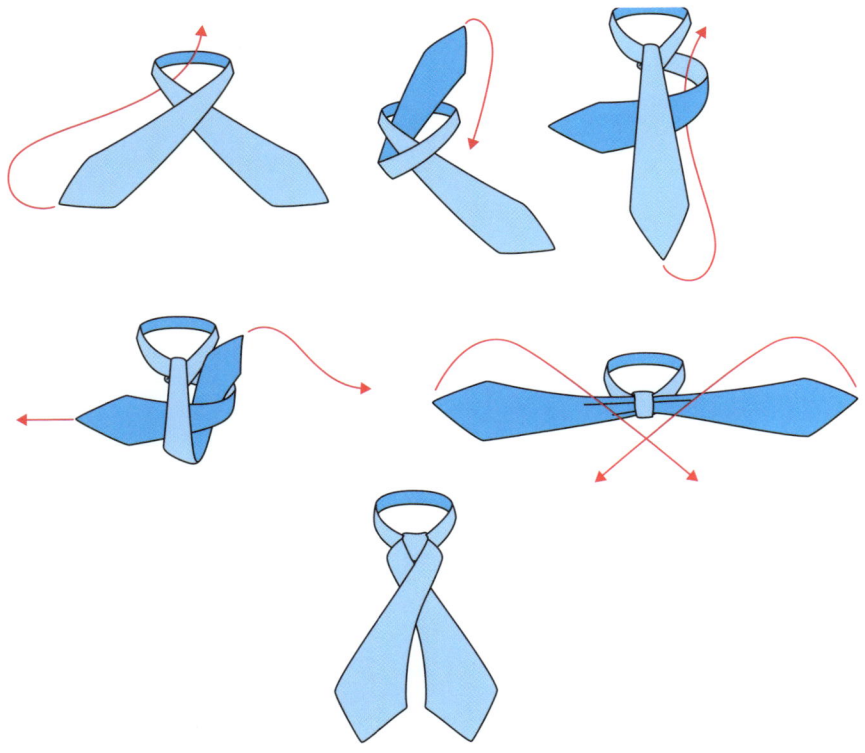

ANOTHER KNOT TO TRY:
The headband knot

The headband knot can be purely decorative or very practical, especially for athletes. To tie it, simply centre a headband on your forehead and make a reef knot with the ends behind your head. Note: if you see an athlete constantly tightening their headband, it's probably because they tied a slip knot that slips a bit before holding, instead of a reef knot!

Bow tie knot

Knot type: Binding

Method for tying the knot: Cross the ends, then bring the front end up under the collar. Fold the bottom end over itself twice and fold the first end, folding it the same way. Tuck the front end behind the other and tighten.

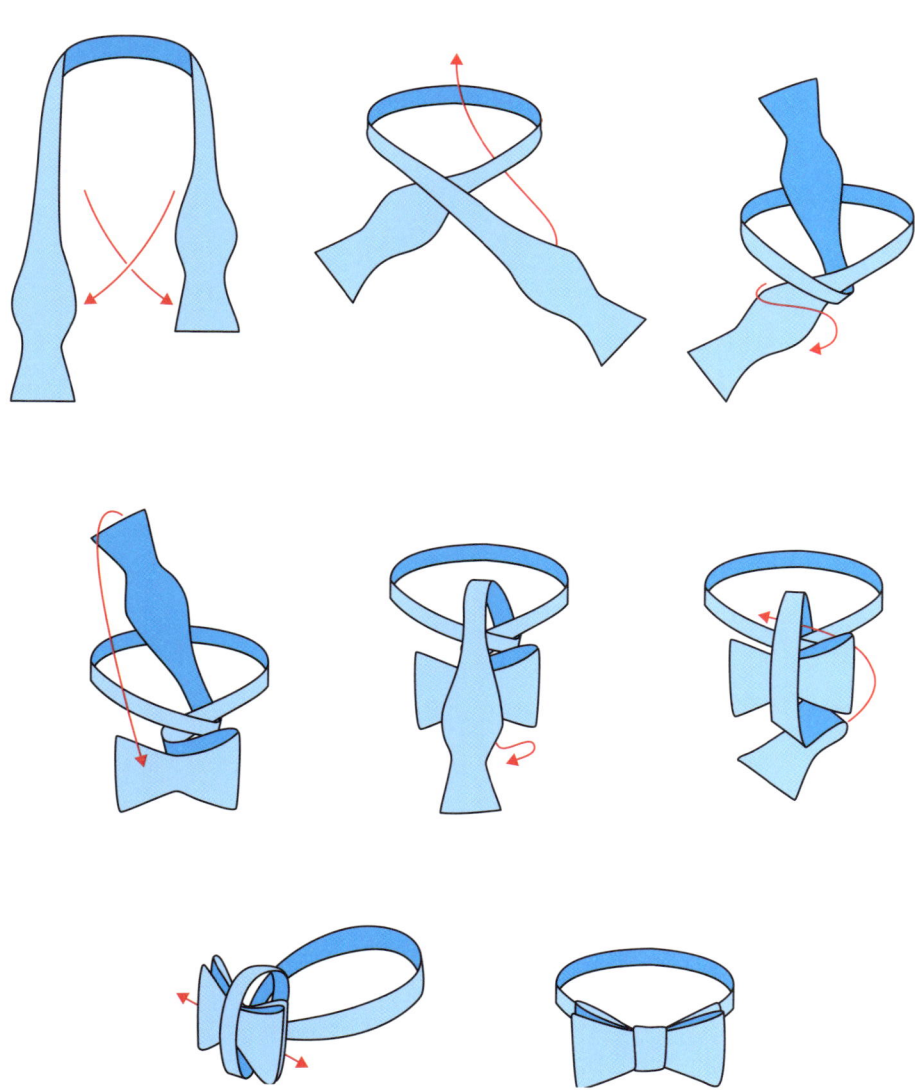

Scarf and headscarf knots

These knots allow you to cover and protect your neck in style!

Simple scarf knot

Knot type: Binding

Method for tying the knot: Cross the ends and bring the front one up under the collar. Fold it down and tighten. Simple and quick, this is a **half-knot**.

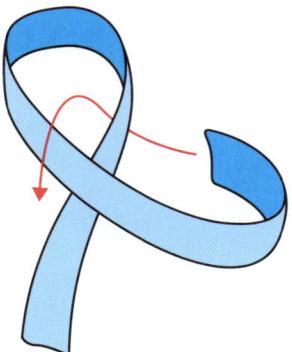 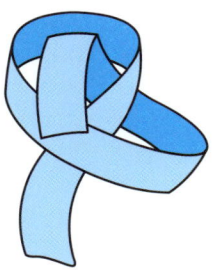 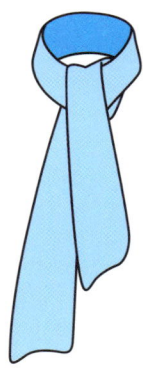

Parisian scarf knot

Knot type: Binding

Method for tying the knot: Fold the scarf in half to form a loop. Wrap the scarf around your neck, then tuck the ends through the loop. Tighten.

Bretzel scarf knot

Knot type: Binding

Method for tying the knot: Start the **Parisian scarf knot**, but pass one end over and the other under through the loop. Tighten.

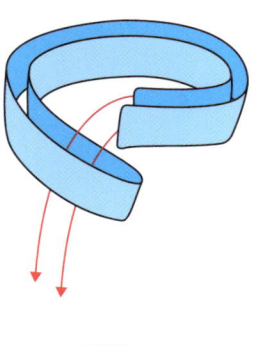

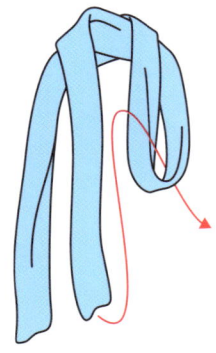

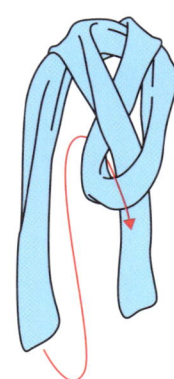

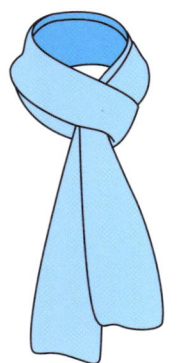

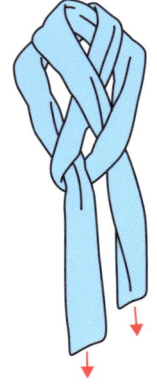

Magic scarf knot

Knot type: Binding

Method for tying the knot: Wrap the scarf around your neck with both ends in front. Slide your hand between your neck and the scarf, then lift the end resting on your shoulder (the lower end) to form a loop. Pass your other hand through this loop and pull the other end through.

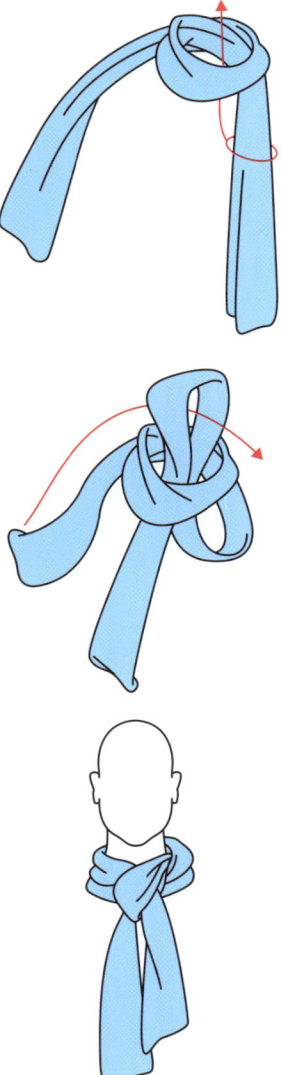

Braided scarf knot

Knot type: Binding

Method for tying the knot: Make a **Parisian scarf knot**, then twist the loop and pass the ends through one more time.

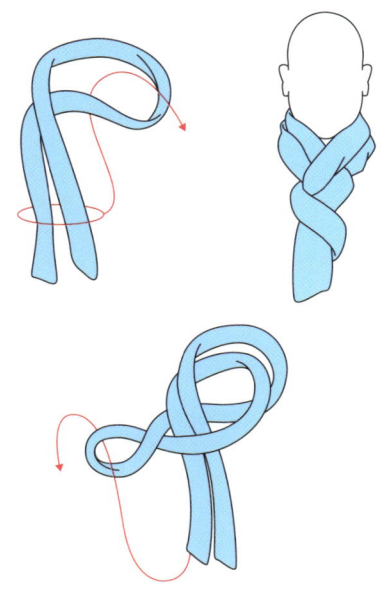

The scarf ring

See the Turk's head with three turns and four loops (page 120). This is the knot used to make the scarf ring for scouts. It looks very pretty when made with leather strips.

Belt knots

These knots will hold clothing in place without using a belt fastened by a buckle.

Trenchcoat knot

Knot type: Binding

Method for tying the knot: Tie the belt with a **half-knot**, then fold the end with the buckle to form a loop. Make a second half-knot with the loop and the other end. Ensure that the end without the buckle is in front. Simple and stylish, this is a **slipped reef knot**.

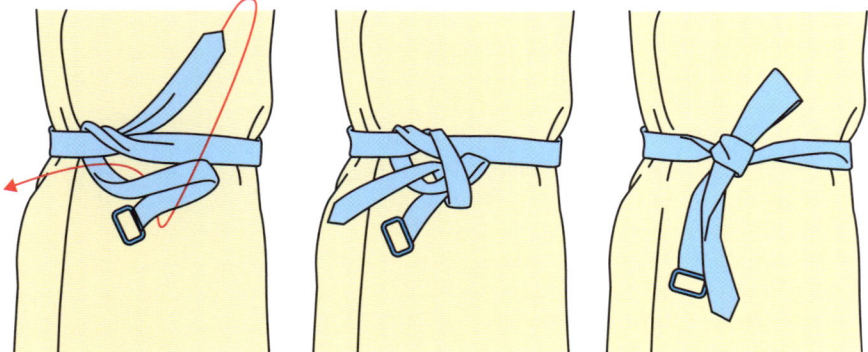

Bathrobe belt knot

Knot type: Binding

Method for tying the knot: Cross the belt, then bring the lower end over the other end and under itself, forming a **half-hitch**. Next, pass this end under the half-hitch, creating an overhand knot. Pull the slack to tighten this half-knot around the other end. The result is a neat triangular knot.

Caution: This knot is not suitable for a flat-section belt.

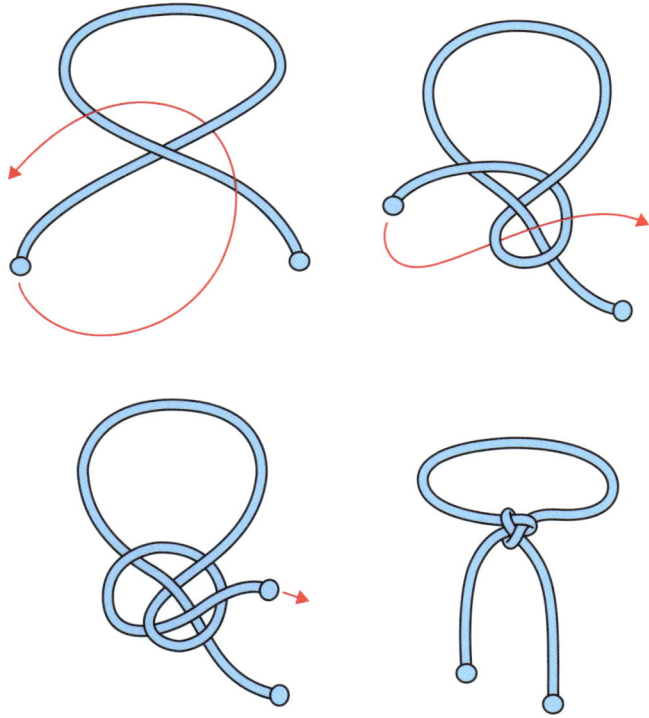

Capoeira knot

Knot type: Binding

Use: Close the belt of a capoeira outfit.

Method for tying the knot: Double the cord and pass it through the belt loops of the trousers. The ends and the loop should rest on the hip, with the loop at the back. Pass the ends through the loop. Bring the ends up under the belt to form a **half-hitch**. Fold the ends through this half-hitch and tighten the knot. Since capoeira is a martial art of Afro-Brazilian origin, the knot is called boca de lobo in Portuguese.

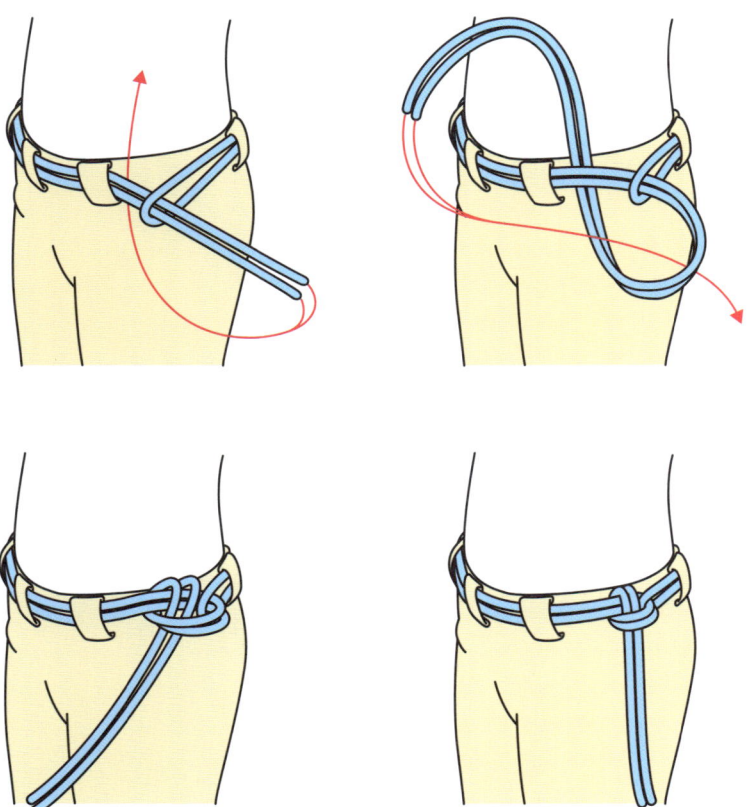

Crossed obi knot

Knot type: Binding

Use: Fasten a traditional Japanese garment using a belt called an obi, such as kimonos or those worn for practising martial arts.

Method for tying the knot: Place one end of the obi on one hip, then wrap the belt around the waist until the other end reaches the opposite hip. Next, bring the front end up under the belt and pull out the back end. There are many versions and variations of the obi knot, ranging in complexity depending on the knot's purpose and the type of garment.

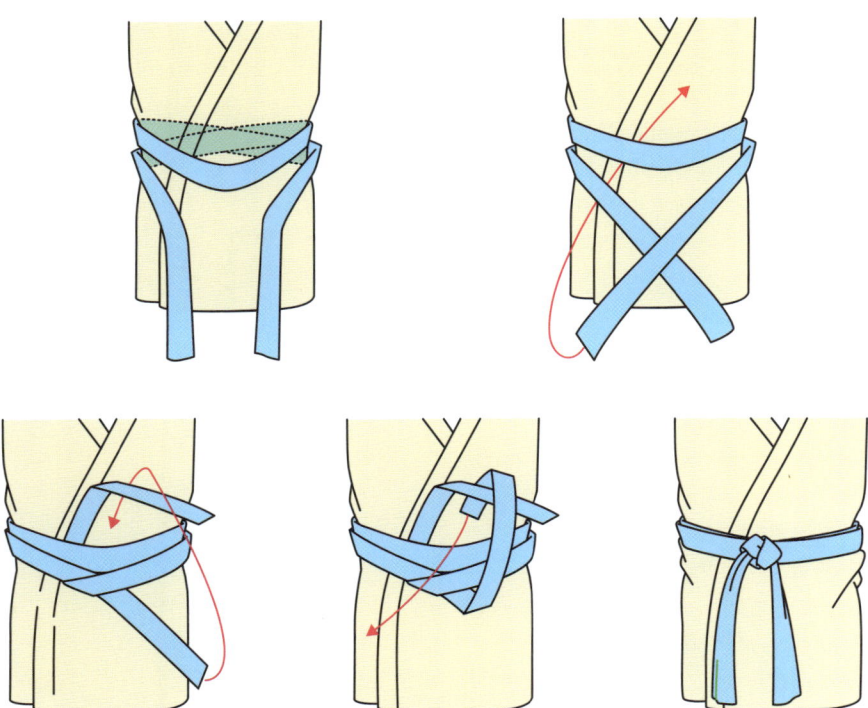

Laces and lacing

These knots are used to tie shoelaces.

Simple shoelace knot or bow knot

Knot type: Binding

Use: Decorative closure for any lace, be it on clothing or shoes.

Method for tying the knot: Make a **half-knot**, then double one of the ends to form a loop. Cross this loop with the other end and pull that end through the knot by its centre. Easy to tie and untie, this knot is actually a double-loop reef knot.

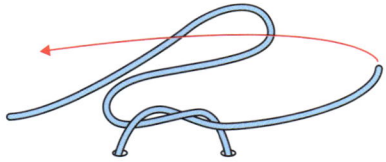

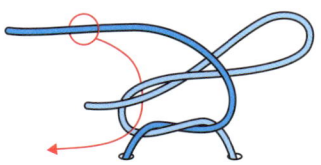

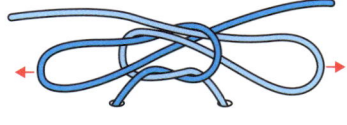

Bunny ears shoelace knot

Knot type: Binding

Use: Teaching young children how to tie their shoelaces.

Method for tying the knot: Make a **half-knot**, then double each lace to form loops. Cross the loops, pass one loop around the other and through the gap in the center of the knot. Tighten.

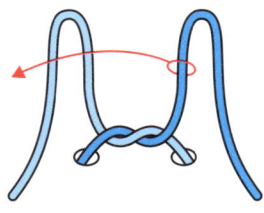

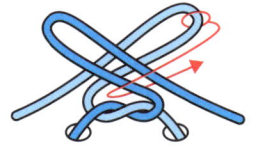

Double shoelace knot

Knot type: Binding

Use: Tie shoelaces that tend to come undone.

Method for tying the knot: Tie a **simple shoelace knot** but make a **turn** around the bow before pulling the end through this loop and the hole in the centre of the knot. Tighten. This knot is hard to untie if the loops accidentally get pulled through the knot.

Double shoelace knot: alternative method
Tie a simple shoelace knot, then pass one of the loops a second time through the hole in the centre of the knot. Tighten. Easier to do, but the result is less neat.

Shoe clerk's knot

Knot type: Binding

Use: Shorten the loops of a shoelace to avoid stepping on them.

Method for tying the knot: Make a **shoelace knot**, then tie the loops one or more times more to reduce their size. Contrary to popular belief, retying the loops does not make the shoelace knot more secure.

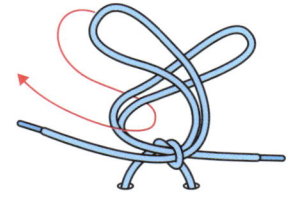

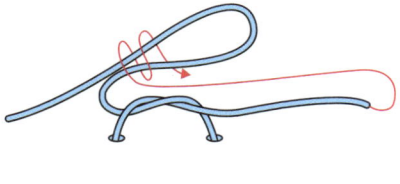

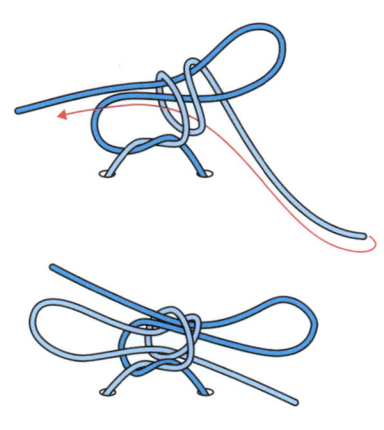

Self-locking shoelace

Knot type: Binding

Use: Hold the tension more firmly before tying the shoelace knot.

Method for tying the knot: Make sure that the last pass of the shoelace through the shoe eyelet goes from the outside to the inside. The lace is then trapped between the tongue and the side of the shoe.

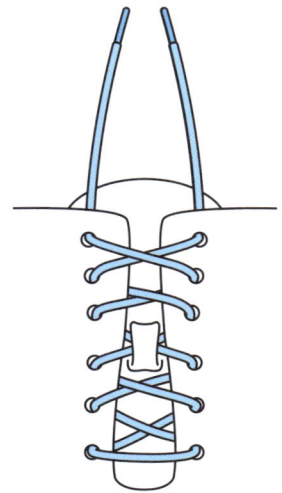

Cross lacing

Knot type: Lacing

Method for tying the knot: Pass the lace through the bottom eyelet of each row from the inside. Thread the left lace through eyelets R2, L3, R4, etc. Do the opposite with the right lace. Tighten and tie.

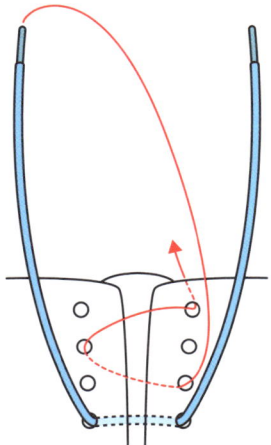

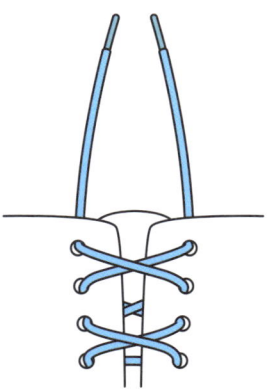

💡 TIPS & TRICKS

Tighten the lacing firmly and pull the ends strongly; the shoe will stay securely on the foot even without a knot. Especially useful for sports shoes.

💡 TIPS & TRICKS

At the start of lacing, both ends should be the same length.

Parallel lacing

Knot type: Lacing

Method for tying the knot: Pass the lace through the bottom eyelet on one side and the top eyelet on the other. Thread the lace through the eyelets from bottom to top, hiding the diagonal sections inside the shoe. Tighten and tie.

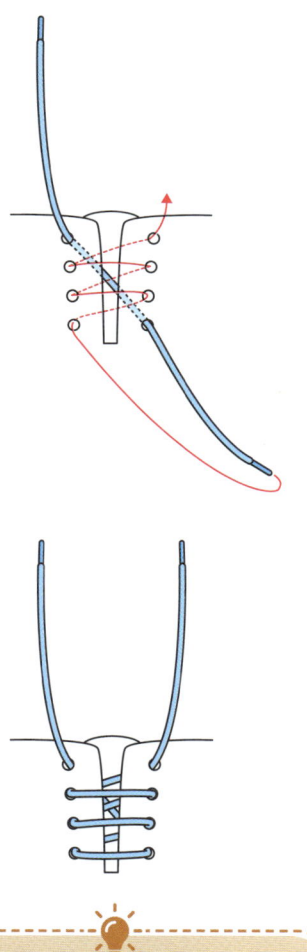

TIPS & TRICKS

At the start of lacing, the bottom lace should be longer than the top one.

Herringbone lacing

Knot type: Lacing

Method for tying the knot: Pass the lace through the bottom eyelet of each row from the inside. Thread the left lace through eyelets D2, G3, D4, etc... moving from inside to outside. Do the opposite with the right lace. Tighten and tie.

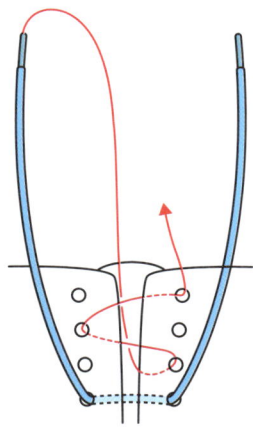

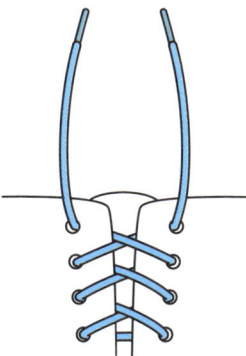

TIPS & TRICKS

At the start of lacing, both ends should be the same length.

One-hand lacing

Knot type: Lacing

Method for tying the knot: Make a simple knot at one end and thread the lace through the first eyelet at the top, from inside to outside. Do a **parallel lacing** down to the last eyelet at the bottom, then bring the lace back up inside the shoe and through the first eyelet on the other side. Make a **slipped half-hitch** around the first parallel lace.

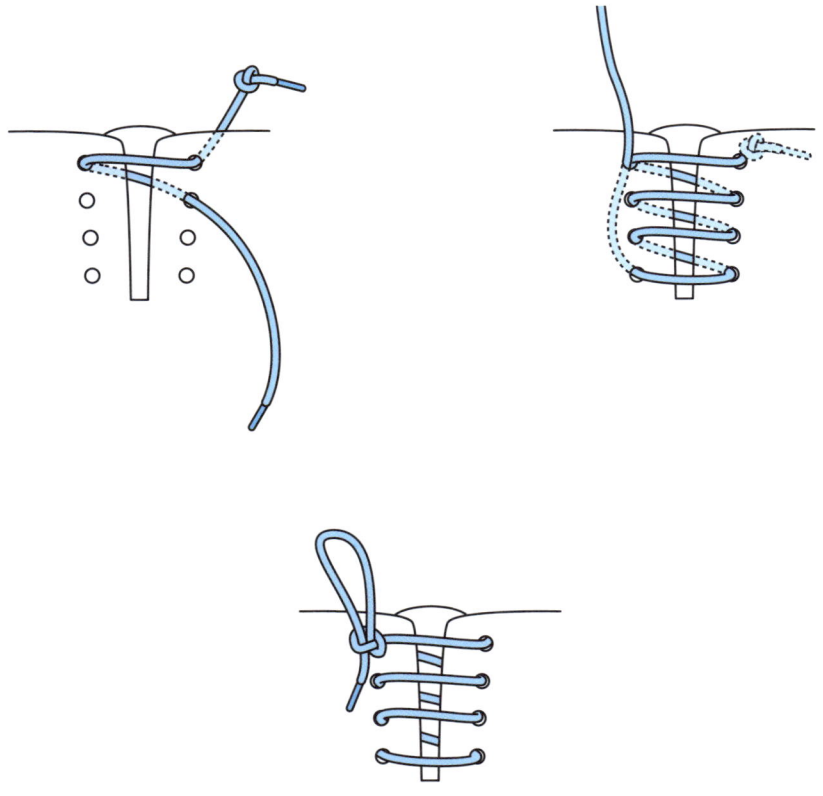

SAILING KNOTS

COMMON REUSABLE KNOTS

Bowline knot

Use: Form a loop at the end of a rope. Among the knots every sailor must know, the bowline is perfectly suited for mooring a boat to a ring, bollard, or cleat (with a collar), thanks to the fact that it can always be untied.

Round turn and two half-hitches

Use: Attach a rope to any support (bollard, ring, railing, tack point, etc.). A knot unmatched in its versatility, it undoubtedly deserves the sailor's saying: a round turn and two half-hitches never fails.

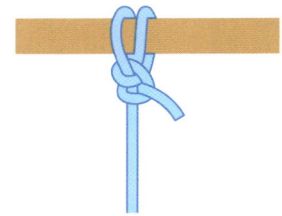

Clove hitch

Use: Attach fenders to the railing. Besides its function as a fastening knot, the clove hitch is a key component of many knots, such as the **constrictor knot**.

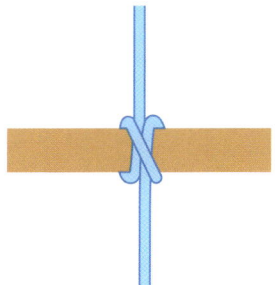

VARIANT
Round turn and two reversed half-hitches

Use: Known for holding as well as the round turn and two half-hitches, but harder to untie.

Sheet bend

Use: Join two ropes together, especially of different diameters. Attach a rope to a flexible loop. The best knot for joining two ropes.

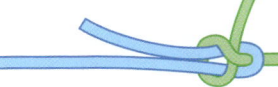

Double sheet bend

Use: More secure than the **simple sheet bend** when shaken or subjected to vibrations. Perfect for attaching sheets to sails rigged in the traditional way.

Figure eight knot

Use: Increase the diameter of sheets and any other line to prevent the end from slipping out of its pulley. This is the best stopper knot suited for sailing.

Midshipman's hitch

Use: Tighten a mizzen shroud, stretch a sun awning, or even make a temporary clothesline. Whip the locking **half-hitch** to make it easier to untie.

Cow hitch

Use: To stow a rope on a support, for example, hanging the mainsheet on a handrail, you can use a cow hitch. A cow hitch can be formed by passing a loop around a support and then feeding the working ends through the loop. If the support is a movable object, like an anchor, and the loop is large enough, pass the object through the loop instead of the rope end; the result will be the same.

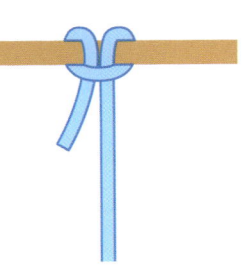

SPECIFIC SAILING KNOTS

Mooring

To successfully dock, you need to stop and secure the boat. The following knots, as well as the bowline (see common knots to reuse), are used for this purpose.

Knot on a busy cleat

Knot type: Fastening

Use: Tie a mooring line to a bollard or post that is already in use.

Method for tying the knot: Passing underneath, thread the **bowline knot** or the spliced eye of the mooring line through the one already in place and hitch the loop onto the bollard. In this setup, each mooring line can be removed independently without affecting the other.

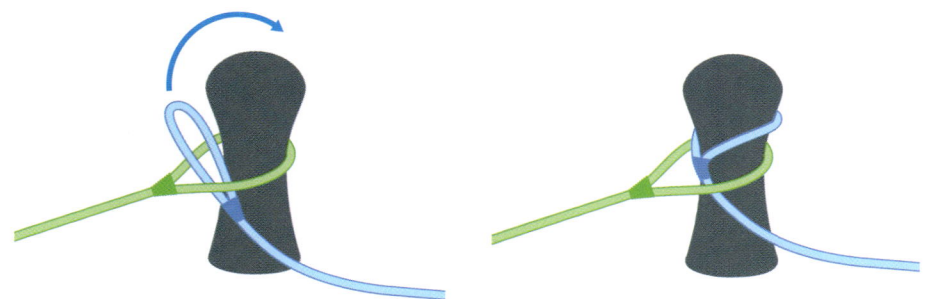

Stevedore knot

Knot type: Stopper

Use: Add weight to the end of a throwing line.

Method for tying the knot: Make a **half-hitch** at the weighted end of the rope, then make a **round turn** around the standing part before passing the working end through the initial half-hitch.

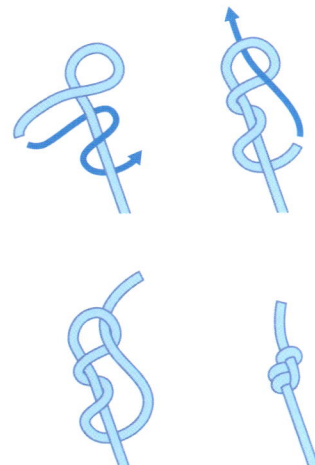

TIPS & TRICKS

On a boat of a certain size, it may be better to pass the mooring lines before the boat reaches the dock. To do this, first throw a small line to a person onshore. To make it go as far as possible, coil a few metres of rope near the end to form a throwing bundle. The stevedore knot ensures that the end flies ahead for the receiver to catch. Don't forget to attach the standing part to the mooring line that will be passed ashore. See also the **monkey's fist knot** on pages 110–111.

Flaking

Knot type: Storage

Use: Prepare a mooring line or anchor chain in anticipation of letting it run out.

Method for tying the knot: Lay the rope in parallel back-and-forth loops. Bring the loops together with gentle taps of the foot to take up less space on the deck.

Figure eight flake

Knot type: Storage

Use: Prepare a mooring line in preparation for paying it out.

How to make the knot: Lay the rope in overlapping figure eights, slightly offset from each other. A rapidly unwinding end can be dangerous, especially the tightest arc between the running end and the standing part. Watch your feet! This is not suitable for chains.

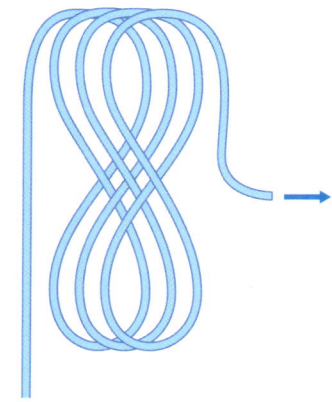

Knot on a hard-to-reach post

Knot type: Fastening

Use: Tie a mooring line to a bollard, ring, or dolphin that becomes inaccessible due to the falling tide.

Method for tying the knot: Make a loop around the post, with the working end underneath. Make a second loop, again underneath, and pass the working end around the turns of the first loop. Double the end and pass the bight through the second loop. Pull on the loop to release. This knot holds wonderfully, but should still be monitored. This is also known as a **picket line hitch**.

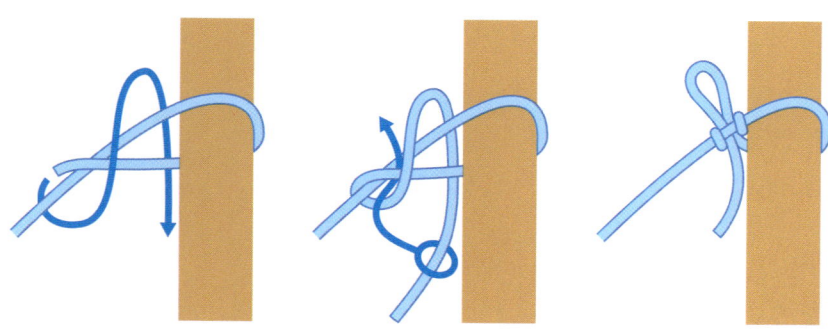

MOORING

The eye splice, the grapnel knot, the cleat hitch, the slipped clove hitch, the running bowline, as well as the clove hitch, the round turn and two half-hitches, and the cow hitch knot (see common knots for reuse), all allow you to secure a mooring line or a tackle to a ring, an anchor, a bollard, or a cleat.

Anchor hitch

Knot type: Fastening

Use: Attach a rope to an anchor ring, buoy ring, or chain link.

Method for tying the knot: Make a **round turn** around the support, then pass the running end around the standing part, through the round turn, and under itself. Tighten and finish with a second **half-hitch** on the standing part.

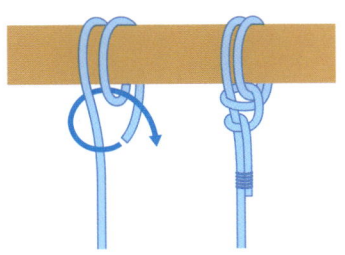

Anchor hitch with loop

Knot type: Fastening

Use: Attach a rope to an anchor ring, buoy ring, or chain link.

Method for tying the knot: Make the anchor hitch, but instead of a second **half-hitch**, tie a **bowline knot** on the standing part.

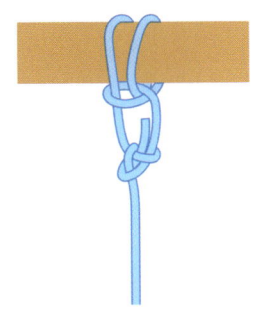

TIPS & TRICKS

Secure further by attaching the end to the standing part using a hitch (see **shear lashing** and **frapping knot** pages 43 and 35).

Cleat hitch

Knot type: Fastening

Method for tying the knot: Pass the rope around the base of the cleat, then make a figure eight using the cleat horns. Make a second turn around the base of the cleat.

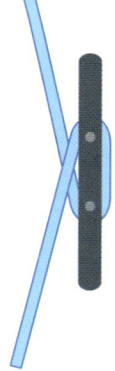 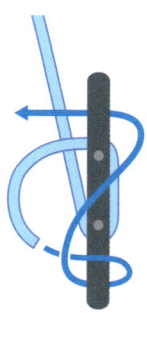

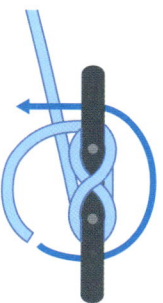 

Slipped half-hitch

Knot type: Fastening

Use: Moor a line that needs to be released quickly (sheet, halyard, towline, or reefing line).

Method for tying the knot: Make a **turn** around the support, double the running end, and tuck the resulting loop under the standing part. Pull the running end to release the line.

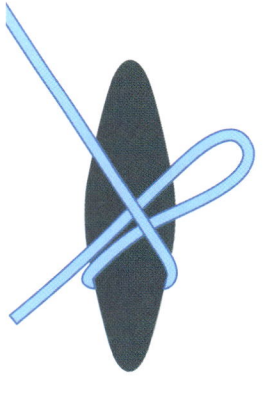

> ### TIPS & TRICKS
>
> On a capstan or mooring bollard, it is customary to make up to three figure eights. Avoid making a half-hitch with the running end underneath, as it might jam on the cleat.

Bowline on the bight

Knot type: Loop

Use: Moor a line at its midpoint (to a ring or tack point) or create a reliable attachment point in the middle of a rope.

Method for tying the knot: Double a section of the rope to form a bight. Place the bight on the standing part and wrap the standing part around the bight. Pass the bight over the loops that will form the knot. Pull on the standing parts and both strands of the bight to tighten the knot.

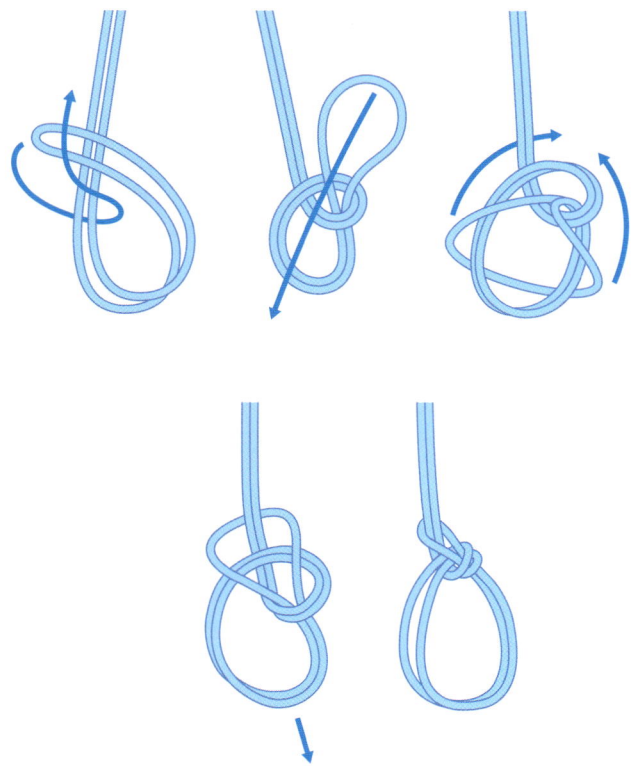

Adjusting

Bowlines and carrick bends, as well as single and double sheet bends (see common knots to reuse), are used to connect two different ropes together.

Bowline bend

Knot type: Bend

Use: Extend a towing line, attach a heaving line.

Method for tying the knot: Make a loop at the end of one of the ropes to be joined, then pass the end of the other rope through the first loop and make a second loop.

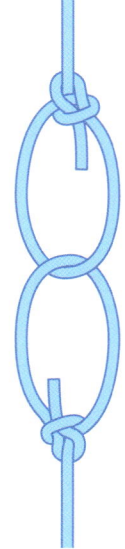

TIPS & TRICKS

Traditionally, the **bowline** is used to make loops, but any other similar knot will do. The **bowline bend** is suitable for joining ropes of different diameters. It's handy and easy to untie.

Carrick bend

Knot type: Bend

Use: Join two large-diameter ropes together (mooring lines, hawsers).

Method for tying the knot: Make a loop with the running end underneath. Pass the end of the second rope under this loop, then lock the knot by alternating passes over and under. The ends must not be on the same side of the knot. Pull on the standing parts to tighten the knot.

Caution: After being subjected to a heavy load, this knot can come undone just as easily as a bowline.

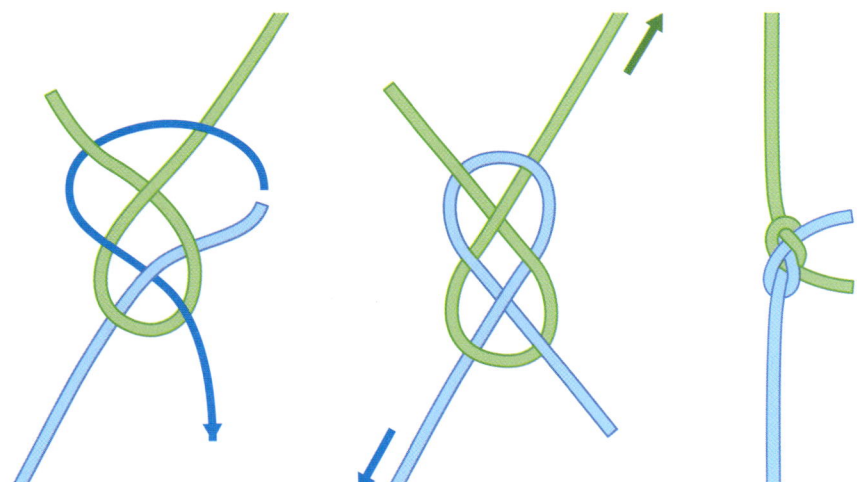

Hauling

Pushing, hoisting, pulling, towing – there so many manoeuvres on board that call for practical, sturdy, and dependable knots!

Rolling hitch knot

Knot type: Fastening

Use: Take up the tension on a line to change cleats or release a winch. Secure a rope to a spar or other rigid support.

Method for tying the knot: Make a **round turn** around the support, in the direction of pull, then pass over it and tie a **half-hitch** on the support. Tighten firmly before putting it under load.

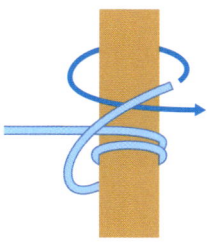 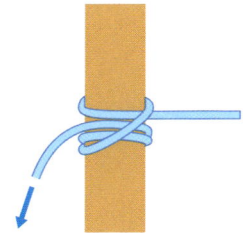

Magnus hitch

Knot type: Fastening

Method for tying the knot: Make a **round turn** around the support, in the direction of pull, then bring the working end back over and finish with a reversed half-hitch around the support. Under load, this knot is less prone to twisting than a standard rolling hitch.

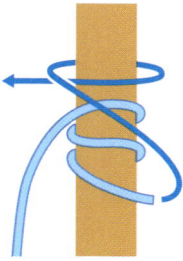 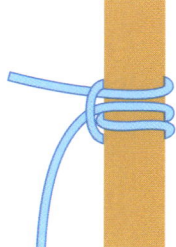

Rolling hitch (prolonged)

Knot type: Fastening

Use: Secure a rope to a thicker rope or a chain. It's particularly well suited to rigging an improvised block and tackle.

Method for tying the knot: Take a **round turn** around the support, bring the working end over the standing part, then make several extra turns around the standing part from beneath. Finish by locking everything with a **half-hitch**.

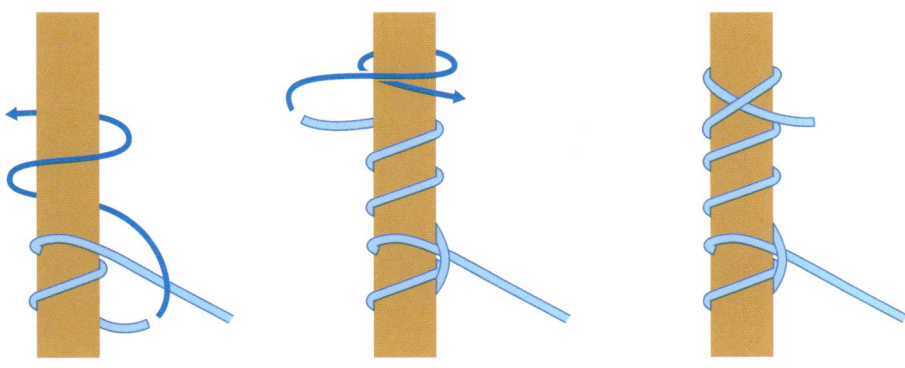

Loop or sling

Knot type: Assembly

Use: Basic component of several knots for hauling a line or lifting a load.

Method for tying the knot: Tie the ends of a single rope, cord, or webbing to form a loop of the desired size. In sailing, the **double sheet bend**, **carrick bend** (see page 257), **Zeppelin bend** (or **Rosendahl bend**) (see page 85), etc., are commonly used to finish the sling.

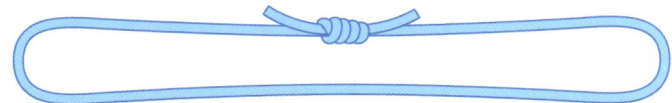

Sling for block and tackle

Knot type: Sling

Use: Haul a large-diameter line, using a **sling** and a block and tackle fitted with a hook.

Method for tying the knot: Centre the sling on the line, then braid the bights around it to form at least two 'X' shapes.

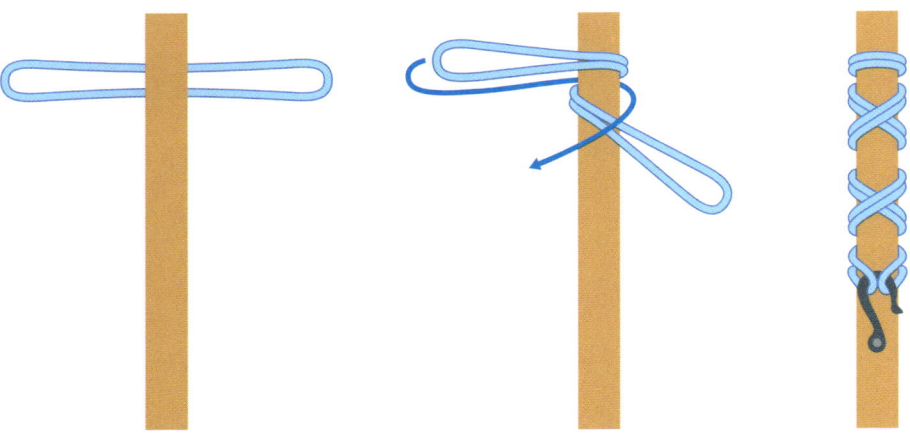

Killick hitch

Knot type: Fastening

Use: Hoist booms and other spars vertically into the mast.

Method for tying the knot: Apply two **half-hitches** around the upper half of the object to be lifted, spaced to suit the support's length, then secure everything with a **timber hitch**.

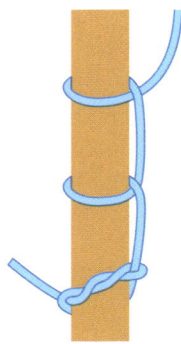

TIPS & TRICKS

If the Killick hitch doesn't hold on a support that's too smooth, use a **groundline hitch** instead. Test it at the start of the setup.

Caulker's bowline

Knot type: Loop

Use: Create an improvised harness for climbing the mast.

Method for tying the knot: Tie a **bowline**, but before tightening it, form a second loop. A quicker way is to make a **round turn**, then pass the running end over the standing part and through the loops. Twist the crossing of the running end and the loops to form a loop in the standing part, then finish the knot as you would a standard bowline.

TIPS & TRICKS

To use as a harness, pass one leg through each loop.

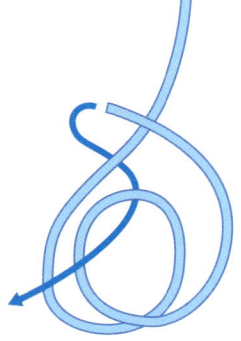

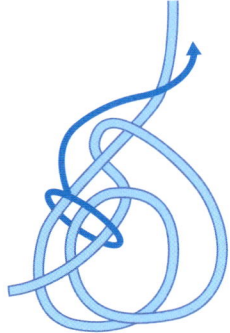

Marlinspike hitch

Knot type: Fastening

Use: Temporarily secure a rope to a marlinspike (or screwdriver) to get a better grip when pulling. Invaluable for tightening a seizing or a lashing.

Method for tying the knot: Place the marlinspike on the rope and hold the end with your free hand. Rotate the spike around the eye from bottom to top to form a loop. Then, bring the spike behind the standing part and slide the half-hitch over the tip of the spike. Pull tight.

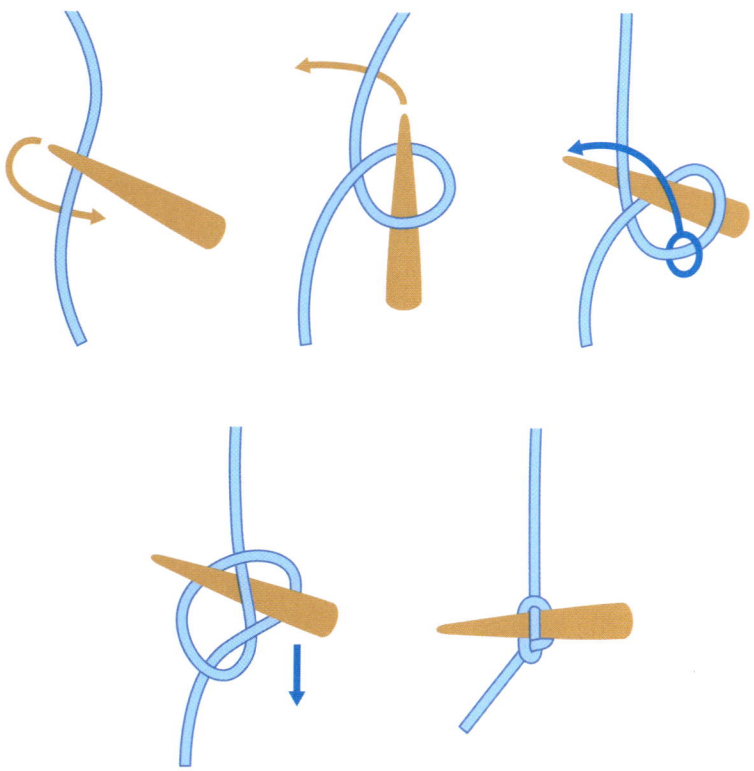

Whipping

The figure eight knot (see common knots to reuse) is used to 'stop'
a line to prevent it from running off a pulley. Whippings are used
to 'stop' a line in the sense that they will stop it fraying.

Sailor's whipping

Method for tying the knot: Form a turn on the rope to be whipped using the end of your whipping
twine. Make at least three turns to lock the working end, then lay the standing part of the
twine along the rope in the opposite direction. Continue wrapping the twine tightly around the
rope, passing the working end through the loop formed by the twine on each turn. Finally, pull
both ends of the twine to snug the wraps firmly. This method uses less twine than the **plain
whipping** (page 84).

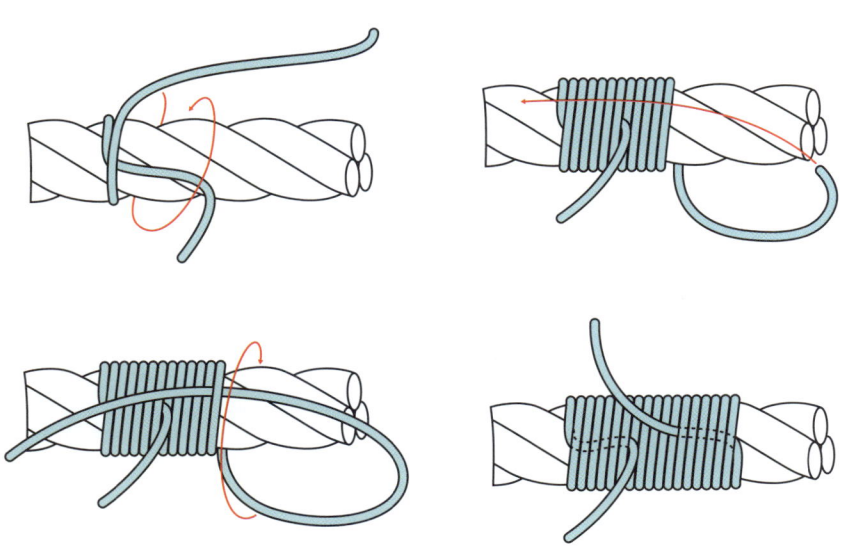

Sewn whipping

Method for tying the knot: Cut a length of whipping twine and thread it onto a sailmaker's needle. Pass the needle through one strand of the rope and make the required number of turns around the rope, trapping the twine's end under the wraps, then pass the needle through another strand. Next, serve the whipping by seating the twine into the grooves between the strands and pass through a strand again. Once the twine has filled all the grooves, tie a **half-hitch** around one of the serving turns and bury the end in the centre of the whipping (use a fid or small wooden tool to push the needle through).

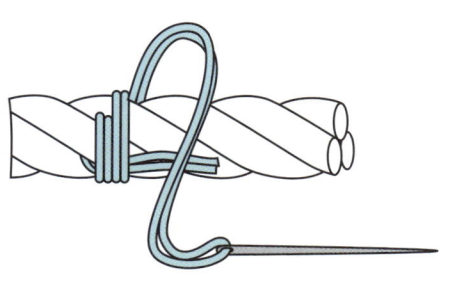
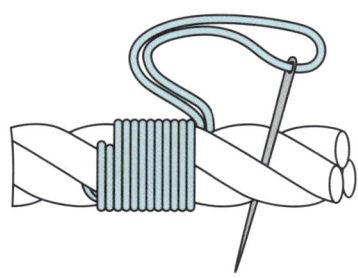

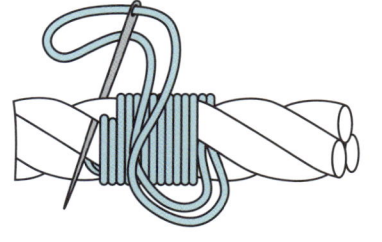
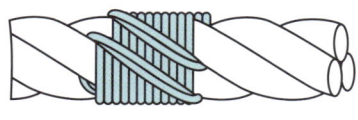

Storage

On board a boat, it's essential to keep everything perfectly stowed and organised. This is especially true for lines: if they aren't stored properly, a crew member could trip over them and fall, or the line could become tangled or unavailable when it's needed for a manoeuvre.

Finger coil

Knot type: Storage

Use: Stow small-diameter sheets and halyards.

Method for tying the knot: Pinch the end between your thumb and forefinger, then coil the line in a figure eight around your little finger and thumb. Remove the bundle from your hand and make one final wrap around its middle. Secure everything by tying one or two **half-hitches** around the bundle.

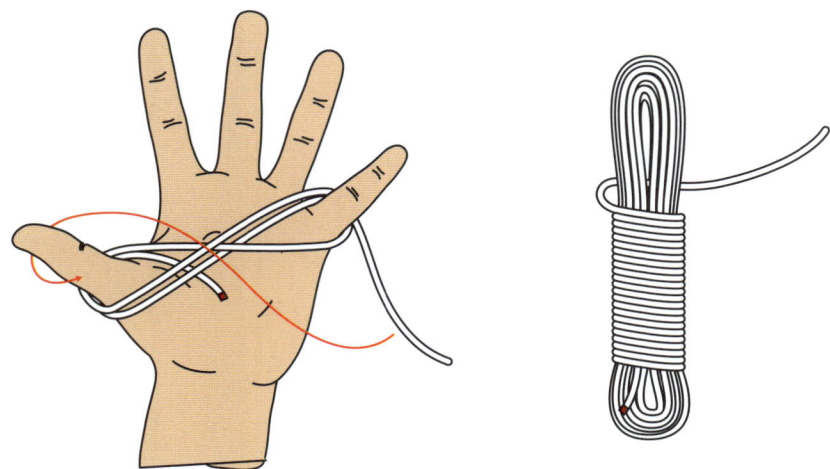

Hand coil

Knot type: Storage

Use: Form the rope into a coil.

Method for tying the knot: Grasp a length of rope and tuck its end into the 'storage' hand. The distance between your hands sets the coil's size, so – to keep it even – don't move the arm of your holding hand. If the wraps start to bulge or form figure eights, give the rope a quarter-turn twist before placing it into your storage hand.

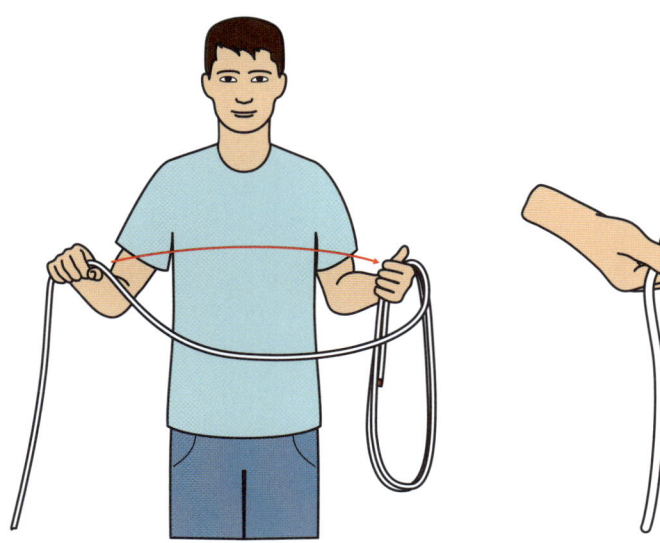

Arm coil

Knot type: Storage

Use: To coil large-diameter or very long rope on the arm.

Method for tying the knot: If the coil becomes too bulky to hold in your hand, slip it over your arm, then continue coiling by draping the rope over the back of your hand before grasping it. To finish with horizontal wraps, instead of winding the end around the last turn, rotate the entire coil by making turns with your storage hand.

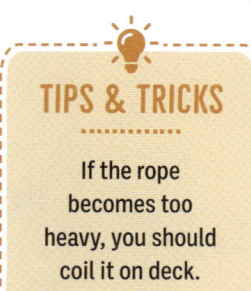
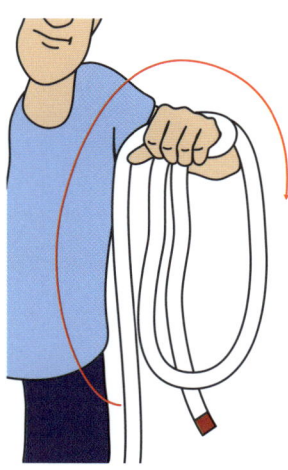

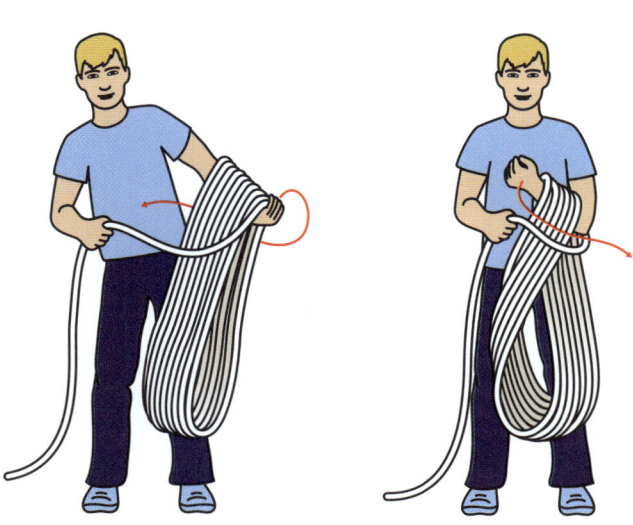

Coil on a cleat or bitt

Knot type: Storage

Use: Hang a coil on a cleat or bitt.

Method for tying the knot: Coil the free part of the mooring line, then slip your hand through the coil and grasp the line where it exits the cleat or bollard. Twist this first wrap to form a loop and belay it onto the mooring fixture. This is also known as a **halyard coil**.

TIPS & TRICKS

If the rope isn't too bulky, you might find it simpler to hang the entire coil directly on the cleat.

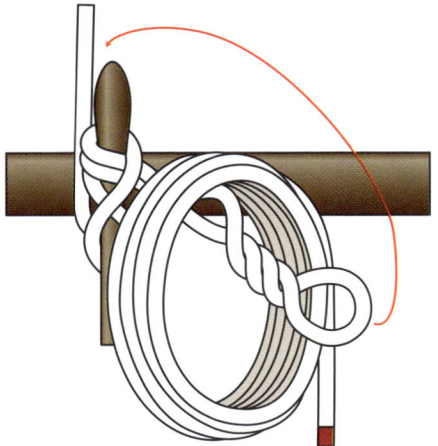

Gasket coil

Knot type: Storage

Use: Hang a coil on a cleat or bitt.

Method for tying the knot: At a suitable distance from the end, wrap the rope around the coil at least three times. Then fold the working end back, pass the resulting bight through and over the coil, and pull the end tight to secure it.

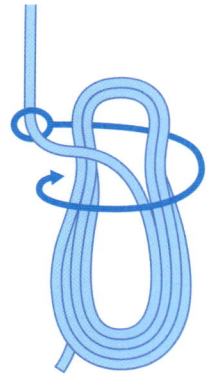

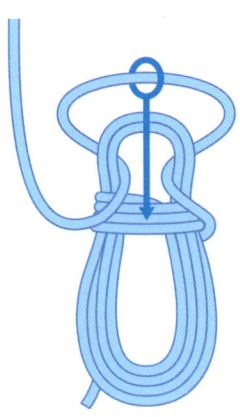

Large coil

Knot type: Storage

Use: Store a large coil semi-permanently.

Method for tying the knot: Once the rope is coiled, take a length of twine and make a **round turn** around the coil, then finish with a **packing knot** (see page 64). Generally, four pieces of twine are enough. This is the method rope-makers use to secure coils.

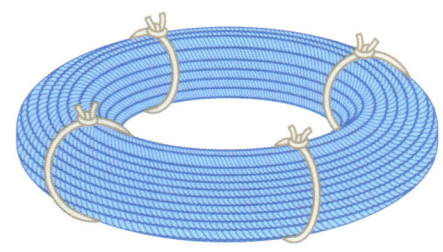

Specific knots

The following knots have very specific uses aboard boats.

Slipped reef knot

Knot type: Binding

Use: Any situation where you need a binding knot that can be easily released, especially when reefing or un-reefing a sail.

Method for tying the knot: Make a **half-hitch** around the spar, fold one end into a bight, then use the other end to tie a second half-hitch just like a **reef knot**. It's essentially the **shoelace knot** without one loop and is also called a reef knot.

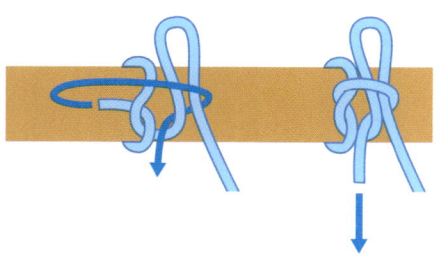

Buntline hitch

Knot type: Fastening

Use: Attach a buntline to the foot of a square or fore-and-aft sail.

Method for tying the knot: Pass the rope around the fitting (the attachment point), then make a **half-hitch** on the standing part with the working end crossing over. Repeat for a second half-hitch in the same manner and tighten firmly. This knot stands up exceptionally well to sudden jerks because, unlike two half-hitches tied in succession, the working end is trapped between the knot (essentially a clove hitch) and the fitting.

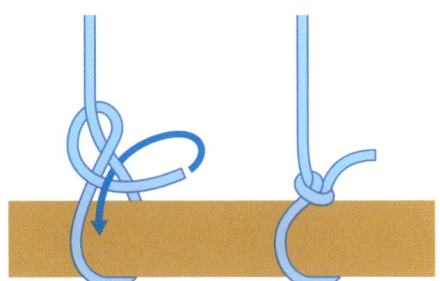

Halyard bend

Knot type: Fastening

Use: Attach a studding-sail halyard to a spar or yard.

Method for tying the knot: Make a round turn around the spar, leaving it fairly slack. Then bring the running end behind the standing part and back through the **round turn**. Tuck the working end under the middle strand of the turn and draw the knot tight.

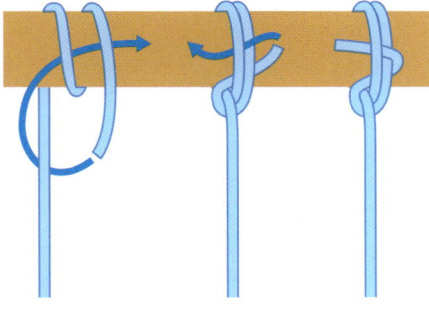

Marline hitching

Knot type: Lacing

Use: Shift a sail onto a spar, and lash bales, packages, and parcels.

Method for tying the knot: Begin with a **timber hitch** (or any other suitable hitch) around the support. Then pass the running end around the support, bringing it over and under the standing part. This knot might look like a half-hitch – it is in fact a simple half knot, which gives it greater tenacity.

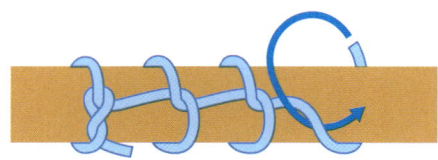

Jury mast knot

Knot type: Loop

Use: Make an attachment point on a jury mast for the forestay and shrouds.

Method for tying the knot: First, line up three loops in a row (stacked so that the leftmost loop sits up front and the rightmost one tucks in behind). Next, take the working end of the first loop and weave it under, over, under through the three strands to its right; at the same time, mirror that move with the working end of the third loop on the left. Draw the middle loop forward, belay its midpoint to your jury mast, then snug everything up by pulling on the standing parts. Finish with a **reef knot** to lock it in place. This is a clever little knot for ocean sailors … or for weary paddlers who fancy turning an oar and a picnic blanket into a makeshift sail!

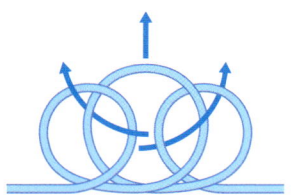

HOBBIES
(GAMES, COOKING, SPORTS, KITE-FLYING, MUSIC)

GAMES

Magic knot

Challenge: Perform a sequence of **simple knots** as if by magic!

Coil the rope by tying a series of **half-hitches**. Tie each half-hitch with the working end underneath, placing each new hitch atop the previous one. Once the entire rope is coiled, pass the standing part through the hitches. Have an assistant pull the standing part slowly while the magician ensures the knots form evenly.

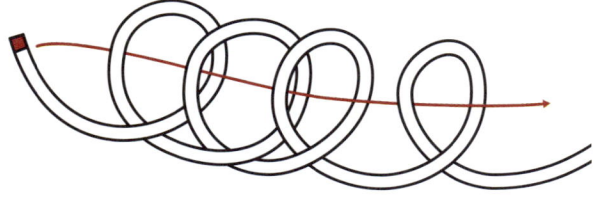

Crossed arm clove hitch

Challenge: Tie a **clove hitch** without ever letting go of the rope.

Lay the rope in front of you and cross your arms. Grip the rope with both hands, then uncross your arms. Slide the lower half-hitch beneath the upper one, and finally belay the knot onto a fixed support.

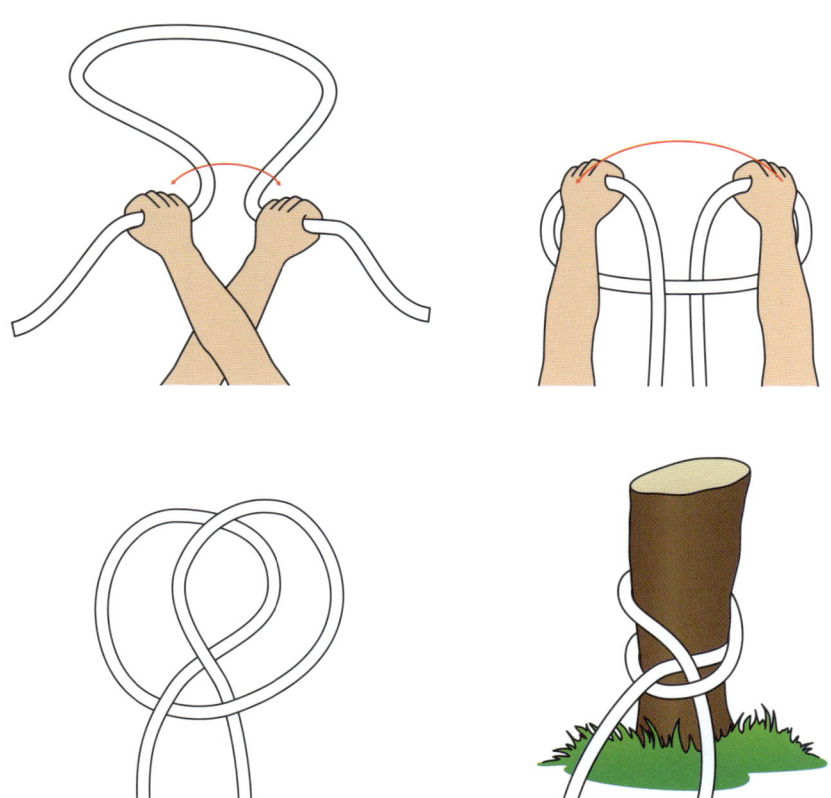

Handcuff knot

Challenge: Take a prisoner in the blink of an eye!

Tie two belayed **half-hitches** on the standing part, then draw each inner bight through the adjacent hitch to form two loops. Invite the 'prisoner' to slip their hands into each loop, pull the standing ends in opposite directions to cinch the loops snugly around the wrists, and finish by locking the knot with a **reef knot**.

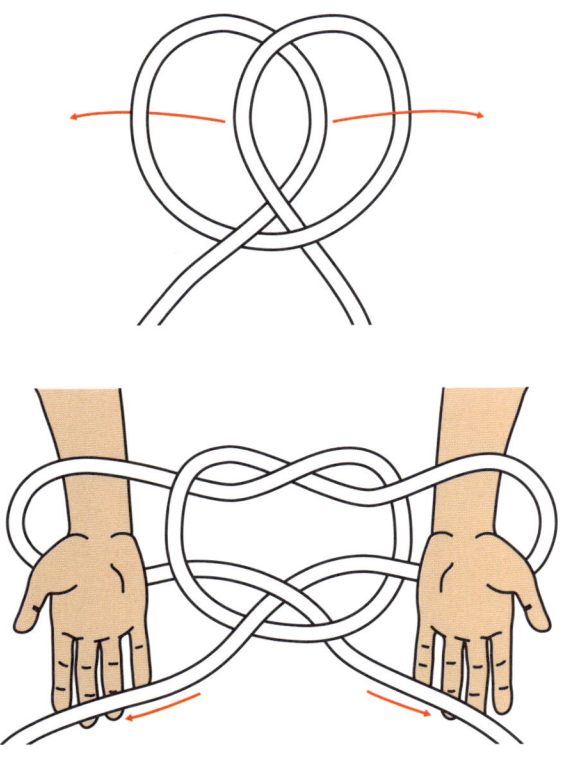

Impossible knot

Challenge: Make a complex knot that comes undone in a single motion.

Tie one overhand knot and then another to form a **reef knot** without tightening. Pass the standing end from above through the lower loop, then through the reef knot, and pull on the ends.

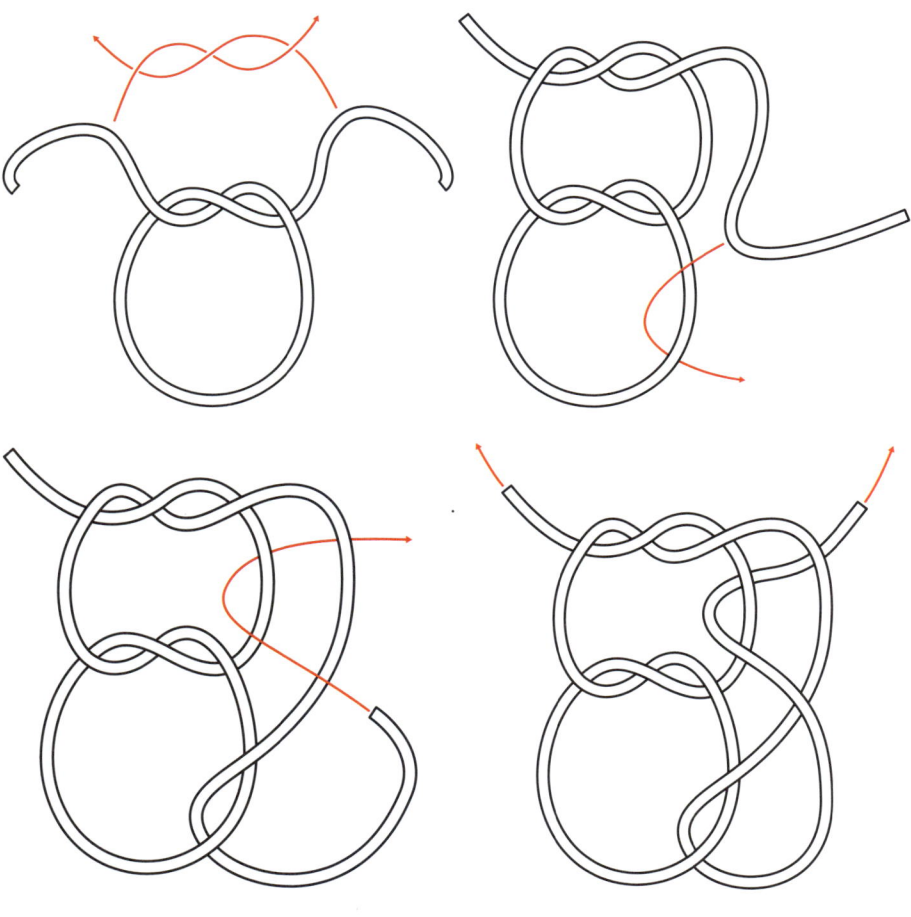

Pass through the bight

Challenge: Thread a ring through a bight, one-handed, without ever letting go.

Form a few wraps of rope around your thumb, then finish with a bight pinched between thumb and forefinger. The end to be threaded must be no more than 20cm long. Twist the bight's end so that it points toward the wraps. Then pretend to aim the end at the bight, but – in one swift motion – let the rope slide over your thumb and catch against your index finger. Magically, the end will have passed through the bight.

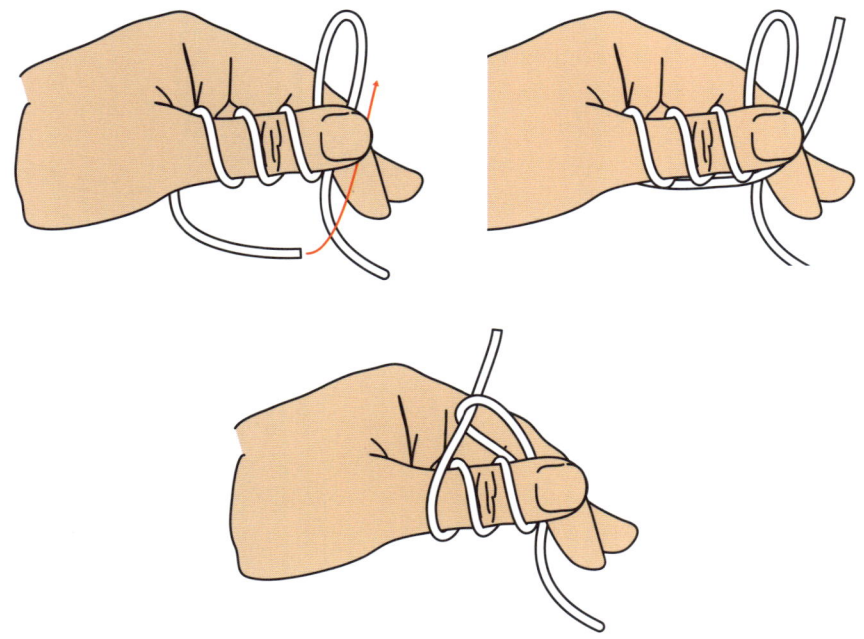

Pass through the fingers

Challenge: Pass a loop through all your fingers.

Make a **sling** from a flexible line, using the smallest possible knot so that it won't snag during the trick. Slip the sling over one hand; then, with your other hand's index finger, reach under the front strand and through the gap between thumb and index to hook the back strand. Twist the rope to the right to form a loop and secure it on your index finger. Repeat this for each finger. Finally, pull the loop off the thumb and tug on the loop on the opposite side of the hand. The ring will magically travel 'through' all your fingers.

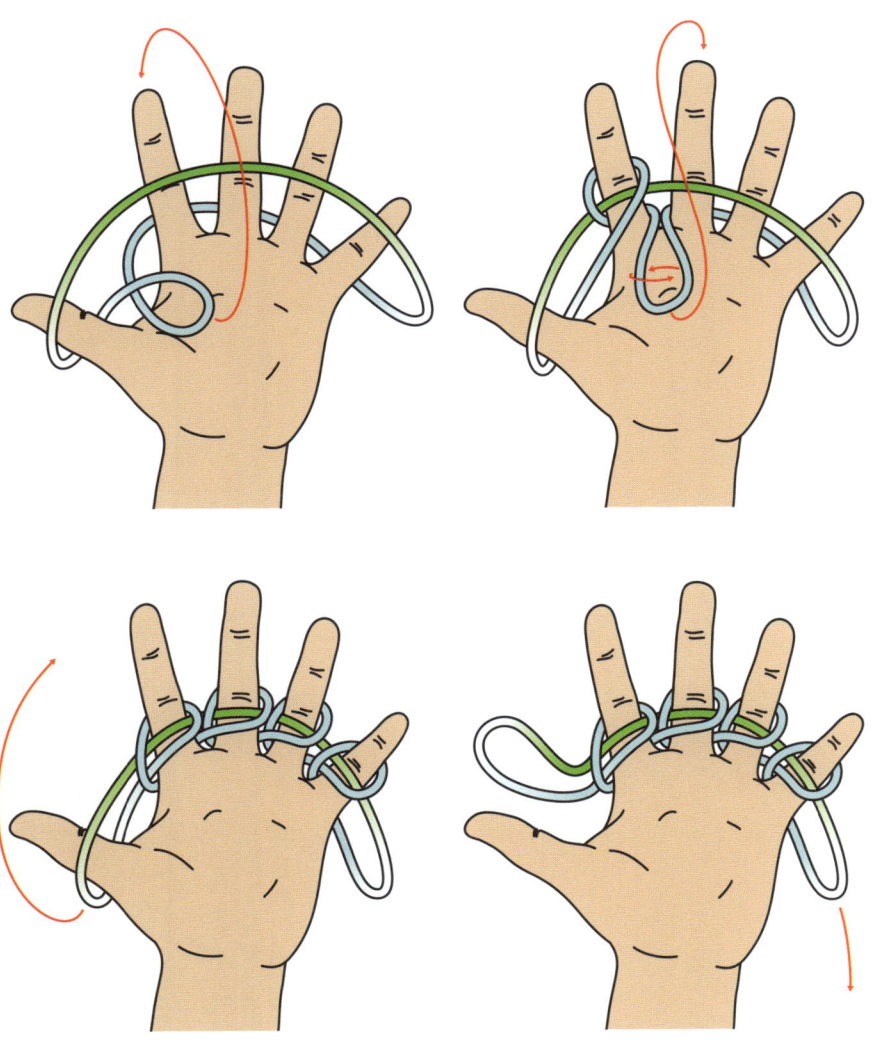

Drop the ring

Challenge: Drop the **ring** without ever letting go of the rope.

Make a flexible loop of rope with the smallest possible knot so that it won't catch during the trick. Thread a rigid ring (a large ring, shackle, or scissors) onto the loop, then suspend the whole assembly between your thumbs. Use your right little finger to hook the strand across from you, and your left little finger to hook the right-hand strand at the front. Release the loops from your right thumb and left little finger. The ring will fall away, but the rope loop will stay wrapped around your fingers.

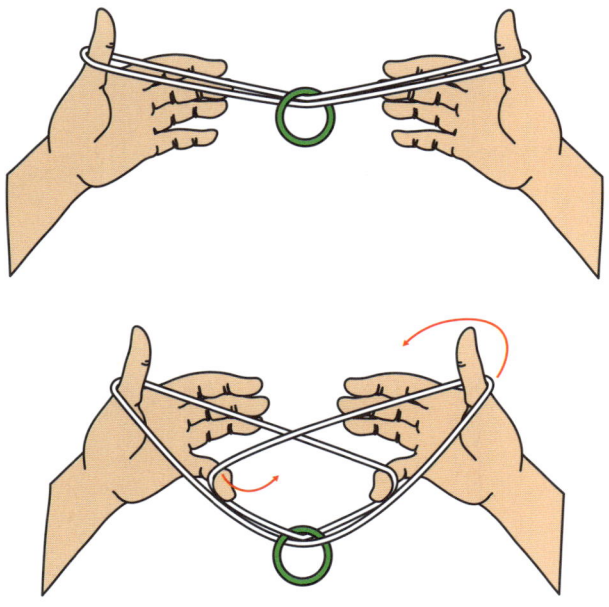

Mariner's quoits

Challenge: Play quoits just like sailors on a long voyage.

To make the **quoits**, craft rope rings in different colours (see pages 134–135). Draw the target on the deck (or floor) with chalk. You can also add a wooden target in the centre, with a base and a peg that can double as quoit storage. The player with the highest score wins.

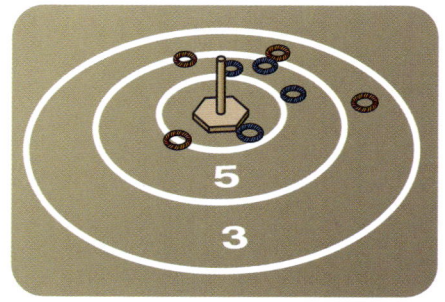

Twirling rings

Challenge: Can your partner mirror your every move?

Make two small string loops and hand one to your imitator. Begin by twirling your loop around your index finger. Your partner must match you exactly. Reverse the spin and see if they can switch directions as smoothly. Next, lay the loop flat and pinch it between thumb and forefinger (one palm up, the other down). Bring your hands together and wait for them to do the same. At just the right moment, open the pinch (keeping each index touching the opposite thumb) and watch the loop.

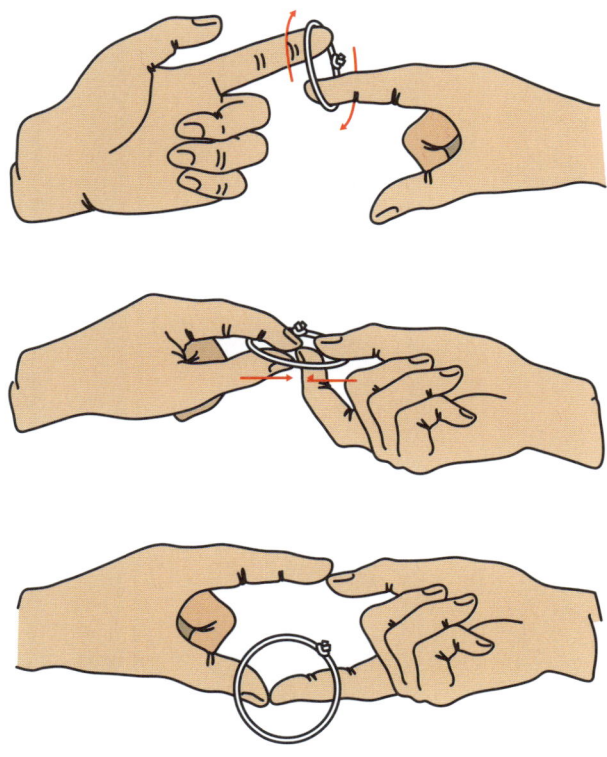

Free the finger

Challenge: Magically remove a rope loop from a finger.

Form a large loop of cord. Ask an assistant to hold out their index finger vertically. Slip the loop onto their finger, then thread your left index through it, pointing downward. With your right hand, make a 'scissors' shape (index and middle finger), then lift the left strand over the right, with your middle finger nestled between the two. 'Shorten' the loop by rotating your left hand clockwise, with your left index riding just to the right of the strands. Reverse the twist and press your left middle finger against the assistant's index. Finally, grip the top wrap with your left hand and let the other two turns drop away. Voilà! The loop slips clean off their finger.

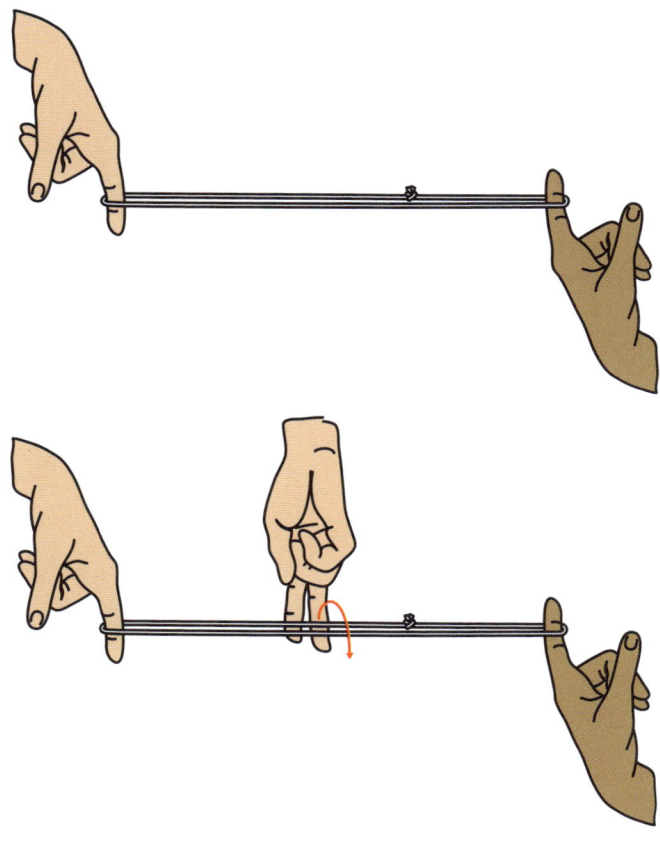

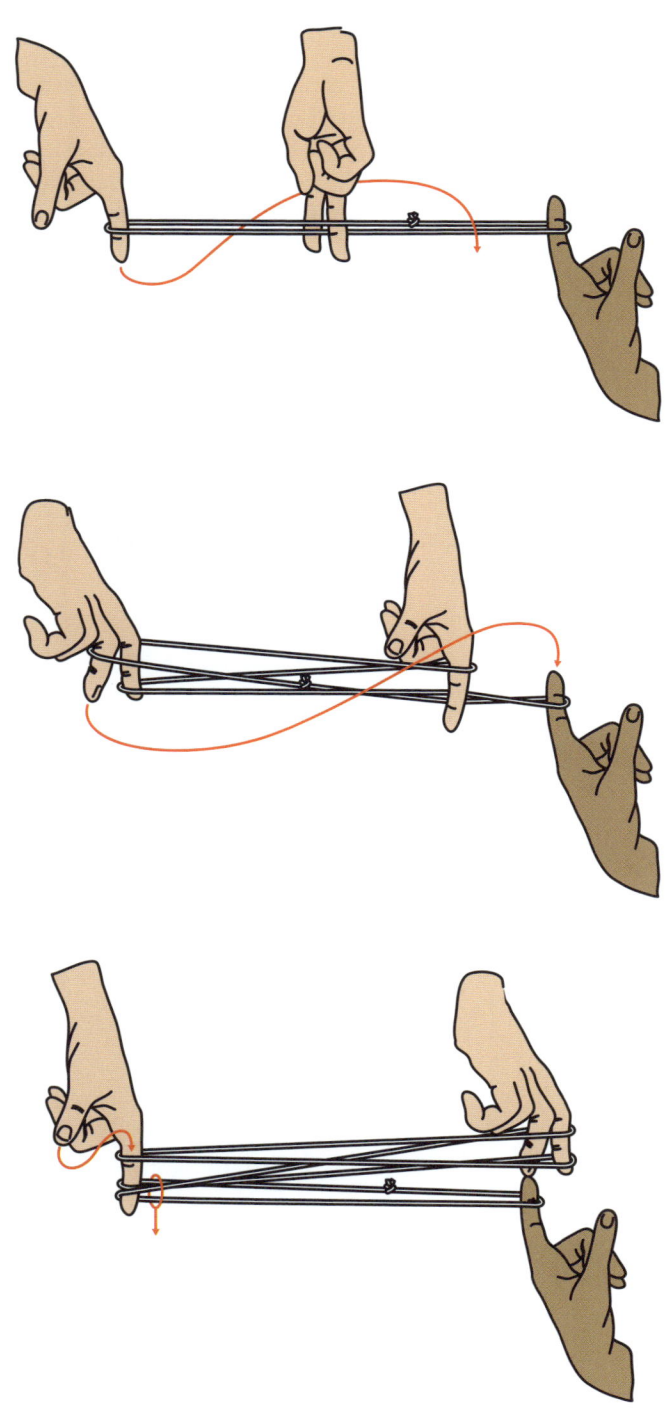

Pass through the neck (the garotte)

Challenge: Remove the loop from someone's neck, without cutting off their head!

Place a large loop of rope around your 'victim's' neck. Pass the left strand around the neck again to form a **round turn**. Twist the main bight in front clockwise. Hold the loop on each side of the resulting crossing, then bring the front bight up and over their head. Let go of the two loops resting on their shoulders, then gently pull on the front bight. The loop will fall away. Take care not to pull too quickly or too hard, otherwise you could burn your assistant's skin.

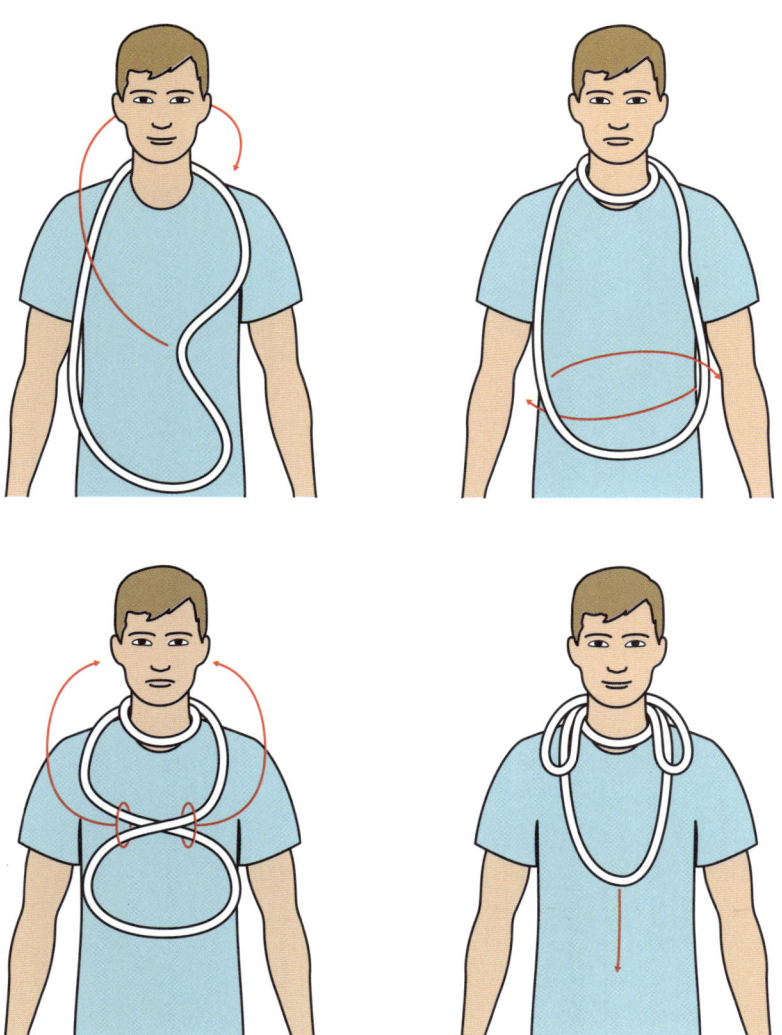

Unreliable knots

Challenge: Find a way to free yourself without slipping the loops off your wrists.

Cut two lengths of rope, about 2m each, and tie a loop in each end (using a **bowline** or an **eye splice**). Pick two people who know each other well, then place the loops over their wrists, crossing the two ropes. The 'victims' must escape by any means, just don't let the loops leave the wrists.

Solution: Feed one rope through the opposite person's loop and slip it over their hand.

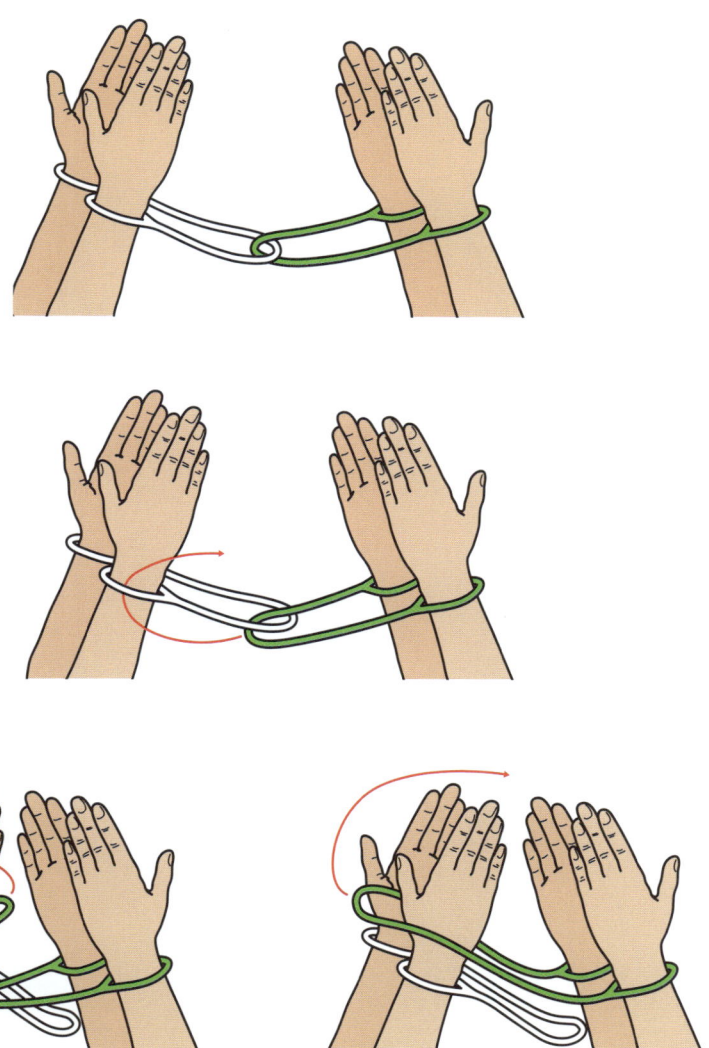

COOKING

Bag knot

Knot type: Binding

Use: Temporarily close a large flour or potato sack.

Method for tying the knot: Circle the neck of the sack once, then cross the working end over the standing part and take a second turn as if tying a **clove hitch**. Instead of passing the end beneath the crossing strand, fold it back on itself and tuck it under the first turn. The result is a knot that's quick to tie and easy to untie, unlike, say, the **constrictor knot** or **miller's knot**.

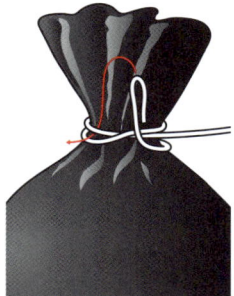

Butcher's knot

Knot type: Binding

Use: To truss roasts and other dishes before baking.

Method for tying the knot: Place a length of kitchen twine beneath the roast so that the ends emerge on top. Loop one working end around the standing part and tie a **half-hitch**; pull it tight. Make a second half-hitch around the standing part and slide it down over the working end. Cinch everything snugly and trim off the excess twine. For a series of bindings, simply make successive ligatures around the joint, securing each with a butcher's knot. For dishes you'll marinate, use the salting knot instead (see page 290).

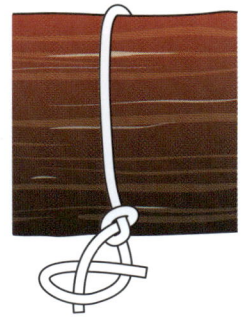

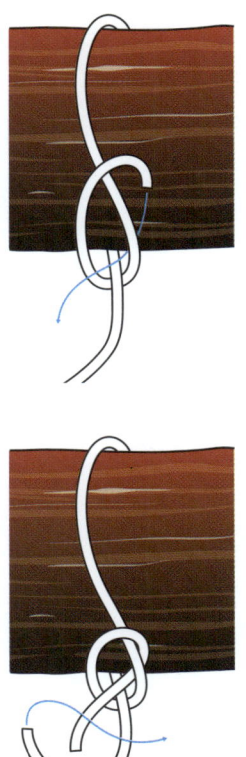

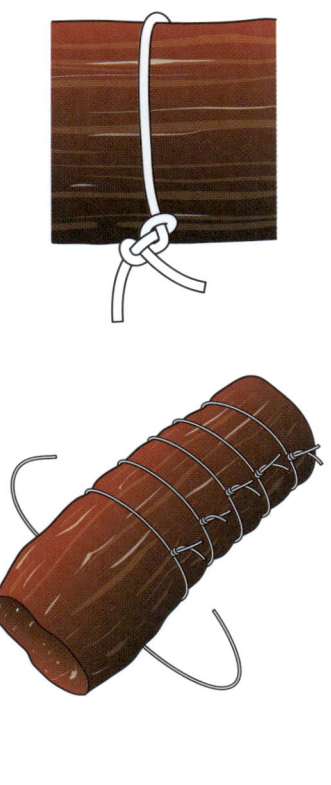

Trussing a roast

Knot type: Lacing

Use: To truss a roast or a rectangular paupiette.

Method for tying the knot: Begin by making a tight binding around the roast and secure it with a butcher's knot. Next, tie **marline hitches** (page 272) around the joint at even intervals. Then, take the free end of the kitchen twine, pass it behind the roast, and tuck it under each binding all the way back to your starting point. Finally, bring the twine behind the first crossing and finish by tying two half-hitches around the twine itself.

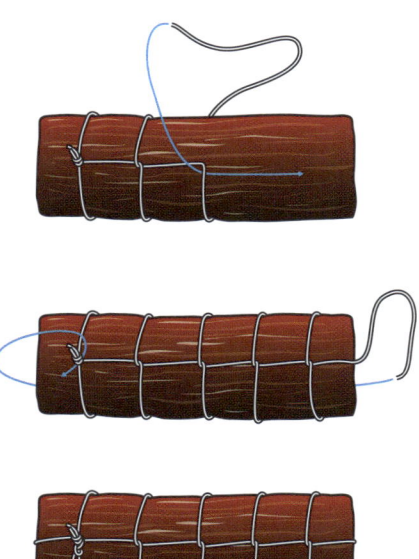

Corned beef knot

Knot type: Binding

Use: Tie up any preparation destined for salting.

Method for tying the knot: Wrap the food with kitchen twine, then loop the working end around the standing part and tie a **clove hitch** on itself. Make sure the end is caught between the first half-hitch of the clove hitch and the standing part. Cinch the clove hitch tight. Next, tie a **half-hitch** on the standing part, slide it over the working end, pull everything snug, and trim off the excess twine.

TIPS & TRICKS

This knot is ideal for things you'll marinate, since meat tends to contract as it cures. Just undo the final half-hitch to retighten the binding around your preparation. However, it's a bit trickier to tie than the standard butcher's knots.

Trussing poultry

Knot type: Lacing

Use: To truss a chicken or other poultry for spit-roasting.

Method for tying the knot: Bring the drumsticks together and loop a length of kitchen twine around them. Cross the strands over the breast and, running under the wings, tie the ends at the back with a **butcher's knot** or similar.

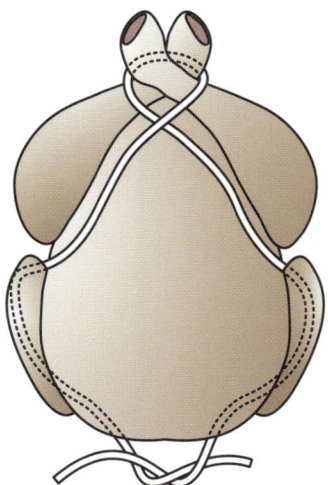

Round paupiette knot

Method for tying the knot: To tie a knot around a round paupiette, wrap the kitchen twine around it, then cross the strands at the front. Lay one strand across the top of the paupiette and tuck the other underneath. Both strands will now meet on top, effectively cutting the paupiette in half vertically. Cross the strands again. Next, lay one strand to the right of the crossing over the paupiette and pass the other underneath on the left, dividing it into four segments. Repeat this process, crossing and laying one strand over and the other one under, creating as many divisions as you like. Finish by securing everything with a **butcher's knot**.

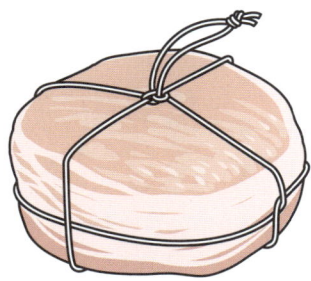

RACKET SPORTS

Tennis or badminton rackets

Racket-stringing

Racket-stringing involves feeding a string through the holes in a racket's frame, going from one hole to its opposite, either top to bottom or side to side, and tensioning it enough to form a sturdy mesh. The mains are the strings that run vertically, and the crosses are the strings that run horizontally.

Two-knot stringing pattern

This stringing pattern lets you string a racket using a single length of cord. Begin by feeding the cord through the hole at the centre of the racket (top or bottom, depending on your setup). Plan your 'short' end (shown in blue) so it's long enough to string half the mains. The 'long' end (shown in red) must reach to string the remaining mains and all the crosses. String the mains gradually, in groups of three or four, to even out the tension on the frame. Once all the mains are done, secure the short end with a knot. Then, use the long end to string every cross, carefully alternating each pass over and under, and finish by tying off with a knot.

Four-knot stringing pattern

This stringing pattern lets you mount a racket using two separate lengths of cord. With the first cord, begin by feeding it through the hole at the centre of the racket (top or bottom, according to your setup). String the mains gradually, in groups of three or four, to distribute tension evenly around the frame. Then, secure each end with a knot. For the crosses, anchor the second cord to one of the mains as close as possible to the starting hole, then string 'downward' towards the handle. This method also lets you combine two different string types. For example, monofilament for the mains and gut for the crosses.

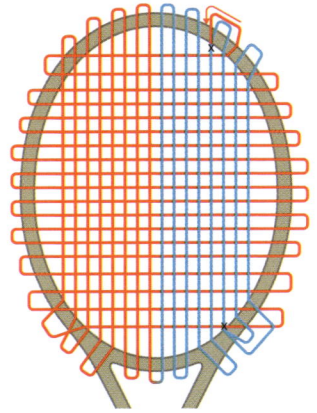 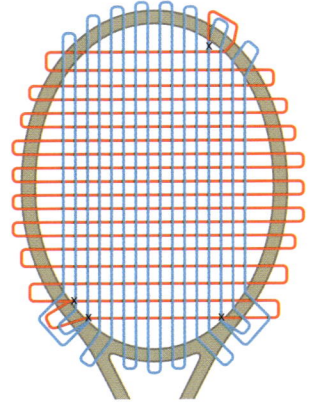

Simple stringing knot

The simple stringing knot is a finishing hitch used to close off a racket's stringing. Pass the working end of the string you've just strung through an adjacent hole (already occupied by a tensioned string), feeding it from the outside towards the inside of the head. Tie a **half-hitch** around that tensioned string and snug it up tightly using calking pliers or by forming a **marlinspike hitch**. Add a second half-hitch to lock it in place. When tying the knot, pull the working string with about 1–2kg of extra tension (for a tennis racket) compared to the other strings, to make up for any future slippage. Be aware that the second half-hitch may not grip well on monofilament strings.

Standard stringing knot

Follow the steps for the **simple stringing knot**, but before tightening the half-hitch, fold the working end around its standing part and pass it back through the half-hitch to form a figure eight. Then, snug the half-hitch firmly without disturbing the figure eight. To finish, pull the working end to draw up the second loop of the figure eight. This yields a tidier finish with the free end aligned along the string, and is the knot used by most racket-makers and professional stringers.

TOOLS

....

Stringing pliers are used to lever against the frame to tension a string.

Lacrosse head

The **stopper knot** used to start the side-wall lacing is simply an overhand knot (1). To do the **side-wall lacing**, attach the mesh to the sides of the cross with a series of **marline hitches** (2). For the **shooting-string lacing** through the mesh, centre the lace on a dedicated hole in the stick, then weave the strands through the mesh (3). To tie off the **shooting strings on the side-wall**, pass each end through its frame hole and finish with a **reef knot** (6). The **anchor knots** that secure each end of the top side-wall lace to the stick are **double overhand knots** (4). The **top knots** that fasten the mesh to the upper rail of the stick are **cow hitch knots** (5). Nowadays, lacrosse mesh comes pre-strung, but you can create your own using the **diamond-mesh technique** (see page 199).

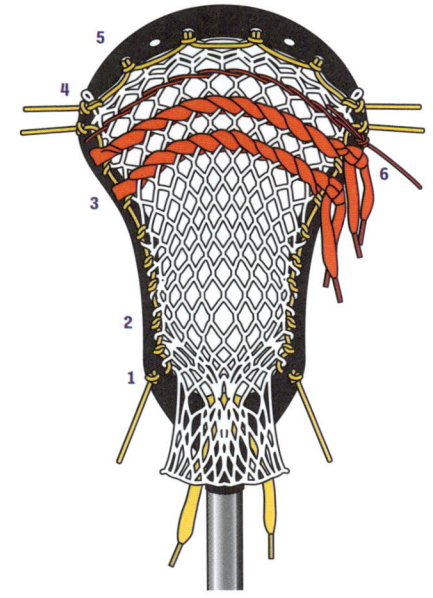

KITE-FLYING

Square lashing

Knot type: Binding

Use: Tie the two spars of a kite together.

Method for tying the knot: Cross the kite's spars, then lay the line in a Z-pattern over the crossing. Finish by tying each end with a **half-hitch** under the diagonal of the lashing.

Although it looks like a kite transom knot, if the top spar is removed, it becomes a strangle knot. Avoid using a **constrictor knot**, which tends to make the spars twist.

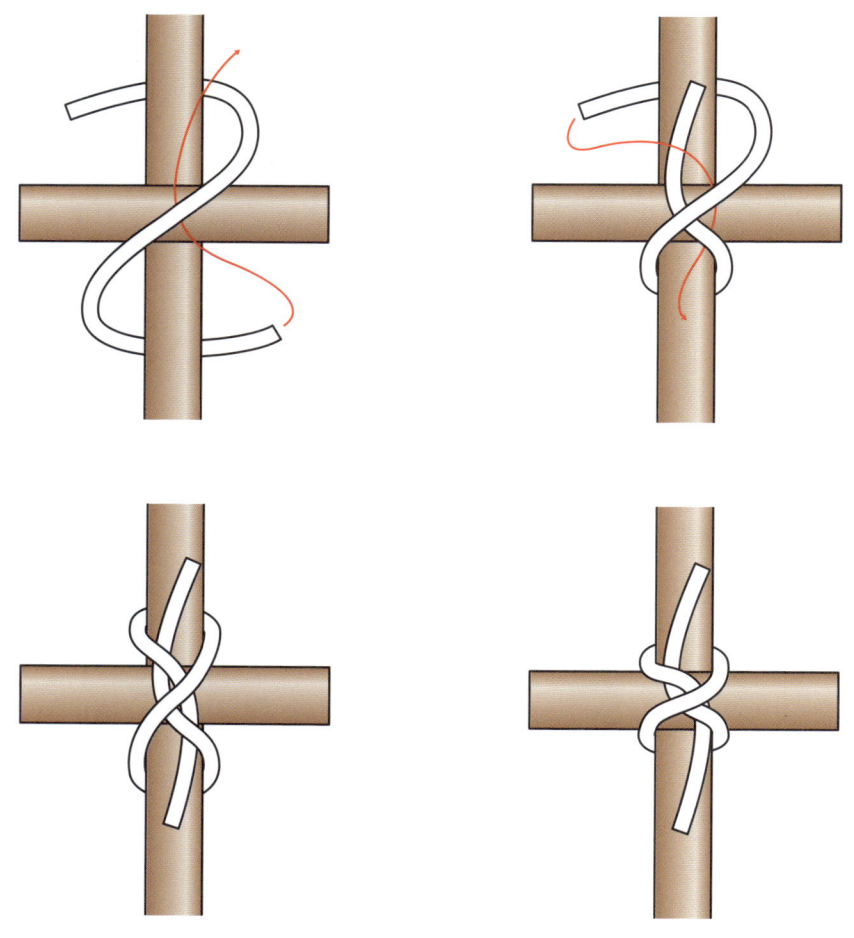

Bridle knot

Knot type: Fastening

Use: Attach the loop to a kite's bridle.

Method for tying the knot: Tie an **overhand loop** at the end of the line, leaving a loop large enough to pass the twine spool through. Slip the loop over the bridle, then wrap the spool around the bridle and back through the loop twice. Slide the knot up or down the bridle until the loop sits in the optimal spot.

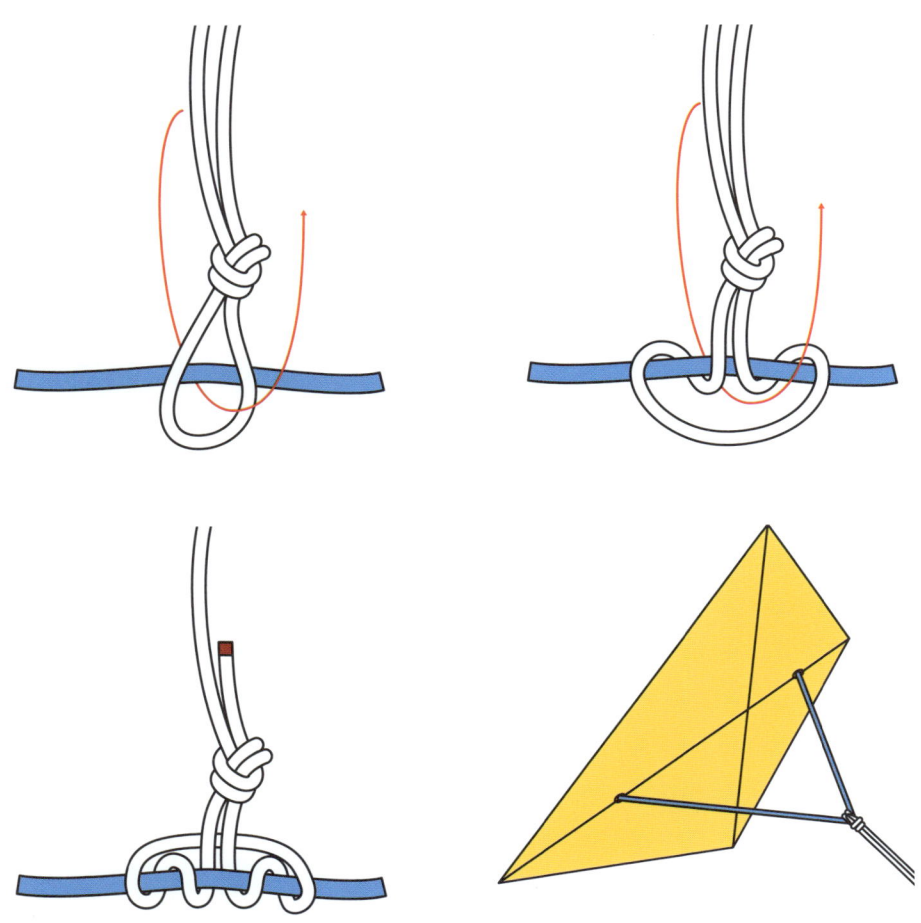

Kite tail knot

Knot type: Stopper

Use: Add decorative **bows** to a kite's tail.

Method for tying the knot: Use the **magic-knot** method to tie as many overhand knots as you like. To form each bow, loosen one overhand knot so that it opens into two loops. Push one of those loops back through the knot. Make sure the knot you end up with is a slipped cow hitch, not a **slipped reef knot**.

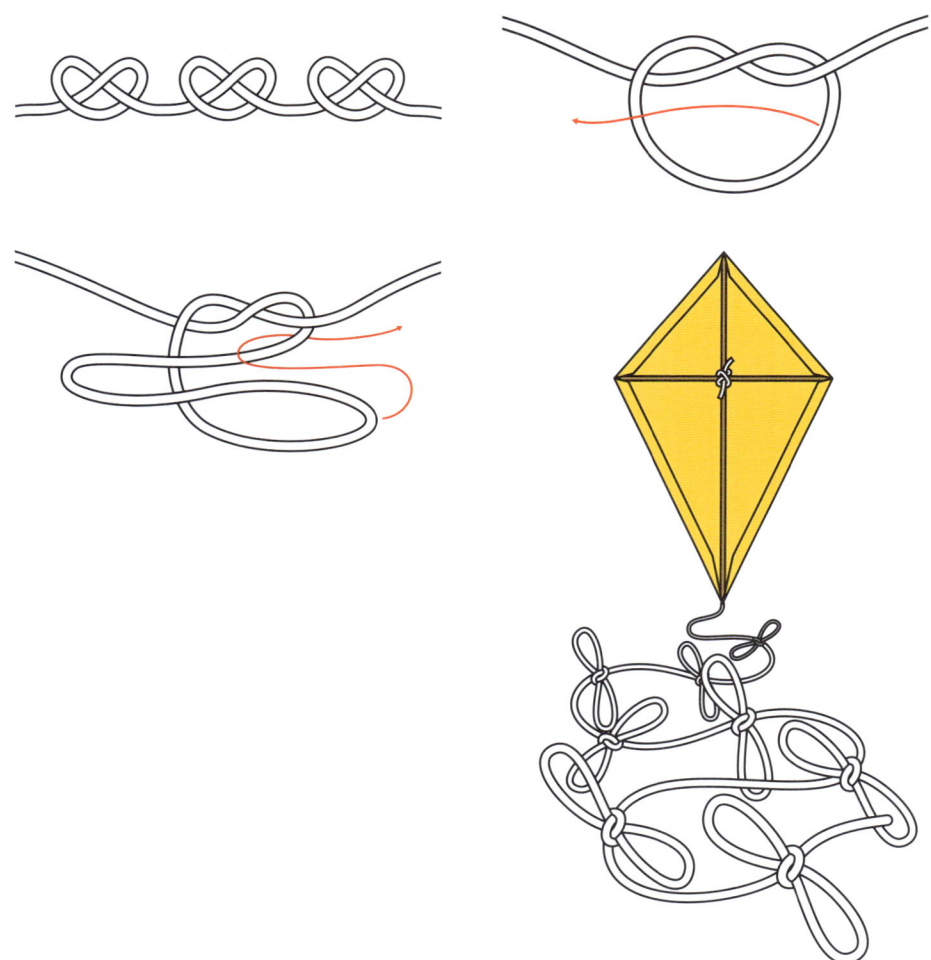

Kite timber hitch

Knot type: Storage

Use: Stow a kite's flying line.

Method for tying the knot: Take a stick of suitable length, then wrap the line around it in figure eight turns. See also the finger-coiling technique.

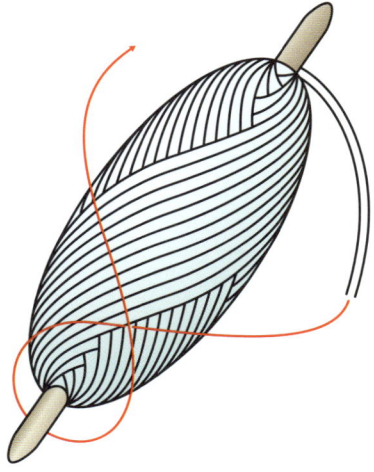

MUSIC

Bridge knot for a treble string

Knot type: Fastening

Use: Attach a treble (nylon) string to a guitar.

Method for tying the knot: Thread the string through the bridge, then tie a **timber hitch**.

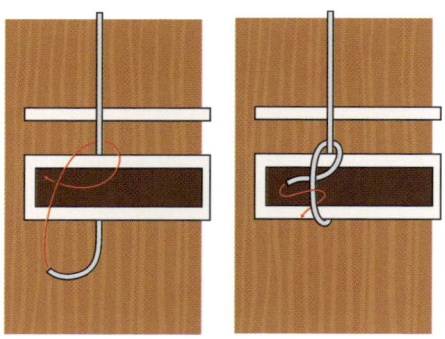

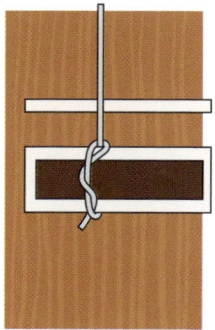

Bridge knot for a bass string

Knot type: Fastening

Use: Attach a bass guitar string to a guitar.

Method for tying the knot: Thread the string through the bridge, then tie a **half-hitch**.

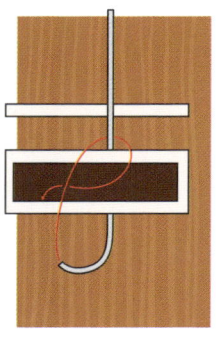

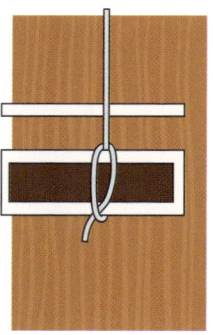

Tuning-peg knot

Knot type: Fastening

Use: Attach a string to the tuning peg of a guitar, violin, ukulele, etc.

Method for tying the knot: Thread the string through the tuning peg, then tie a **half-hitch**. Make sure that the string pulls snugly against the loop of the hitch as you turn the peg.

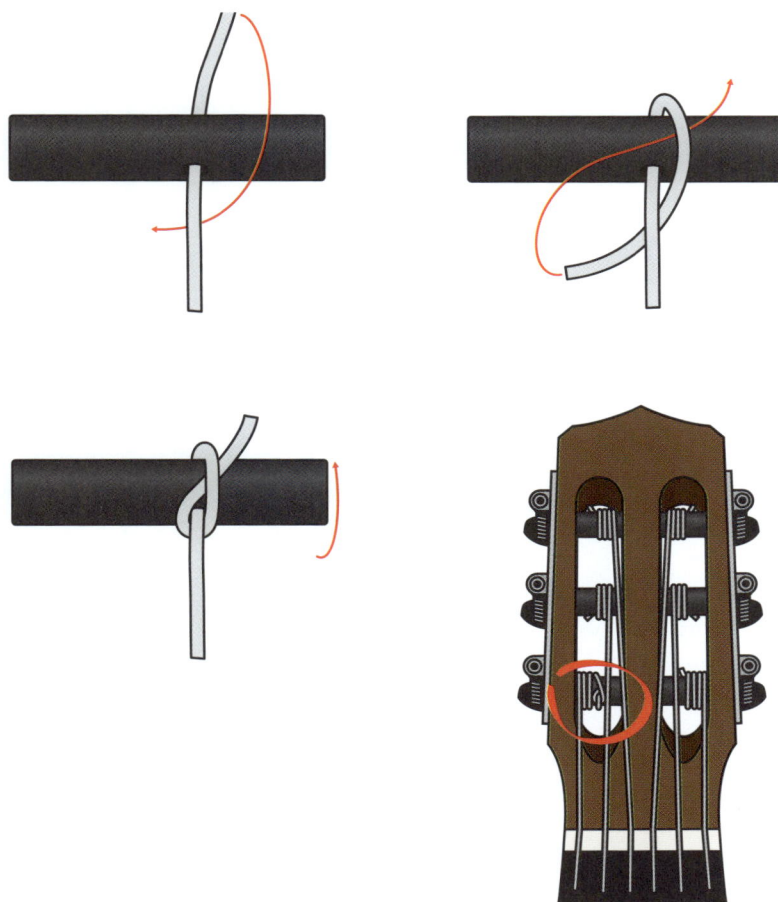

INDEX